Being Humans for Horses

The Power of Being with Horses

Andrew-Glyn Smail

Dedication

To our horses, **Gulliver**, **Farinelli**, **Anaïs** and **Pip**, and all the other horses with whom I have been privileged to be and interact with.

To **Klaus** and **Janosch** for pointing the way forward.

To **Michael** for introducing me to the challenge of choice with horses.

To **Vicki**, my partner and best friend, for opening doors for me which I might otherwise never have passed beyond.

Contents

FOREWORD

The approach to horses that I describe in this book has its origin in the intrinsic nature of the horse. An understanding of the true nature of the horse points to the opportunity to employ a completely new paradigm in our approach to the horse, one based on choice rather than control, connection instead of coercion, and communication as opposed to conditioning. In all of this energy is the key. As such, this approach seeks to avoid the use of instruments of coercion, tools of restraint and any form of conscious training. It is an approach that seems to come so naturally to some humans that they require little in the way of self-development to act accordingly. As such, they have no need of this book. Unfortunately, the number of humans involved would appear to be negligible. I myself know of only a tiny number of such humans and have been privileged to have been greatly helped by one of them.

The rest of us humans need to work on ourselves, if we wish to adopt and live up to the approach which I have set out. This book is for us and I am first in line. In fact, what I have written is based on my own self-development since I first set out to seek a relationship with a horse based on trust and friendship. You may know the story.

It was 2007. I saw a video. The opening scene showed a young man astride a brown gelding moving swiftly along a forest trail at the head of a group of grey riderless horses. Downhill and uphill they moved at varying paces. Horse and human put their trust entirely in each other, for they used no tack or tools. The human trusted that his horse would carry him safely. The horse trusted that his human would guide him safely. Their connection was profound. It was not the riding that drew me but the bond between horse and human. It was the most powerful that I had ever seen on various levels. And I knew there and then that I also wanted such a relationship with a horse. So I went in search of it. And I found it. This book synthesises the essence of what I have learned in the process.

What I have learned from horses by listening to them when they have spoken over the years has led me to raise highly critical questions concerning some of the ways we humans interact with them. This criticism I have levelled at such approaches with every intention of exposing the issues involved but with absolutely no desire to judge an individual who pursues any of them.

Ultimately, there is only one human to whom any of us have to answer on behalf of ourselves and the horse(s) in our care and that is the one who stares right back at us when we examine our face in a mirror. When all is said and done, no one else can usurp our place or assume our responsibility for what we choose to do or not to do with the horse(s) in our care.

Possibly as important is the realisation that in the journey that we are each embarked on with a horse, whatever method or approach we pursue may amount to the equivalent of one human's poison being another's sustenance. By way of example, let me mention a development taken from my own journey. I have been known to be highly critical of the 'natural horsemanship' approach to training (but not its approach to horse husbandry). Yet I will never forget my appreciation when it became the next 'big step' forward on the path that I have shared with our horses, for it gave me the means to feel entirely safe with horses for the very first time in my life. And once I achieved that, a path opened which I would never have believed possible.

Similarly, I am aware that what I am critical of at any stage may represent a 'big step' forward to another human, perhaps you. If this is the case, please do not interpret my words as a judgment of you, for I have probably been where you are now, relishing that 'big step' forward and eagerly seeking the next. Instead, why not simply question what I write but, above all, why not look to your horse to show you the way forward to your next 'big step' on the journey that you are taking together?

In Search of a New Way of Being with Horses

Around the world there is a growing tide of humans in search of a new way of keeping, being and interacting with horses, one that is in tune with their needs and requirements as equines and which also contributes to their psychological and emotional well-being. No longer are these humans prepared to accept conventional horsemanship's insistence on horse care and training regimes which are utterly opposed to the horse's intrinsic nature as a fellow sentient and cognitive being, and a highly sensitive and sociable one at that. As far as possible these humans seek to keep their horses in conditions which are in line with their understanding of the nature of the horse. Stables are abandoned in favour of keeping horses in 'herds' with access to effective shelter against the elements, the metal studs masquerading as 'shoes' are pulled off to allow them to move barefoot as they were born, and bits, whips, spurs and other metal and leather restraints and instruments of coercion are left in the hands of trainers committed to coercive control or practitioners of the deviant sexual behaviour inspired by it. These developments are accompanied by talk of 'natural horsemanship', references to a 'partnership' between horse and human and even allusions to connection, choice and love.

All of this is commendable and to be encouraged, if for no other reason than that they hold the promise of a more humane future for our horses. But how far do we dare to go? Taken to their logical extreme, these developments must inevitably give us cause to pose the question as to what type of relationship we seek to have with our horses. They raise the question as to whether we are going to base the relationship between horses and humans on control or choice. Put another way, is this relationship to be based on control by the human for the human's benefit *or* choice, that of the horse and that of the human for the horse? And if it is to be based on choice, does this then not imply a major challenge to the human? For if we abandon control for our benefit, both physical and mental, how are we to ensure that the horse makes choices which are not only conducive to their well-being but ours as well and that we do so too?

Perhaps more to the point, is it possible to do so and, if it is, what does this require of the human?

At the risk of walking a plank into ridicule, I claim that it is. This I do, not on the basis of some pie-in-the-sky, air-fairy fantasy but rather actual achievements in my management of and interaction with horses, not to boast of them but to reveal just a little of what is possible if we rise to the challenge of choice.

Let me say at the outset that I am not a great horse trainer, rider or show person. Neither do I 'break in' horses or participate in equestrian competitions, although there was a stage in my life when I travelled the world to attend the World Equestrian Games and the equestrian components of the Olympic Games to cheer on the Dutch and Australian teams.

Instead, like millions of other ordinary humans around the world, when it comes to horses I am first and foremost a carer, a role which is probably one of the most underrated in the domain of the horse in captivity, if the amounts paid to grooms in many professional yards represent a reliable yardstick of appreciation. Not that I am paid anything to care for our horses. Like other committed carers, I do it simply because I really care. I check on our horses and provide them with feed and water several times a day, separating them where necessary to ensure that all have as much as they require. As and when needed, I pick out their hooves, apply salves and lotions to any part of their body, including under their tail and between their legs, and slap horse flies and other 'nasties' which settle on them (these slaps can be pretty hard), often when the horse 'requests' this themself. All of this entails leading or guiding the horses to specific places, or asking them to move backwards and/or sideways on their own or amongst each other. And all of this I do at liberty, in some cases while clutching one or more buckets of feed as I gently but firmly make my way amongst them (no bribery). I feel no need to resort to training or the use of tools of restraint or instruments of coercion in order to do any of this. So how do I manage to do it all without resorting to training or the use of such tools and instruments while avoiding injury or the risk of any?

Simply by adopting and maintaining the approach described in this book, which is based on choice.

Over and above this, I trim our horses' hooves under the guidance of an equine podiatrist about every three to five weeks, depending on their wear and tear. I have done this in Australia when we still had horses there. I have also done and still do this in Europe. Such hoof care I have done at liberty and still do. And I have done this with our horses on their own and with my mare, Pip, in a herd of up to forty horses. (You can find some examples of this in my blog post entitled *Lessons Taught Me by My Horse, Lesson 4. Trust is the strongest bond between horse and human!* at http://horsesand humans.com/blog/2018/01/26/lessons-taught-me-by-my-horse-lesson-4-trust-is-the-strongest-bond-between-horse-and-human/) Again, there is no need to resort to training or the use of tools of restraint or instruments of coercion for this purpose. So how do I manage to do all of this without resorting to training or the use of such tools and instruments while avoiding injury or the risk of any? Simply by adopting and maintaining the approach described in this book, which is based on choice.

The Equine Touch is a form of soft tissue vibrational equine bodywork, which I share with our own and other horses mainly in horse rescue centres. I do this in my capacity as a qualified practitioner and instructor. This type of work involves raising and holding a horse's legs where possible and advisable, and even placing a hindleg over my thigh while performing certain proce-dures. With our own horses I usually perform this equine bodywork at liberty and I have also done this with some rescue centre horses when I have felt that it was called for. You can find some examples of this in my blog post entitled *Equine Bodywork and the Challenge of Choice* http://horsesandhumans.com/blog/2020/02/19/equine-bodywork-and-the-challenge-of-choice/. And again, while working at liberty I have never felt a need to resort to training or the use of tools of restraint or instruments of coercion. So how do I manage to do all of this without resorting to training or the use of such tools and instruments while avoiding injury or the risk of any? Simply by adopting and maintaining the approach described in this book, which is based on choice.

Then there is the interaction which occurs between horse and human but is not part of everyday care. What do you do, if you drive down the driveway to open the gate so you can go shopping and your two mares, who just so happen to be dallying next to it, decide that an open gate is an invitation to greener grass on the other side of the fence? Simple, you just enjoy the beauty of the moment with them and then, using a combination of gestures, words but predominantly energy, you calmly motion them to step back without in any way touching or driving them and then head back to the car to drive through. Being the horse she is, Anaïs feels that my absence from her side is a renewed invitation to walk through the open gateway, so I have to repeat the exercise but this time emphasise the need for her to stay back (yes, I actually speak to her and stress the importance of staying on the property). This time she does and both mares watch as I drive through and close the gate, promising to be back soon. There are other experiences I can cite (see for instance my blog post entitled *Horse Training: Do We Not Hide Behind It?* at http://horsesandhumans.com/blog/2019/08/17/horse-training-do-we-not-hide-behind-it/) but this is enough for the moment to show that there really is no need for all the hard, rough or conditioned control that we humans all too often insist on in our dealings with creatures who are not only sensitive to a fly alighting on their coat or the energy accompanying a half-cocked ear emanating from another horse that is fully present in the moment but are also capable of understanding and communicating with a human. And yet again, the secret to achieving this lies in adopting and maintaining the approach described in this book, which is based on choice.

Although I do not resort to training, I readily admit that equine behaviour modification does occur to some extent through habituation and even conditioning, albeit not consciously on my part. In all cases though, the horse is the author of their own learning. And yes, there are times when some type of restraint is called for, such as when the vet or dentist comes. I normally use a softly lined webbing halter if I do require one and it is attached to a light rope lead of no less than two metres which always has slack in it between my hand and the horse. I avoid driving the horse with or without physical contact.)

When I used to ride my mare, Pip, it was usually with a soft leather cavesson on Pip's head and a bareback pad without stirrups (in the absence of any restraint, instrument of coercion or other device) on her back. As a qualified master saddle-fitting consultant, I would have preferred a saddle to distribute my weight more evenly but I could not find one to accommodate her imbalance (her left shoulder is higher and further forward than the right). The lack of an appropriate saddle is one of the reasons why I stopped riding Pip. Riding was replaced with walks in the countryside on our own or together with my partner, Vicki, and her mare, Anaïs. Initially, I used a soft leather cavesson attached to a two-metre lead rope along with a dressage whip to ensure safety in public places. In the course of time the whip was no longer required and was ditched. Not long after the cavesson went the way of the whip. It was replaced with a comfortably lined webbing halter, the lead rope always having a 'smile' in the in it. Unfortunately, the temptation to lose the halter as well had to yield to public safety and insurance requirements. I no longer use gimmicks or gadgets to move or stop Pip. Nor do I rely on training.

The bottom line is that, if Pip chooses not to be with me when we are together, I have no desire to oblige or compel her to change her mind. Ultimately, she is free to go whenever she wants to. At liberty she is free to walk away at will. On the lead, the moment she expresses any urge to be somewhere other than me, I trust that I am sensitive enough to sense that and, if any light-hearted attempt fails to persuade her otherwise, I remove the halter and she is free to go. Pip weighs as much as a compact car but moves with far greater agility. Consequently, even if I were to be foolish enough to play the boss and try and confine her to my presence, I would not really have the means to do so. In the absence of any other tool, restraint or some kind of trigger to elicit conditioned behaviour, a comfortable webbing halter linking my mare to me with nothing more than a relatively thin lead rope attached via a small connector would simply not suffice. Pip would either attempt to bolt or shut down. Pip remains with me and within the field of the slack in the rope, because she wants to. She exercises choice. If Pip really did not want to stay with me, I would have very little in my hands to persuade her otherwise.

So what keeps Pip with me when we do anything that would not normally accord with her natural inclinations in the absence of the bond that binds us? Just that: a bond that binds us but one which is not only paradoxically based on choice but which is also equally paradoxically much stronger than any that is not while still having the horse entirely present. So what exactly is this bond? How can we achieve it with our horse? And once we have such a bond, how can we ensure that our horse does what we would like them to do or refrains from doing whatever it is that we would prefer them not to do in the absence of control?

THE RELATIONSHIP BETWEEN HORSES AND HUMANS

By this stage you may be fidgeting a bit uneasily. No effective tool or restraint, no conditioned behaviour, does this not suggest the absence of human control over the horse. And if it does, is not chaos the only alternative to such absence of control? After all, at the most immediate level of day-to-day practice, that is, the way we relate to our horses and secure their cooperation in our daily care for and interaction with them, can we really afford to run the risk of such chaos by pursuing a relationship with our horses which seeks to abandon control and to give our horses a choice instead? Do we dare to do so? Of course not, surely?

Control

But what if I were to challenge such conventional wisdom? What if I were to claim, not only that there is a far greater risk of chaos occurring if we rely on control which is ineffective but also that the more control we attempt to exercise over a horse, the greater the likelihood there will be that such chaos will occur if our control remains ineffective? In addition, what if I were also to claim that the more effective we are in exercising control, the less likely it will be that we will have a spontaneous, sensitive and sentient horse to care for and interact with. This is a lesson that my mare, Pip, taught me. Unlike her mate, Anaïs, who actively resists attempts to control her with restraints and coercion by rearing spectacularly, amongst other things, Pip simply escapes. She does this by doing everything demanded of her while simultaneously shutting down and withdrawing, until all that is left in the human's hands is a hollow shadow of the magnificent horse that she is. Yes, she seems to be obedient. Yes, it would appear that there is communication and connection between horse and human. Ultimately though, there is nothing. The real horse has gone absent without leave.

Yet control seems to be a straightforward, logical option doesn't it? Indeed, it is quite probably the very first thing that we notice and learn, when we take our first steps towards the horse, how to ensure that this huge creature does not hurt us while doing what we or our trainer insist they do. Safety, that of the horse and ours, if it is not a sound enough reason for controlling the horse, what is? Of course, I do not dispute the need for safety. Being of sound mind, what human would? And is there any way of ensuring safety other than by controlling the horse? If there is, we may not be aware of it now and in all likelihood we were not familiar with any when we started out with horses.

Control, as you know, can take many forms and it extends from how we breed and keep our horses through to how we interact with them. In its crudest form it is first and foremost physical, although such control almost always has a mental, psychological and even emotional dimension or effect, even if unintended. In its most refined form as evidenced in training, it also relies on behaviour modification and/or psychological manipulation. Such conditioned behaviour is activated by means of the 'aids' in the case of negative reinforcement and a trigger (for instance, a gesture or a word) where positive reinforcement is pursued and while the horse exhibits it, they have little or no control over their physical and mental faculties. Put another way, the spontaneous, sensitive, sociable sentient being that is the horse is utterly incapable of behaving fully as such a being while exhibiting conditioned behaviour. Effectively, the horse has bolted and all that remains is a hollow shadow of themself, a look-alike puppet in a human-orchestrated pantomime.

<hr>

MYTH BUSTER

The myth: it is possible for a human to control the actions of the spontaneous, sensitive, sociable, sentient creature that is the horse.

The buster: if attempts to control a horse are ineffective, the human runs the risk of having to contend with the chaos of a horse resisting or evading the attempts to control them. On the other hand, where control is effective, it usually produces a horse that is to some or other degree no longer the spontaneous, sensitive, sociable, sentient creature which they are capable of being either because their behaviour is conditioned (due to positive reinforcement and to a limited extent negative reinforcement and/or punishment) or because the horse has shut down psychologically even to the point of learned helplessness.

<hr>

Control need not be harsh and dominant or cruel and vindictive. Control can also appear to be as soft as silk or as splendid as a glowing sunset. The effect though is the same. When we control our horses, we humans do so for our benefit first and foremost and, by doing so, disempower and deprive them of much, if not all that allows them to be as much a sentient being as we are, a creature that in the absence of such disempowerment and deprivation is also far more spontaneous, sensitive and sociable, in short, all that attracts us to horses. If a horse has a soul, control smothers it when that control is exercised, no matter how well-intentioned.

The internet abounds with images and videos of horses exhibiting such conditioned behaviour while interacting with their human in some or other jaw-dropping, gob-smacking rendition of 'closeness' and 'connection' between the species. Almost invariably the audience is treated to a heart-wrenching portrayal of the most intimate, trusting relationship between horse and human or the latter has the former perform laudable feats of classical dressage with little more than a neck rope, often with a forest, a shoreline or a lake as a romantic backdrop. Struck by the immensity of the dream come to life on the screen before us, we immediately share such a portrayal with all our friends on the social media platform of our choice and they do likewise. And before the day is done a new 'horsemanship' star is born with no camera around to capture the collapse of the dream once the conditioned routine has run its course and the horse returns to being just that: the superbly spontaneous, sensitive, sociable sentient being to whom we are drawn. It is simply impossible to control a horse without destroying what we seek to control. Ultimately, the real reason why we need an alternative lies in the compelling nature of the failure of control.

Choice

At first glance it may seem that there are many aspects of human control of horses which are simply not susceptible of change, let alone choice. After all, horses in captivity cannot be offered a choice in relation to the way they are kept. Surely not? We need to be realistic, don't we? Horses need to be taught how to survive in our world, don't they? Such concerns do have the ring of incontestable truth about them. Yet if we dig beneath the veneer of logic and rationality, do they retain that quality? Yes, it is true that horses cannot be offered a choice in relation to the way they are kept. After all, we are in full control of that. But if we are, don't we have a choice as to how we keep our horses? And if we do, why do we insist on keeping horses in ways which are utterly alien to their true nature? Is it for our convenience? Do we really benefit from it? Do not the ways in which we keep horses create so many problems that we spend far more time, energy and resources trying to find solutions to them than we would do if we were to keep them in ways that are commensurate with their essential nature? And don't those problems make it so much more difficult for horses and humans to relate to and interact with each other? Would it therefore not be better for both species if we humans were to refrain from keeping horses?

Questions suggesting a similar degree of futility may also be posed with regard to the way in which we relate to and interact with horses. After all, if we are only able to relate to and interact with horses with the aid of training and the use of tools of restraint and instruments of coercion, methods and devices which at best effectively reduce horses to hollow shells of themselves in the course of relating to and interacting with them, is there really any point in doing so, unless our purpose includes reducing them to such hollow shells?

Questions suggesting such futility in the way we keep horses and how we relate to and interact with them clearly beg a question in themselves, as you probably suspect. And it is this: Is there an alternative? By now, you would probably also suspect that there might be and that it lies in choice. First of all there is the choice which we can allow our horses to make as to whether they wish to relate so and interact with us, assuming that they would like to do so. Then there is the choice that we can make as to whether we should keep horses and, if we choose to do so, whether we should not do so in line with their intrinsic nature.

I propose that, instead of trying to control our horses solely or mainly for our own benefit, we empower and energise them by allowing them first of all to choose to be with or follow us in our endeavours and, by doing so, to truly share them with us and, secondly, by opting for a way of keeping them which enables them to exercise such choice more readily. You may be one of the few who are aware that such a proposal is not new. There is a small but growing number of humans who are committed to allowing the horse to exercise the choice which they would normally do as fellow sentient beings. Perhaps you are one of them. Or quite possibly you are open to exploring this option. Alternatively, you might be a sceptic who is simply intrigued to see where such a crazy idea could lead. Whatever the case, the question begged by allowing the horse to choose whether or not to be with you, me or any other human, is this: What can we humans do to help the horse choose to do just that of their own volition either in response to a human invitation to do so or entirely of their own accord? This is the challenge of choice and essentially what this book is about.

HORSES AND THEIR DOMAIN

The horse is first and foremost a prey animal, a creature of flight. How often have we not heard this statement? Everyone who has anything to do with horses seems to trot out this conclusion with the solemnity of the faithful religiously reciting their creed. And the members of the equestrian congregation who hear it nod unthinkingly in agreement, as though acknowledging the first tenet of equine doctrine. This is how we humans define the essence of the horse. No one questions this definition. It is taken as given, a bit like acknowledging that the earth is round. There is a difference, of course. We do not base our approach to the earth on our acknowledgement that it is round. Nor do we use the fact that it is round as the basis for a human approach to the earth which is devastating the planet (mainly through a combination of human induced and facilitated global warming, pollution, mass extinctions, the destruction of biodiversity and related conditions). However, we do use the claim that the horse is first and foremost a prey animal, a creature of flight to justify a human approach to horses which is premised on domination and control to the human's advantage. Perhaps it is time to question this statement and to establish whether it is indeed an accurate reflection of the essential nature of the horse. Is there a better time to do this than when considering the question of choice?

If we are to offer horses a choice as to whether and how to relate and interact with us or to make a choice in the way we keep and raise them which accords with their intrinsic nature, then we need to have a reliable idea of what that nature is and what it entails. Yet how many of us actually do? How many of us have really taken the time and have made the effort to find out just what this creature, horse, really is? How many of us understand what a horse is in physical, mental and emotional terms? What do we know about their capabilities? How much do we really know about a horse's natural inclinations, how they would choose to live and relate to each other, their environment and other species in the wild or if they had a chance to do so in captivity? What do we know of their capacity for learning, their natural curiosity, and their feelings and emotions?

The vast majority of humans who have much to do with horses may feel that we can answer these questions with confidence based on our knowledge and experience of them in captivity. Yet we must question whether such knowledge and experience are reliable, which they need to be if they are to serve as the basis of choice. The reason for this may be found in the potential for major discrepancies to exist between our evidence of the essential nature of horses in the wild and their behaviour in captivity. Because horses are at liberty to exercise greater choice in the wild, it is to their behaviour in this domain that we must turn if we are to obtain a reliable indication of their intrinsic nature.

The horse in the wild

There is a tendency amongst some humans to romanticise the wild. Let us resist the temptation, for the wild can be a hard, uncompromising place. We may also want to bear in mind that the truly wild horse is extinct. All the horses that currently live in the wild are actually feral. This is to say that they or their ancestors used to live in captivity, if only briefly, as in the case of the Przewalski horses.

This may appear to be a shortcoming, a detraction from what might otherwise have been a living historical record of horses that are truly wild. And perhaps it is.

Yet the existence of feral horses is perhaps far more important to those of us who keep and interact with horses in captivity than their original wild counterparts. This is because it allows us to see how our own horses might actually live and organise their communities were they themselves to return to the wild or be given the chance to do so in captivity. In other words, the existence of feral horses in the wild affords us an opportunity to observe and familiarise ourselves with the natural tendencies and characteristics of horses at this point in their evolution, including those who rely on us for their health and well-being in captivity. For this reason we need to turn to equine studies and ethology, in particular, to help us learn and understand the true nature of our horses, and their essential inclinations and requirements. Yet, while we do so, we need to bear in mind that, as in the case of any science, these are fields of study which are constantly evolving as new discoveries are made and former conclusions are ditched or revised. As such, it would be advisable for us to keep abreast of developments in these fields, while simultaneously conducting our own observations of and experiments with horses in captivity, especially where they are kept in conditions which resemble those of the wild. We may also want to resist any temptation not to be critical when assessing field studies conducted by others, especially in relation to the conclusions which they draw from their observations. In addition, we may also wish to consider the quality of the actions which we or others observe and not merely the empirical data.

It is predominantly in the wild, where human influence, al-though still present in natural resource management practices, is rather limited, that many of the salient features of the horse are far more easily discernible than in captivity. Let us therefore start by examining the key features of the intrinsic nature of horses in their natural habitat while reflecting on some of the implications for our dealings with those in captivity.

The physiological horse

A brief survey of key aspects of the horse's physiology will suffice to provide important clues as to how we may want to keep and raise horses, and relate to and interact with them, if their physiological needs and preferences are to be accommodated appropriately. For the sake of convenience I have grouped my observations into logical categories.

The Imperative of movement

From the very first moment when we clap eyes on them, it is clear that horses are designed to move and to do so fairly rapidly if necessary over varying terrain. Relative to their body, their legs are long and are driven by powerful combinations of muscles, while their hooves are hard enough to withstand tough, uneven surfaces, simultaneously absorbing shock through the frog and deep digital cushion.

This initial impression is confirmed by the existence of a relatively small stomach, which suggests that, given their bulk, horses are designed to eat small quantities of food frequently rather than a limited number of large meals.

Confirmation is also obtained from an examination of the hoof mechanism, which not only plays a vital role in protecting the horse in the course of frequent movement but also facilitates circulation in the hoof and legs, compensating for the absence of muscles in the lower legs. Although the circulation of blood to remove waste and introduce nutrition is vital to the health of the hooves, and gravity makes it possible for the blood to drain down the legs and enter them, there are no muscles in the lower limbs to pump the blood back out. This is where the hoof mechanism plays a vital role, allowing the hooves to expand and complement gravity by sucking the blood down when they hit the ground and to then force the blood out and up the legs, when the hooves leave the ground as they contract to their original shape. The expansion of the hooves occurs mainly to the rear of their structure, allowing the horse's natural shock absorber (the frog and the deep digital cushion above it) to absorb much if not most of the shock of impact with the ground, thereby protecting the joints and other tissue in the legs and elsewhere.

Taken together, all of these factors show unequivocally that, not only is the horse made for movement, they depend on a good deal of it at frequent intervals, if they are to remain healthy. The reality of horses in the wild confirms this. They are known to move anywhere from fifteen to thirty-five kilometres (just over nine to a little under twenty-two miles) a day and to the extent that the conditions of the wild allow, they are generally pretty healthy and fit. Reflection on these factors also suggests a pattern of a relatively brief period of foraging, followed by a snooze repeated throughout most of the day and interspersed at various intervals with, amongst other things, social interaction, movement to water and better pasture, at least one brief period of REM sleep and the relatively few times when they need to evade predators. Observations of horses in the wild largely confirm this.

Highly developed senses

Perhaps the sense that is most obvious to us humans in horses is that of sight. With their eyes situated on either side of their head, it is clear at a glance that horses have a huge field of vision compared to us. In addition, although humans can discern colours and still objects more easily than horses, horses can detect movement, even the slightest, far more readily than we do and they can see in conditions which are far too dark for us to see much, if anything. They are also capable of discerning the slightest subtle movement at relatively short range, especially when it is coupled with a change in energy, for instance, where another horse does little more than tighten their mouth and harden their glance.

Perhaps as legendary as the horse's capacity for sight is their hearing. Not only does their sense of hearing cover the entire range of a human voice better than a dog's, it also extends well beyond.

Who has not been out hacking or walking with their horse and not noticed that the latter can detect a presence well before it is visible?

Not as well-known perhaps is the horse's sense of smell, which is arguably as well-developed as that of a dog. Smell helps horses find feed but also plays a vital role in their busy social life, helping them to identify friends and family along with the condition in which they find themselves. As in some other species, there is a neurological link between smell and taste, the two frequently reinforcing each other.

Touch is also a sense in the horse which we humans vastly underestimate. Although some of us point out that a horse is so sensitive to tactile stimuli that they can detect a fly alighting on their coat, so too can we feel one come to rest on our skin. Horses though are also capable of sensing a tactile stimulus which is too light for humans to detect.

Hard-wired response to physical pressure

When it comes to horse training which involves negative reinforcement, such as classical equestrian pursuits and more recent approaches masquerading as 'natural horsemanship', there is a common assumption on the part of the instructors and practitioners, namely, that horses yield to pressure by nature. Yet a closer examination of how horses physiologically respond to pressure paints a very different picture.

Where pressure is applied through physical contact, horses tend to do the very opposite of yielding to such pressure, at least initially before training has advanced far enough to successfully demand the requisite response of yielding, although it should be borne in mind that the horse's response will then be a conditioned one and not how they would respond of their own volition in the absence of such training. The untrained natural response of horses to physical pressure is not to yield to it but to resist it and to do so with increasing force until that pressure is removed or is strong enough to overcome the horse's resistance. When such physical pressure is initially applied, the horse's muscles automatically resist it. The horse is physiologically primed to respond in this way. As such, it is not an instinctively informed or a cognitively ordered process but rather a physiological reflex.

Limited load bearing capacity

More often than not horses are acquired for the purposes of riding them. Yet veterinarians are often amongst the first to acknowledge that horses are not made to be ridden. The very first thing that my saddle-fitting instructor said to our class at the beginning of our practical training is this: 'Riding is harmful to horses,' no ifs, buts or maybes. She was also a vet. A saddle, she explained, was designed to reduce the harm inflicted on a horse due to riding.

So why is this the case? Essentially, it is because a horse has limited load bearing capacity. A rider sits on the back of a horse but not all of the back is capable of supporting them. Only a relatively small part is, namely that part behind the withers which is supported by the ribs, and then only to a limited extent. This means that a rider is confined to the small area from about the twelfth to no further than the eighteenth thoracic vertebra. Even then, the rider needs to ensure that their weight does not press down on the spine, especially because, if it does, it is likely to occur mainly through the small area of their sit bones, thereby creating pressure points, which would compromise the horse's back to some or other extent depending on the weight of the rider and the strength of the horse. From the horses' perspective, the primary purpose of a saddle is to distribute the rider's weight evenly over the paraspinal muscles, while clearing the spine of any pressure and freeing up the shoulders. Yet, depending on the weight of the rider and the saddle, the superficial tissue may begin to be compromised within as little as a quarter of an hour even with the best fitting saddle.

And we have not even mentioned the nature of the horse's back in relation to its primary supports, the four limbs. Picture if you will a trestle table whose top has a width equivalent to one fifth of its overall length, the distance between the trestles being roughly equal to their height but with the trestle at one end situated markedly further towards the centre than the other, so that it bears a load twice as much as the other, the overall weight of the top being roughly three times more than that of both trestles taken together. Then imagine that the top is as about thick as the height of its legs at that end and noticeably thinner at the other, the horizontal beam of the trestle providing firm support for the table top at the latter end but not the former, where the horizontal beam has been replaced with a thick rubber band. This is roughly how the weight and volume of the horse's body is distributed and secured, although in the horse the two pairs of sloping legs at the end of each trestle have been replaced with a single thin leg ending in a hoof. Now ask yourself where the weakest part of the table top is located. Precisely ... between the trestles. And now ask yourself where, if you were to sit on that trestle table, it would be safest for the horse for you to do so. Given the distribution of the table top's volume and weight, your answer is likely to be above the trestle at the thinner part of the table top, so as to address the obvious imbalance and to rely on the secure join of the trestle to the table top at that end, is it not? Now consider where you would normally sit if the trestle table was a horse. Perhaps this position is not very helpful to the horse? Naturally, there are the ribs which support the back up until the eighteenth vertebra but is this enough?

Classical dressage seeks to remedy this imbalance by employing a range of tools of restraint, instruments of coercion and techniques to collect the horse, so as to induce the animal to raise the base of the neck, round the back as far as possible and have the hind legs step further under the torso to shift the horse's weight towards the rear, all for the sole purpose of enabling the horse to carry a rider more effectively to accommodate the latter's needs or desires. The drawbacks are self-evident if one looks carefully. Because the collection is false in that the horse is not collecting themself but rather the human is collecting the horse, everything falls apart when the tack is removed. More insidiously, as the horse is not collecting themself, their body is effectively forced into a frame and their body parts are pushed into positions where they would not naturally go.

The result is discomfort for the horse at best. It is small wonder that one therefore sees so much tension in horses ridden at the summit of equestrian sport, even those of world champion equestrians.

Having said all this, we should confess that a horse's capacity to bear a load largely depends on their size, strength, conformation and condition in relation to the weight, size and shape of the load. Many horses would easily be capable of bearing a load equivalent to a lightweight human, especially the larger breeds and, in particular, if the load is alive and capable of moving together with the horse in the absence of tools of restraint and instruments of coercion.

Capable of great speed and highly responsive

The allure of the equine back, whose apparent length and shape so many humans have interpreted as an invitation to ride rather than the confession of fragility which they actually are, is enhanced by the horse's capacity for speed of movement, one which is not confined to very short distances. It is a capacity which is legendary in human history and culture, and which still serves as the basis for an entire industry in some countries. Such speed is initially evident in horses' responsiveness. Once a horse has identified the need or desire to move, it may take a split second for them to turn it into a reality.

Not only are horses highly responsive but they are also not confined to a slow start-up, going from stationary to walk and then trot before easing into a canter and then a gallop. On the contrary, they are able to leap into a faster gait at the outset, depending on their intent, conformation and physical condition. Similarly, they are also capable of coming to a rapid halt, for example, from a gallop to motionless within a few strides in natural conditions. But this is far from being 'all'. Perhaps one of the most fascinating examples of a horse's capacity for almost instantaneous response lies in their ability to influence and be influenced by spontaneous action on their or another horse's part in the middle of frenzied flight at the gallop. Such a response occurs too rapidly for the rational mind to be directing proceedings. Clearly this is an example of spontaneous consciousness at work.

The cognitive horse

Most of the 'horsey' humans whom I know will readily concede that horses are capable of learning from each other. All of us seem to have a story to illustrate the point. One of my favourite stories concerns Pip learning to step up onto a pedestal after watching Anaïs do it under Vicki's guidance. For ages I had tried to get Pip to do the same but every time she simply walked off almost shaking her head as if to say, 'You're crazy'. Caring for Pip while she was having problems with one of her hooves was a watershed experience for us. Her attitude towards me changed completely. I did not realise just to what extent it had, until I took her to the pedestal, put my foot on it and uttered the cue, 'Step', as I had vainly done so many times before. She lifted her hoof slightly. I then bent down and raised it on to the edge of the pedestal to show her what I meant and then we tried the whole thing again. This time Pip simply put her foot on the pedestal and turned her head towards me as if to say, 'Oh that's what you want? Well, here you are then.' Although it was only one foot, I was suitably impressed. Then I took Pip to watch Anaïs put both front feet on the pedestal but my mare did not seem to be overly impressed. A week later I discovered why. Asking Pip to put one foot up onto the pedestal and trying not to expect anything, my mare looked at me, turned back to the pedestal and simply stepped up onto it with both front feet. The next time I asked her a week later, she promptly walked right up and over the thing. An illustrated version of this story may be found in my blog post titled *Towards Riding 1: The Horse*, which can be found here: http://horsesandhumans.com/blog/2014/03/19/towards-riding-1-the-horse/.

This story also points to what is perhaps the most significant observation we may make about humans' scientific knowledge of horses' cognitive abilities, namely, how little we know about their capacity for social as opposed to individual learning. Here 'social learning' refers to horses' ability to learn from each other, as opposed to how they learn on their own or from humans. Any information that is available on the subject appears to be largely anecdotal. Given the highly sociable nature of horses, we should perhaps be alarmed by our lack of knowledge of social learning amongst horses. After all, it reflects a level of ignorance on the part of humans about what is arguably the most important aspect of the horse's cognitive abilities – given the horse's excessively sociable nature – which is simply inexcusable in relation to a species that we claim to know and which has played and still plays such an important role in human history and culture. Yet this shortcoming on the part of humans is perhaps entirely understandable when viewed within the context of how we keep and relate to horses. The type and level of care that we provide to our horses is largely defined by our individual convenience and requirements, as is our approach to equine learning and human training. Our research into horses' cognitive abilities generally reflects this preoccupation with the individual and the human, with the result that we know far more about how horses learn individually and from human training rather than what and how they learn from each other and even from us when they are authors of their own learning. The few attempts that have been made to study social learning in horses have suffered from similar limitations or worse.

Ultimately, it is only in the wild, where horses are fully capable of being the highly sociable creatures that they are, that it is possible for horses to engage in the full gamut of social learning available to them and hence for humans to study this as extensively. While some work has been done in this respect, it also suffers from a serious limitation in that studies of horses in the wild tend to focus on agonistic (conflict-related) behaviour rather than affiliative (companionship-related) behaviour, with the result that sociability, which is by its very nature affiliative, is largely ignored.

Consequently, what we know about horses' cognitive capacity is rather severely limited. Nevertheless, the relatively little that we do know reveals that horses have fairly advanced cognitive abilities which go well beyond the rather rudimentary mechanistic behaviour modification techniques which humans generally resort to for the purposes of 'horse training', be they of the positive or negative variety. Yet it is precisely the type of modified behaviour achieved through such techniques which is often cited as evidence of the horse's cognitive abilities. We are told that horses excel in both non-associative learning, such as habituation, and associative learning, which takes the form of associating stimuli (classical conditioning), such as the opening of feed bins with actual feeding, or associating a stimulus with a response (operant conditioning), which can be reinforced by removing an adverse stimulus when the desired behaviour is presented (negative reinforcement) or by rewarding the desired behaviour (positive reinforcement). Still it could be argued that, to the extent that cognition is the mental action or process of learning, knowing and understanding, any behaviour modification that occurs through such horse training is not an example of cognition in the horse or at least not fully so, as it involves little or no mental action or process, or at any rate only partially so and often only initially. This is particularly true in the case of triggered behavioural changes, which involve modified behaviour that is automatically reproduced when the trigger is invoked, thereby effectively precluding any cognitive process while the rote behaviour occurs.

It is possible for us to go on to cite examples of far more complex forms of cognitive ability in horses. For instance, we may mention their ability to generalise and discriminate between what they experience. They are capable of applying knowledge acquired through the performance of one particular type of action for the purposes of carrying out a related task, an example of learning to learn. Categorisation and conceptualisation are not entirely alien to them either. Horses have also been found to have excellent memories, which is the basis for learning to learn. There are also indications that horses are capable of adducing routes through terrain that they have not yet fully explored, which would suggest that they have some prospective learning potential.

Pip also showed me once that it is possible for a horse to infer meaning from a combination of original utterances expressed with the appropriate energy from a distance. She was at the top of a hill looking for her friend, Anaïs, who was gorging carob beans behind a tree towards the base of that hill. Indeed, so intent on filling her belly was Anaïs, that she did not even bother to reply to Pip's urgent whinny. Fortunately, I saw this happening from some way off and called out directions to Pip. How she responded and eventually found her friend is described in my blog post titled *Horse Training: Do We Not Hide Behind It?*, which you can find here: http://horsesandhumans.com/blog/2019/08/17/horse-training-do-we-not-hide-behind-it/.

Ultimately though, the true test of the potential complexity of horses' cognitive ability should focus more closely on the animal's capacity for learning from and together with members of their own species. This is because sociability is arguably the horse's predominant character if we base such an assessment on the time, energy and effort devoted to it in the course of interaction with other living creatures. Although human study of such social cognition amongst horses in the wild is sparse and focused primarily on agonistic behaviour, the vast extent of intensive sociability amongst them suggests that such social cognition occurs on a relatively large scale. Given that all horses in the wild are essentially feral, it would therefore be difficult not to conclude that horses in captivity could achieve and realise a similar potential in appropriate circumstances.

The energetical horse

Although the energetical nature of the horse appears to me as something which is so utterly obvious and self-evident, I have yet to come across its mention in any ethological study of horses in the wild in spite of the fact that it is so clearly present in the audio-visual documentaries dealing with the subject matter. For this reason most of my observations and conclusions are based on my experience with horses in captivity, albeit in situations which in some small way seek to emulate the horse's natural habitat.

If you have access to a group or herd of horses, you can learn much about their energetical nature by watching them communicate with each other. Like me, you will probably have been told that horses communicate with each other using body language. While this may be true to a certain extent, does this represent the full picture? We have learned that certain subtle movements mean certain things but do they really do so on their own? For instance, you are probably aware that when a horse moves their ears back, they may be giving a warning. Yet horses do the very same thing when they doze. And when we see a horse perking up their ears, we tend to conclude that they are content, yet they also do this when detecting potential danger and preparing to flee. Clearly the same sign may have not only different but even opposite meanings. So how do we know which one applies? The energy with which the sign is expressed, surely?

But let me play devil's advocate. It could be the context in which it occurs rather than the energy behind it, couldn't it? After all, the dozing horse is calm, while the creature flashing a warning is strident. Yet is this not indicative of the energy behind the sign? After all, if the horse flashing a warning was not strident but instead exhibited the energy of dozing within the context of warning, would anyone really take that warning seriously? Indeed, there are times when a horse need not even move their ears back to issue a warning. A look may be enough. We know this too from our observations of horses. Again though, is it not the energy that is communicated through the horse's presence and actions, however subtle they may be, which 'speaks', as it were?

As always, intent is the driving force of the energy with which a horse expresses themself. Intent determines the nature, intensity and direction of such energy. As such, the energy with which a horse expresses themself communicates their intent through the form of that expression. It is precisely this use of energy which explains why horses are able to communicate with each other using signs which are sometimes so subtle that they are barely noticeable. The hardening of the eyes is an example of this.

The nature of horses as energetical beings is particularly evident in their interaction with each other and members of other species. This is especially true in relation to their response to what they perceive to be physical pressure and what they treat as an energetical request or demand. As already noted, horses are hardwired to respond to what they perceive to be physical pressure (and this can vary somewhat from one horse to the next) by resisting it. If we push, they push back and if we pull, they pull back. These are reflexive responses and the energy with which they are expressed is precisely that, reflexive. This may of course change. In a particular situation the energy may turn to that of panic, for instance, where a horse at the end of a lead rope frantically realises that they cannot escape and blindly starts to thrash around. Alternatively, the horse may realise this and resort to resistance and even attack. This energy is very different from that of panic.

The type of energy with which any action occurs is arguably as, if not more, decisive than the body language employed to articulate it. For instance, horses may treat a sharp slap or smack very differently depending on the situation in which it occurs. Because it descends upon them at speed and with force, they are likely to perceive it to be threatening and may start moving away from it before it lands, hence, before any physical contact occurs. But will they do so if our energy is not threatening but concerned? Let us take slapping as an example, and here I am referring to a pretty hard slap anywhere on the horse's body with the exception of the head and between the hind legs. What would normally happen if you were to slap your horse nice and hard? They would move away, would they not? Of course they would but only if they perceive the energy accompanying the slap to be threatening.

What if I were to tell you that I slap my horse and not just mine but my partner's too? What if I were to tell you that my partner slaps her mare and mine too? And what if I were to tell you that both mares come to us when they want to be slapped and position their bodies in front of us, so that we can deliver the slap to exactly where they require it? Actually, our horses do not normally do this. They only do so in the warmer months when horse and other flies descend upon them, reducing their lives to fly-bitten misery. Even when wearing fly mesh, there are still occasions when a horsefly alights on the mares' thin summer coats and the only sure way of liquidating it is to slap it smartly. Our horses know that we are helping them when we do this and they are willing to accept the slaps – and even beg for them – if this is what it takes to eliminate the pests. And how do they know? By the words we speak? By our energy? If not by our energy, what then?

Then there is the energy which accompanies physical contact but without any physical pressure being exerted. This type of energy I discovered entirely by chance while trying to ask a horse in my care to raise their head from their pile of hay to allow me to clean their eyes (I preform a good deal of physical care while the horses eat, as they seem to be much calmer and more amenable). Describing how I do this may perhaps illustrate what I mean more graphically than an abstract attempt at explanation. Essentially, I place my hand under the neck or jaw of the horse while standing just to their side. Fully present in the moment, I suddenly stand up erect, all my energy and intent directed at ensuring that the horse raise their head but my hand below their neck or jaw, while remaining present, does not itself exert any physical pressure and merely serves as a conduit for the energy. This action I might accompany with a verbal request, such as 'Head up'. Although I do not usually need to employ this technique as the horses habituate themselves quite quickly to routines, it does illustrate horses' sensitivity to energy and the resultant difference in their response to the physical contact.

Where energy is not accompanied by physical contact, horses tend to respond differently on the whole. Instead of resisting such energy, they appear to be more inclined to yield to it and to do so far more readily than in the case of physical contact, provided that the source of the energy is a creature who has presence or inspires fear. In this case too the reason is quite straightforward in that it lies within the nature of horses to do so. On the odd occasion when a horse is faced with a perceived danger, they almost instinctively seek to flee first. Well this is precisely what explains in part why horses are likely to yield to such energy in the absence of physical contact where it is perceived to be that of an actual or potential threat.

Horses also appear to respond very differently to contact-free energy, depending on whether they perceive it to be focused on them or not. Indeed, it is precisely this distinction which is so clearly discernible in herd behaviour. By way of an example, in one of the 'herds' in which my mare, Pip, spent part of her life there were two geldings, a heavily built Dutch warmblood gelding called Bentley and a grey Polish quarterhorse dubbed Duke. At the top of the pecking order (this was an arbitrarily chosen 'herd' in captivity), Bentley could pass calmly through the herd without causing any consternation and any horse in his path would defer to him and move out of the way with a similar degree of calm. All the other horses acknowledged his status as the dominant (as in further up the 'pecking order' as opposed to dominating) presence in the 'herd' and yielded to that presence in the knowledge that any pressure which they may have experienced was not directed against them.

Duke, on the other hand, was an aggressive, maladjusted individual who felt a constant need to charge any horse that he felt was entering his rightful domain or was close enough to do so. As a result, all of the other horses with exception of the acknowledged 'leader', Bentley, were frequently sent scattering, almost always creating potentially dangerous situations. Duke directed his aggression towards his herd mates and they responded by ducking out of the way and rushing off to escape his perceived reach. Instead of simply moving out of his path, as they did with Bentley, safe in the knowledge that no aggression was being directed towards them, they immediately felt Duke's focus on them and responded accordingly.

It is precisely this difference in focus, this indirect energy (the energy being directed towards the path, as it were, and not against any horse obstructing it) which lends itself to creative interaction with horses. By assuming the energetical presence of a creature with presence, hence one who does not entertain any doubts about that presence and who therefore has no need to resort to dominant behaviour, it is possible to indirectly induce a horse to acknowledge our presence and ultimately choose to follow it. Those humans, on the other hand, who fail to acknowledge this important difference in focus are left with little choice but to adopt the presence of a Duke, securing compliance through the threat of force. And like Duke, the source of such aggressive behaviour ultimately lies in impotence. Powerless in the absence of any meaningful alternative, the human resorts to unsocial behaviour towards one of the most sociable creatures on the planet.

I find this indirect energy particularly useful when distributing hay in a small 'herd' of horses. Sometimes holding my hand higher than and in front of my head to create the illusion of a 'bigger me' with the hay held in my other arm away from the horses, I move determinedly through the herd without looking at any horse directly and they generally back or turn out of the way, although on occasion I may need to motion them away with a slight but 'intentful' (full of intent – a word waiting to be invented) wave of my erect hand.

There is another form of energy in the absence of physical contact which horses respond to without feeling threatened. I call it 'oblique' energy, as it is a combination of aspects of direct and indirect energy. In this case the energy is directed at the horse but without facing the animal or looking them in the eye. Although the horse is aware that they are being challenged, they do not experience this type of energy as threatening, because it does not appear to be directed at them personally, as it were. I find this form of energy particularly useful for asking a horse to reconsider their decision to abandon their pile of hay to chase a fellow species member away from theirs because they perceive it to be bigger or better. In this case I position myself between the dominant horse (as in higher up the 'pecking order' at that particular point in time) and the subordinate animal (as in lower down the 'pecking order' at that time) and respond to every step of theirs with one of my own, blocking access to the other pile of hay. Calmly and patiently we conduct our little dance, until the message sinks in and the dominant horse returns to their own pile of hay.

Ultimately, all these forms of interaction with the exception of physiological reflex responses are expressions of energetically laden behaviour. In the absence of any restraints or instruments of compulsion, a horse with presence relies predominantly on the energy of their intent when interacting with other members of their species. Other horses respond energetically to the energy which they sense. It is this creative use of energy which defines the energetical horse and nowhere is this more clearly illustrated in the horse than in their capacity for cohesion and synchrony.

Cohesion refers to the tendency of horses to move together, especially when doing so at a pace in excess of more than just walk, particularly at a canter or gallop and to do so dynamically. When they move in this way, they edge close together but without jostling each other, even at speed. Clearly this requires a particularly finely tuned sense of other horses' energy. Analyses of video footage of wild horses fleeing a predator reveal that in such a situation the herd appears to act as a unit, much like a shoal of fish, capable of switching direction at any point through any of the creatures involved even in the frenzy of flight. This they manage to do without colliding with and crashing into each other. Again, this suggests that horses are not only keenly aware of each other's energy but are also able to respond to it instantaneously.

Closely tied to such cohesion is the horse's innate predilection for synchrony. In its most basic form, synchrony denotes simultaneous action, movement or occurrences. In the horse it is most clearly discernible in the natural way in which horses move together, whether in walk, trot or canter, or at the gallop. Such movement occurs in unison or so it seems, even where a change is suddenly evident in their pace, direction or equilibrium. As noted in relation to cohesion, any horse moving in synchrony with another may initiate such a change, even in a herd in flight. The horses gallop together as though they comprise a single living creature, even though their pace, direction and energy level may be altered en masse simply by virtue of any one of their number initiating such change and the rest following suit. It is this capacity for interactively altering synchrony that I wish to reflect in the use of the term, 'dynamic'. In horses dynamic synchrony refers not only to the movement of horses in synchrony with each other but also to their ability to influence its nature – pace, direction, energy level and so forth – dynamically.

The horse's innate energetical nature, could it not be of profound significance to those of us humans who find joy in interacting with them? Does it not also imply that, if another living creature is capable of being influenced by the horse's energy, that we might similarly be capable of doing so if we learned to be open to that energy? Does it not suggest as well that such a being might also be able to influence the horse's energy by using their own to do so? And given humans' extensive knowledge and experience of shaping personal energy, especially in Eastern experiential disciplines and more recently in the West's growing embrace of such practices, does this not point to an avenue which has the potential to completely transform the dynamics of interaction between horse and human if we only learned how to harness our own personal energy?

The sentient horse

The ability to perceive and experience everything that we are capable of perceiving and experiencing within our immediate surroundings is called sentience. This capacity for awareness is something which horses share with us as fellow sentient beings. Except when they are asleep or dozing, they are fully aware of their immediate surroundings. They tend to live more in a state of spon-taneous being, with rational consciousness only kicking in, for instance, when they need to make a decision in relation to their health and well-being or try to determine what it is that we are asking of them. Is it time to find water or food? Is what they sense benign or a threat? What do I do now?

Sentience is something in which horses excel thanks in large part to their physiological and energetical sensitivity, which is far superior to that of us humans. As such, they are far more intensely aware than we are and the scope of the immediate surroundings of which they are aware extends much further than in the case of humans.

There are also other reasons why horses are far more aware than we are. For instance, we humans are frequently paralysed by a dichotomy of our own creation between the mind and the creature of whom it constitutes part, with the result that we all too frequently allow ourselves to be controlled by our mind even if it is anywhere but present in the ever unfolding now. Horses do not suffer from such a debilitating condition. Unlike us, they are always fully present when they are awake, their mind being fully at the service of their awareness of their immediate surroundings and responses to it, be they spontaneous or rational. To the extent that horses do not allow themselves to be hijacked by a wayward mind, as we frequently do, it could also be argued that their presence as sentient beings is far more the norm than in the case of humans for this reason.

Similarly, when given the chance, horses show themselves to be exceedingly curious creatures giving full range to their capabilities as sentient beings. Once they have satisfied themselves that a new phenomenon is not dangerous, for example, by observing the interaction between a trusted creature – another horse or in captivity a dog, cat or their human – and the object in question, they are keen to approach and inspect it using various senses to do so. In some cases such inspection may lead to play, for instance where the new object is capable of being rolled around. We humans tend to be more hesitant or reluctant to engage our capabilities as sentient beings, often because of the demands of our daily agenda or, especially in cities, due to fear of the unknown and the likelihood of encountering another human with dubious intentions. The curiosity of being is snuffed out by the fear of no longer being. We would be forgiven for concluding that humans are predominantly prey animals. Perhaps we could learn from the horse just what it is to be a sentient being ourselves, if we simply started to appreciate their presence as fellow sentient beings instead of prey animals whom we superior humans need to lead and control?

The rhythmical horse

Sentient and simultaneously physiologically and energetically sensitive as they are, horses are readily receptive to anything remotely resembling rhythm. Not only do they pick up on rhythm, they are also capable of employing it as a means of spontaneous communication and connection. As part of their interaction with each other, horses exhibit the use of active and passive rhythm in situations varying from the mundane of everyday grooming in captivity to the drama of fleeing predators in the wild.

Being something that is capable of being felt and experienced at different levels, rhythm represents an essential part of equine bonding. It is both reciprocal (simultaneously active and passive) and synchronised (the movements of the horses involved mirror each other). As such, it is eminently suitable for both expressing and enhancing social rituals and activities. Not only is it evident in mutual grooming but also in play, courtship, grazing and other activities.

Flight too is an exercise in synchronised rhythm to the point of establishing social cohesion through energetical connection and synchronisation on the part of the horses fleeing a predator at and in one and the same time and place. We may wish to recall that in flight the individual bands which make up a herd dissolve and their members merge with each other in synchronised movement. This sees the herd flow over the countryside like a single organism with no apparent leader and any horse within it seemingly capable of changing the pace and direction of the flow.

Have we ever considered whether the horse's innate rhythmical nature could have implications for the way in which we humans interact with them? And have we ever wondered just what those implications might be?

The emotional horse

Whereas sentience refers to the ability to experience things using our senses, such experiences may also have a subjective impact on us to the extent that we may feel joyful or sad, upbeat or disappointed, hurt or mean, elated or angry, or any of a range of other emotions. Much has been written about the difficulties of proving that horses experience emotions. Yet the vast majority of the horse owners and carers with whom I have had contact would be more likely to be astounded by news to the effect that horses do not experience emotions than that they do. Although we always have to contend with the temptations of anthropomorphism (attributing a human rationale to the actions of other creatures), there is enough anecdotal and scientific evidence to conclude that horses also experience emotions, albeit not as many as we do. Some of the main emotions which are common to both horses and humans are fear, anger, sadness and joy. So-called 'secondary' emotions, such as jealousy, revenge, pride, shame and guilt, are the ones that seem to be peculiar to humans and, as such, are not found in horses. Perhaps this says more about human dysfunctionality (where the abnormal becomes the norm) than about equine shortcomings.

Of all their emotions joy is the one in which horses revel. They exhibit joy in their natural playfulness with each other as well as members of other species. It is also the emotion which inspires them when they strut and preen themselves. Indeed, the energy of joy in a human is something which can even flick a horse out of any other emotion, so contagious is it to them. In fact, so powerful is the emotion of joy to a horse, that it is not only capable of being used by a human to overcome equine resistance but can also serve as the horse's self-created reward in the sense that the reward is in the doing. Experience with our own horses has shown this to be the case.

Anaïs is a very 'honest' horse in that she will quickly let me know if I am acting like a horrible, bossy little human. She will resist me with multiple times the force of my insistence that she do or refrain from doing something. And if any human dares to persist in such foolish behaviour, she will rear with or without the individual on board. Yes, I may be able to show her who is boss but all I will have left to deal with is a seething mass of suppressed hostility. Over the years we have learned to inject joy into the equation by turning anything which could remotely be interpreted as resistance on the part of the mare into a celebration of *joie de vivre*. And every single time it works as every self-rewarding exercise does. Anaïs simply softens like butter and actually derives pleasure from the experience, with the result that the entire process reoccurs more readily on each occasion.

The sociable horse

Horses are highly sociable creatures, almost obsessively so, and devote a great deal of time, effort and energy to social pursuits. This is particularly true if we bear in mind that eating is frequently also a social activity and that a great deal of eating occurs in communities of horses. There are some equine ethologists who argue that horses are instinctively sociable for the sole purpose of self-preservation in the face of the constant threat posed by predators, for it is in the herd that they enjoy the best chance of survival. Yet, if we examine the amount of time, energy and effort which horses devote to flight expressed as a percentage of their everyday life when compared to sociability, I wonder whether this is not an example of humans turning reality on its head. While self-preservation is a natural instinct of most, if not all, relatively advanced living creatures, it is far from being a constant conscious preoccupation. In the wild, for instance, flight may consciously preoccupy horses for as little as a tiny fraction of the time which they devote to social affairs, probably consuming a proportionate part of their energy. As such, it beggars belief to imagine that what consumes so little of the horse's conscious time, energy and effort should dominate and hence determine their entire way of life. Of course, this in turn begs the question as to why horses are sociable and what their sociability entails.

Studies of horses in the wild reveal much about their sociable nature and the social structures through which their sociability is channelled. Perhaps the single most obvious factor which differentiates human from horse society is the absence of one of the most powerful barriers to sociability, namely, competition and hence the pursuit of individual advancement at the expense of others. Here

I refer to competition between individuals for resources not merely for survival but also in relation to material pursuits, such as those of power, status and wealth.

Priorities differ in a band of horses in the wild. Individual advancement takes the form of improved well-being rather than the accumulation of material excess, and that of the individual depends on that of the group. With limited exceptions, instead of competing with each other, horses express their sociability by helping each other find feed and water, tend to and educate their young, and groom and play with each other. There are no resources or other material interests to compete for with the exception of stallions challenging each other for access to mares and some of the latter attempting to thwart a stallion from mating with another mare. Even then, the expressions of such forms of competition are highly limited in terms of time, energy and effort.

As telling as the relative absence of competition in communities of horses, so too is the absence of another barrier to sociability in their social structures which we experience in human society, namely, coercive or bought leadership. Humans either vote for leaders every once in a while, following which they are unable to exercise much, if any, influence over them or they succumb to self-proclaimed leaders who employ a combination of fraud, corruption and/or force to assume control over them. And those leaders, whether elected or not, rely on force or the threat of force (law and its enforcement) not only to maintain control over the humans in their power but also to compel them to surrender vast amounts of personal wealth in the form of taxes to fund the prosperity of those leaders and the projects which they have decided on by threatening them with a denial of liberty or some other form of punitive action if they refuse. While some of that wealth may filter back to the humans from which it is effectively appropriate in the form of improved social facilities, much of it is invested in weapons of mass destruction, propping up ineptly run big business operations and funding tax breaks for seriously well-off private individuals and businesses. Yet even in those human societies where there is a semblance of democratic power sharing, the bulk of human preoccupation during the working week is dictated by a tiny elite who have effectively bought their leadership and exercise their decision-making power autocratically with the aid of managers who rule over their relatively powerless subordinates with the aid of the carrot of as little in the way of a wage or salary that they can get away with paying and the stick of financial insecurity through the denial of such income, thereby reducing the primary purpose of everyday life to the pursuit of things material.

While this is a highly simplistic portrayal of human society, it captures the essence of it in its reliance on coercive or bought leadership. Such forms of leadership – and indeed any type of leadership – are utterly alien to horses in their natural environment. Ultimately, a horse is not led, persuaded, cajoled, coerced or blackmailed into following another of their kind, as humans frequently are. There is no horse that promises another the equivalent of a reward if that other horse yields to the first one's wishes, and none that threatens them with retribution if they fail to do so. Such methods of control represent the way of the human. The concepts of 'leadership' and 'leaders' are alien to horses and the model of interaction between horses and humans which is based on them is not only unhelpful but is also potentially harmful to horses in that it is easily misused to abuse horses. This I have dealt with in some detail in the article entitled 'Horses and the Myth of Leadership' in my book, *When Horses Speak and Humans Listen* – see http://www.horsesandhumans.com/mainsite/whsahl.htm for more information).

Contemporary equine ethology has convincingly debunked the myth of rigid hierarchies with top-down authoritarian social structures in communities of horses in the wild. Horses seek to be part of their tightly knit social structures of small bands comprising a larger herd not merely to maximise their chances of survival but predominantly – based on the relative amount of time devoted to it – to indulge their desire for the well-being that social contact and shared endeavours afford them. Yes, the stallion of a harem band does employ force or the threat of it to keep the band together especially at times of perceived danger but he does not lead its members. Rather, it is usually any of the more senior mares in the band who head off to water or other resources and who are followed by the rest of the band, with the stallion taking up position in the rear to protect the weaker, slower horses and round up stragglers. And although the desire to live together in a band may be instinctive in the case of horses in the wild, they do exercise choice in deciding on the band of which they wish to constitute part or in the case of mares the stallion with whom they wish to live and mate. (You may read more about this in the article entitled 'Horses and the Art of Followership' in my book, *When Horses Speak and Humans Listen* – see http://www.horsesandhumans.com/mainsite/whsahl.htm for more information.)

MYTH **BUSTER**

The myth: one horse follows another because the first is higher up the pecking order and, as such, displays leadership by leading the other.

The buster: overall, equine ethology field studies reveal that in their natural surroundings horses do not have fixed hierarchies or pecking orders, nor do they lead each other in the generally accepted human sense of being in charge, commanding, guiding or showing the way. Instead, a horse *chooses* to be with or to follow another of their species. Similarly, a horse may *choose* not to be with or follow another of their kind and this also applies in the case of mares, many of whom *choose* to leave their stallion and join another.

We have already noted the extent to which horses accompany each other in flight. They do this so closely that they cohere into and act as a single organism. Once the perceived threat disappears, the herd comes to rest and then disintegrates, as the horses seek out those socially closest to them and return to their respective bands. This is also an ideal opportunity for any horse inclined to do so, to join another band. In one instance a study revealed that up to thirty per cent of mares actually desert their band to seek a stallion of their choice, although not necessarily only at a time such as this.

Essentially, there are four main reasons why one horse will choose to follow and/or be with another. The most compelling of these is friendship but perhaps not as an enlightened human might care to define it. It is basic and involves feeling, bonding through the gut. Unfortunately, our awareness of friendship amongst horses is largely based on our observations of domestic rather than wild or feral horses. Ethological studies have largely focused on agonistic (conflict-related) behaviour amongst wild horses rather than affiliative (companionship-related) conduct, with the result that this subject matter has not received as much attention in the wild as it has in captivity. Nevertheless, observations of horses in the wild reveal that close friendships may occur between stallions and between stallions and mares but not usually between mares. Essentially, as I experience it with horses and my best friend and partner, friendship is an energetical and emotional confluence of two life forces, which can become more important to the creatures involved than even food. Indeed, they will even risk safety and security to be with each other or to pine. So too with horses.

INSIGHT

Friendship is an energetical and emotional confluence of two life forces, which can become more important to the creatures involved than even food, safety and security. This is true for both horses and humans.

———

Then there is that special form of friendship which also involves a sexual relationship. An example may help here and our mares, Pip and Anaïs, have provided one together with Pingo, a gelding who was castrated late and still behaves like a stallion right down to recruiting his own harem band within a herd of a little under forty horses within twenty-four hours, the only time I have ever seen anything like this occur amongst domesticated horses. Although Pip and Anaïs have been close friends for years now, when Pip was in season, she constantly left her female companion to go in search of her male lover. While the relationship between Pip and Pingo was largely of a sexual nature, they displayed a great deal of tenderness and caring in the way they interacted with each other. Amongst other forms of endearment, they brushed their muzzles against various parts of each other's body, spend time standing close together even to the point of touching, resting the underside of their heads on each other's necks and gently rubbing up and down each other's mane. From time to time Anaïs tried to intervene. She literally moved between them, faced Pingo and pawed the ground. Initially, I thought she was doing this in order to protect Pip but later on I noticed that she herself had come into season and was clearly demanding attention. A little astounded and nonplussed at first, Pingo would ultimately have none of that. He had set his heart on Pip and Anaïs simply had to go. So he chased her away and she withdrew smartly, looking very subdued. Within twenty-four hours Anaïs was no longer in season, yet she again tried to intervene between the lovers. She remained in their vicinity marking her time until the two female friends together returned to being the core of Pingo's harem band after Pip came out of season.

Where such close friendship is not involved, safety and security represent the next compelling reason why one horse will choose to follow and/or be with another. This is why mares and juvenile horses usually acquiesce in a stallion's desire to round them up and take them elsewhere. In this sense the stallion plays the role of a guardian. The need for safety and security are also the reason why horses will readily abandon the immediate bonds of their band to coalesce with other members of their herd in flight. This need will override horses' desire to be socially active with other members of their band but only in circumstances where they perceive it as such.

The third reason why a horse will readily follow or be with another has everything to do with their immediate physical requirements. Horses need feed and water and it is not their stallion who will lead them to it. Usually, it is any one of a number of more senior mares in the band who will do so. They are horses who have earned the trust and confidence of the rest of the members of the band. They have shown that they are capable of finding food and water for the band. In this sense they play the role of provider. Any kind of movement which such a trusted horse makes in a direction which makes sense to other senior members of the band is likely to result in them *choosing* to follow that horse with the foals, adolescents and the stallion taking up the rear.

Finally, there is partnership. The horses that comprise a band treat each other as social partners. This is particularly true in the case of the mares within that band and may explain why there is little evidence available of mares forming close friendships with each other. When they are not eating or sleeping, horses channel the bulk of their time, energy and effort into social activities within their respective bands. More often than not, they revert to their bands once the herd breaks up after flight and similarly choose to remain with them.

There are several conclusions which we can draw from our observations of horses choosing to follow other horses, especially in a captive herd. They may be summarised as follows:

- horses choose whether to follow and/or be with another horse or not;
- horses choose which horse to follow and/or be with;
- similarly, horses can choose not to follow another horse, whenever they want to;
- horses choose to follow or spend time with a friend (and even more so one with whom they have a sexual relationship), partner or a trustworthy horse that serves as a guardian or provider;
- horses exercise this choice as and when the occasion arises;
- following does not imply the existence of a leader;
- as such, followership is a more appropriate model for understanding equine interaction than leadership.

There is a temptation to view following and followership as passive activities. However, because choice plays such a crucial role in determining whether a horse will follow another of this species or not and because such choice is so fully in line with horses' active commitment towards sustaining and preserving the communal nature of their social structure, we need to view following and followership as what they really are, namely, active undertakings with a hidden power which would equate to the subversive in human society.

The pronounced, almost obsessively social nature of horses raises important questions in relation to our understanding of them and what is required of us humans if we would like them to be and interact with us. This is particularly true when viewed in terms of the time, effort and energy which horses devote to being sociable. Perhaps the most important of these questions is this: Is the horse not first and foremost a sociable being rather than a prey animal and a creature of flight? Secondly, if this is the case, would the horse not be open to being and interacting with a human who has the qualities which draws the horse to a guardian, provider, partner and friend? And thirdly, if the horse is open to this, how could we ensure that we have those qualities?

The trusting horse

Given the extensive sociability to which horses are predisposed, it would be surprising if the degree of intimacy which this implies were not inevitably accompanied by trust. After all, being in the close proximity to each other which such sociability not only implies but also entails would as inevitably expose them to risk. Like us humans, horses have a basic need to feel safe and any creature whom they perceive as one who can offer them safety is one whom they will trust to do so. Yet the perceived satisfaction of their desire to be safe is only one of two key aspects of trust in the horse, although it is the basic one.

Horses though are not content to be safe. They do not simply seek to exist. Rather, when given the chance they are intent on living and on doing so well. Mental and emotional well-being are as, if not more, important to them than physical health and safety in some cases. And this they find in their relations with members of their own species but may also do so even with creatures belonging to others. Such relations may take the form of immediate family and wider fraternity (the band of which they comprise part). Amongst their family and fraternity members there are those horses who are followed because they have shown themselves over time to be capable of finding feed, water or refuge from predators. This too is a form of assured trust. In this case it is trust in the dependability and reliability of such horses.

Then there are the close friendships of which horses are capable. When two horses bond with each other, they enthusiastically indulge in mutual intimacies which involve a pronounced degree of personal risk, one which they would not readily assume with any other creature in the absence of such a bond. In that the participants in such a friendship, whether also sexual or otherwise, make themselves vulnerable to each other and the risk of severe disappointment – through no fault of their own or otherwise – this is the type of relationship which we humans can readily comprehend and feel. It involves a degree of self-exposure which suggests the existence of a considerable measure of trust on the part of a horse that is party to such a friendship.

So far in this discussion of trust I have confined myself to proven trustworthiness. The guardian has shown themselves to be dependable and reliable in this capacity, so the horse therefore trusts them. The provider has done the same in relation to food and water, the partner with regard to all that a partner contributes within the band, and the friend in respect of friendship. This begs an important question. How does trust arise in the absence of such proof? After all, there must be a point where a horse decides to trust another of their species before that other horse has had an opportunity to prove their trustworthiness. We know that horses are capable of deciding to trust another creature and that they can do so within minutes. But just what is it that would encourage a horse to do so?

There are a growing number of humans who believe that horses are capable of trusting another creature, even one of another species. But do any grounds exist to sustain such a conviction? To answer this, we need to clarify what we understand 'trust' to mean. The British English dictionary definition usually refers to trust as a 'belief', for example, in the 'reliability, truth, or ability of someone or something' (the Oxford-powered online Lexico dictionary at https://www.lexico.com/en/definition/trust – consulted on 4 November 2019). This implies that trust is always a conscious determination and not a spontaneous response, a conviction arising in response to a cognitive activity rather than a feeling prompted by perception. Yet this is not how we humans experience trust, let alone horses. Very often we listen to another human eloquently enunciating eminently sensible views but instinctively mistrust them, whereas we may intuitively trust someone who is far less articulate but who exhibits meaningful behaviour. Clearly trust is something which we first and foremost feel, at least initially before it extends to also being a belief. In this sense, the Merriam-Webster definition of trust captures its essence more accurately: 'assured reliance on the character, ability, strength, or truth of someone or something' (https://www.merriam-webster.com/dictionary/trust – consulted on 4

November 2019). In this case such reliance may be either rationally or spontaneously assured, and it is more likely to be the latter, at least initially. After all, can the decision to trust another creature in the absence of any proof of their trustworthiness be prompted by anything other than feeling?

The horse in summary

So let us return to where we started, namely, with the claim that the horse is first and foremost a prey animal, a creature of flight. If we take all of these salient aspects of the horse and view them as they are, the essential features of the species, we may summarise them by saying that overall horses:

- are highly responsive and are capable of moving at great speed;
- can cover considerable distances while foraging every single day – if allowed to live freely – something which is essential for their physical well-being;
- are hard-wired to resist rather than yield to physical pressure;
- have a back which is capable of limited load bearing capacity;
- have considerable cognitive powers;
- are a source of and are highly sensitive to energetical influences;
- have highly sensitive senses, more so than humans;
- are always fully aware of their surroundings;
- have a finely tuned predilection for rhythm;
- are as capable as humans of experiencing emotions such as fear, anger, sadness and joy, especially the latter;
- are highly sociable, almost obsessively so, but from the bottom up rather than the top down, inclined – almost subversively – to follow rather than to lead;
- are capable of trust at various levels.

Reading this summary, would we really conclude that we are dealing with a creature that is first and foremost a prey animal, a creature of flight, and that their status as such is decisive in determining their intrinsic nature? Is it not perhaps time to debunk this clichéd definition which is all too often trotted out by way of an introduction to the species?

The myth: the horse is first and foremost a prey animal, a creature of flight and their status as such is decisive in determining their intrinsic nature.

The buster: there is nothing comprising part of the physical, mental or emotional characteristics of the horse which even suggests that the prospect of them falling prey to a predator or of resorting to flight in order to avoid this could be decisive in determining their intrinsic nature. Rather, a review of the primary features of the horse's intrinsic nature reveals that the horse is essentially a creature that is extraordinarily sensitive physically, energetically, rhythmically and emotionally, has fairly advanced cognitive powers, is physically primed for frequent regular and infrequently rapid movement, and relies primarily on social connection for not merely their survival but also their well-being.

It is difficult if not impossible to conclude that horses are very special creatures with whom humans should have relatively little difficulty being and interacting with them while establishing and maintaining mutually beneficial relations without the constant need to resort to tools of restraint, instruments of coercion and behaviourist training. Both species are capable of sensitivity, awareness, cognition, communication through body language and energy, emotion, sociability, rhythm and trust at various levels. Of course, such a conclusion assumes that humans would be willing to exercise such capacity at least almost as readily as horses normally do. And if this were the case, there would be no grounds to sustain Jonathan Swift's depiction of the yahoos in the land of the Houyhnhnms, would there? Instead, might we not all be following in Lemuel Gulliver's footsteps to some or other degree when we discover the intrinsic nature of the horse and start acting accordingly?

Unfortunately, most of us humans have never had the chance to experience the full range of what horses are capable of in the wild. In the vast majority of cases this is because we have never seen them in their natural environment. Where we have seen horses is in captivity and what we see in this abnormal (to the horse) situation is what we assume is normal but is it really?

The horse in captivity

It is probably impossible to address every different way in which we humans keep, train and interact with horses in captivity. Nevertheless, it is possible to draw conclusions about the manner in which horses are generally kept, trained and used in the service of humans. In most cases horses are kept, trained and used as beasts of burden or servitude for the benefit of humans, be it to eke out a living, yield a modest income, generate handsome profits through equestrian sports or otherwise, to provide safety or security, to serve as accessories to the human ego, for recreational purposes or to comprise part of a human meal. There are very few instances where horses are kept in captivity for their own safety and well-being in the absence of such pursuits. And even in some of the few cases in which they are, we may want to ask ourselves whether they are kept, used, related to and interacted with in a manner which is commensurate with their essential nature as horses.

Husbandry

It usually starts before they are born, doesn't it, the impact that human husbandry has on horses? We breed them for one reason or another, in most cases to benefit ourselves. In many cases we create monstrosities through poor breeding choices. I recall sharing a session of The Equine Touch bodywork with a black mare in the south of the Netherlands. She was as massive of physique as she was majestic in presence, so much so that she was quite literally unable to support her own body without experiencing pain. Almost inevitably, the horse was condemned to a premature death. Aside from the equine Frankensteins we create, there are also the vast numbers of horses which we breed in captivity primarily for the pursuit of fame and gain through equestrian 'sport'. In many, if not most, cases we fail to breed horses that are physically capable of the career which we have chosen for them. And even if they are, there is a huge likelihood that they do not have the mental and/or emotional capacity to cope with the huge demands made of them in the name of equestrian 'sport'. The few horses that are deemed suitable for 'sport' are snapped up by the equestrian establishment to serve as a source of human earnings and a bearer of human fame, while the rest are unleashed on an army of would-be equestrian stars, often at rock-bottom prices, without any warning as to why they are rejects.

And just how are horses raised in captivity? If they are lucky, they may spend their entire, most or much of their time as foals with their dam and perhaps with one or two other horses of varying age as well but almost never with their sire. And if their luck holds, they may just learn some of the equine social graces that are handed down to varying degrees despite human attempts, witting and unwitting, to inhibit this. In such a situation they will almost inevitably grow up in physical conditions which do not permit the range of movement (and perhaps even nutrition) which they would otherwise have enjoyed had they been raised in the wild, movement which is indispensable for optimum healthy physical development, their bones and muscles in particular. In some cases foals are rounded up and carted off to rearing farms, where they are kept together in age groups, the yearlings on their own, the two-year-olds on their own and so forth in the absence of any older horses of varying sex, age and experience, with the result that they grow up without the social graces common to horses held in a herd. It would be difficult not to produce a socially dysfunctional horse in conditions such as these.

Whichever way horses are raised in captivity, it is highly likely that they will be weaned prematurely and will not be brought up in a harem band within a herd, as they would have been in natural conditions, with the result that they may be traumatised or their social and physical development is likely to be stunted to some or other degree at best.

As adults, horses are generally kept either on their own or in groups of varying size. Such groups are often euphemistically referred to as 'herds' but this is a misnomer as a herd or band within one is a phenomenon which occurs in the wild and is formed organically and ultimately on the basis of choice rather than human whim (however well-intended) as is the case in captivity. Being the subject of arbitrary human decision, horses in captivity are often forced into close proximity with others of their species whom they would not ordinarily be drawn to were they in the wild. Alternatively, a horse may develop a very close friendship with another one, only to have it broken up by a human exercising the rights of control which they have abrogated to themself.

An animal – in this case a horse – that is designed to move great distances while interacting closely and almost constantly with their own kind as part of an organically selected group of members of their own species, is effectively cut off from the social contact that they instinctively seek in order to ensure not only their well-being but also their very survival. This occurs not just anywhere but in a relatively tiny confined space in which, unlike in a herd or small band comprising part of one, the horse has no choice but to urinate and defecate in the place where they eat and sleep. Their forced living quarters become their 'toilet' in which they are held in solitary confinement – in a worst-case scenario – being released for controlled exercise with a human one to two hours a day if they are more fortunate than those whose training regime offers less frequent interaction. And in many cases such solitary confinement also entails no access to fresh air and daylight.

Of course, this is an extreme, albeit all too frequently practiced, example of human control over a horse's living conditions. Let us assume that most horse owners are more enlightened and that their horses are turned out during the day with other members of their species. Those horses will certainly be much better off than their counterparts in solitary confinement in their loo. Nevertheless, we need to be aware that they will still spend up to half or more of their lives locked up in their toilets.

Even in those parts of the world in which space is abundant enough to allow horses to be kept outdoors all of the time, horses' living conditions are compromised. If such horses are not held in a field or paddock on their own, they are kept in the company of others whose company they have not sought but which has been dictated by some or other human. They may or may not have shelter available and they may or may not be rugged. If they are rugged, the chances are that the rug is not changed to accord with the prevailing conditions as and when they change. In some cases they may even be 'over-rugged', the implication of the term being that the horse is wearing an excessively warm rug or too many rugs. It is assumed that a rug is a natural and welcome protection for the horse, even where science shows otherwise. More often than not, the size of the field or paddock to which such horses are confined, is too small to permit the range of movement which horses ordinarily require. This is also true in fields which, although very large, still fall well short of that range.

The relatively recent emergence and spread of the 'natural horsemanship' movement in many parts of the world has ushered in a welcome change to horses' living conditions and, as such, has eliminated many of the behavioural problems humans took to be the norm as part of the conventional approach. As far as possible horses are increasingly kept in conditions which try to emulate what they would ideally experience in the wild, chief amongst them being liberty to move at will and to do so as part of a herd of sorts without any metal on their feet to restrict the essential pumping mechanism of the hoof. True, it is far from ideal. The area in which such horses are confined is a tiny fraction of what they would have access to in the wild, where their free-living counterparts cover huge distances by comparison every single day while they forage. Nevertheless, such horses live barefoot in the open with access to shelter, where they have space to move and opportunities to interact with others of their kind, the physical and emotional benefits contributing to their overall well-being and helping them avoid most of the behavioural problems which their stabled counterparts still have to contend with.

Given the fact that horses in captivity do not move sufficiently over appropriate surfaces to ensure optimum health, we humans are used to the fact that the quality of their hooves is inevitably impaired. After all, the hooves consist of tissue which adapt to their nutrition, use and the conditions in which they move. As such, they need to be cared for and protected. Apart from the various dressings which we apply to horses' hooves, usually in vain (as their essential quality comes from within and not from without) and often to their detriment, the most beneficial way in which we can protect them is to put protective but flexible shoes on them – or at least only on the forehooves, which bear most of the horse's weight – so as not to compromise their pumping mechanism. There is a drawback to this option though and it is that these shoes cannot be kept on the hooves permanently. Preferably, they are only used when required and are removed for at least a few hours a day to allow the hooves to dry and harden. Of course, this is a source of inconvenience to us humans, so we prefer to have metal studs nailed to their hooves permanently and euphemistically refer to them as 'horse shoes'. The rationale for this is that the hooves require constant protection because they are weak or have excessively thin soles. Yet this is a condition which is usually caused precisely by the use of metal studs and the lack of movement. After all, it is frequent contact with the ground which causes soles to thicken, as every human who has spent much of their childhood going barefoot can tell you. When I was a kid, my soles thickened and hardened to such an extent that I could walk on stony paths and roads with little difficulty. This was due to frequent movement over precisely such surfaces. The soles of horses' hooves thicken in more or less the same way. Deprive the horse of frequent movement over hard ground and their soles will simply not thicken and harden. In addition, little imagination is required to understand the extent to which metal nails damage the hoof wall, the degree to which rigid metal studs compromise the hooves' pumping mechanism and the extent to which they constrain the hooves' overall development.

Training

Perhaps the area in which we humans are more aware of the control that we exercise over horses than in any other lies in our interaction with them. We feel a need to control horses, so as to ensure that we are safe when we care for them and in order to use them for the purpose which we have assigned to them. Over the years we have devised a myriad of devices, tools, gadgets, gizmos, structures and methods to confine, restrain, immobilise and move horses, all of which rely on a mechanical and mechanistic approach involving – at least initially – the use of force or the threat of it, or a bribe in the form of a treat. Training is perhaps the most vivid example of this in action. We may train our horses to enable us to look after them and we may train them to perform in the field of activity that we have chosen for them. Usually we feel a need to do so, because our horse seems to be far from wanting to be a willing partner. And often we fail to understand why this is the case. Could it possibly be because of the conditions in which we force them to live and interact with us, conditions which are utterly alien to their nature? And then we resort to training to address the problems created by those conditions only to compound the problem by the very nature of the training that we employ. To resolve the problems created by control, we resort to even more control.

And what exactly is the nature of conventional training? Is it geared to the needs of the horse or the deficiencies of the human? More often than not, humans 'break in' and 'work' horses long before their physiques have formed well enough to enable them to withstand the physical demands made on them. 'Breaking in' (aptly named and disarmingly honest) is usually a process whereby a horse is taught the futility of resistance to a human's desire to ride them or use them for some other purpose and is normally accompanied by an array of practices designed to numb the horse's natural sensitivity, crush their equally natural curiosity and instil what could come spontaneously to the horse if only the human knew how to elicit it, namely, the horse's acceptance of and cooperation with the human.

Then finally the training itself can begin. More often than not in the conventional tradition it is referred to as 'work', a concept which many, if not most, humans use to describe the daily, soul-deadening drudgery they tolerate in order to earn enough money to escape from it during weekends and holidays (often with their horses). Yet it is precisely more often than not that humans inflict a similar daily, soul-deadening drudgery on their horses, which takes the form of negative reinforcement or even punishment using various implements taken from their armoury of metal and leather restraints, and instruments designed to inflict various degrees of discomfort or pain, more often than not for little more than the human's personal leisure, pleasure, status or gain.

Well before any horse training commences, humans generally find that horses are often anything but the overall calm, sociable and playful – albeit alert – creatures that they are in their natural surroundings. And this is often evident in their approach to them. Generally speaking, such humans are either supremely confident or exceptionally cautious. Such caution is evident in the efforts they make to stay out of their horse's dynamic zones, a euphemism for the areas deemed close enough to the hooves or teeth as to be in danger of being kicked or bitten. And when they are required to move in close and run the risk, they generally stay to the side close to their horse's head, one hand firmly grasping the lead rope or reins immediately under their chin, as though they really do have a remote hope of controlling a collection of living bones, muscles and potentially dangerous surfaces weighing the equivalent of a smallish car should it decide to resist.

At the other end of the scale are those who have sufficient confidence either in their ability to dominate their horse with the aid of a toolbox of rope, leather, plastic and metal restraints and instruments of coercion which have come to inspire an entire branch of sadomasochistic practices amongst humans known as 'ponyplay', or in their ability to secure a 'bomb-proof' equine through training or psychological manipulation to the point of inducing learned helplessness in their equine friend. Those who rely on these implements make frequent reference to 'lightness' or 'softness', as in the 'lightness of the aids' (using a double bridle, two bits, steel spurs and a whip) or 'softness' of the horse (using a harsh rope halter, a stick-cum-whip device and repressive psychological manipulation). I say this not to disparage the practitioners who employ such implements but merely to illustrate the futility of much of their efforts, for long before any training begins, we humans usually have to contend with horses that are severely traumatised to a greater or lesser extent by what we inflict on them through the way we keep them in captivity, let alone what we do in the name of training, with the result that we need to ask ourselves just how much of the sensitive, sentient horse is left by the time we are finished.

At this point I can almost sense the indignation which such an unflattering synopsis and conclusion may arouse. But pause for a moment and consider the essence of the horse which I have sought to describe above, their physiological bias, potential and limitations, and their capacity as cognitive, sentient, energetically communicative, emotional, sociable, rhythmical and trusting beings. And then reflect on the way that we breed, raise and keep horses, as well as the extent to which this conflicts with their essential nature. If we weigh everything up, would it not instead be startling to discover a horse in captivity that is not traumatised by what we humans do to and with them?

And we have still not examined horse training in any detail yet. It is time that we do. If we go in search of horse training alternatives, it would seem that there are so many types, methods, approaches and techniques available, that it is extremely difficult, if not impossible, to assess what horse training is along with its impact on horses in captivity. Yet, if we dig a bit deeper, it soon becomes apparent that on the whole the training which we humans undertake is solely designed to influence or modify horse behaviour and to do so for the sole purpose of ensuring that horses do or refrain from doing precisely what we want, and how and when we want it. This also applies in those cases where we insist that the purpose of such training is to benefit the horse. Ultimately, it is we who decide what will be of such benefit and not the horse.

Before we even consider the nature of such behavioural (and 'behaviourist' in that it is an example of behaviourism in action) horse training, it is imperative that we note the limitations which we place on both ourselves and the horse by confining both species to this type of training. Why is it imperative that we do so? Quite simply because these limitations are so severe as to render it utterly impossible for horses and humans to communicate with each other freely, spontaneously and authentically while the horses are exhibiting the conditioned behaviour which such training produces and – in the case of negative reinforcement or punishment (and arguably to some extent in the case of positive reinforcement) – while such training occurs.

Yes, it is true that much of what a horse learns may condition their behaviour and that, as such, no training is required for this purpose. However, learning is not the same as training. Indeed, it is important that we draw a sharp distinction between learning and training. This is because, when a horse learns in the absence of training, they are the author of their own education either wittingly or unwittingly and it occurs spontaneously. When a human trains a horse, the latter is no longer the author of their own learning. Rather, their learning is controlled by the trainer and what they may learn through the trainer's control is not necessarily what the trainer intends. Such learning is not spontaneous and, because it is not, it almost inevitably elicits resistance from the horse, unless it is accompanied by the joy factor, which we have already discussed. In such a situation the horse is not a willing partner by definition.

There are many humans who are far more familiar with conventional training theory than I am and who are more capable of explaining it to you. In the course of such an explanation you are likely to hear terms bandied about, such as 'associative' or 'non-associative learning', 'habituation', 'sensitisation', 'operant' and 'classical conditioning', 'positive' and 'negative reinforcement' and 'punishment', amongst others.

Broadly speaking, conventional training theory draws a distinction between 'associative' and 'non-associative' ways in which horses learn. Associative learning may occur through operant (also sometimes called instrumental) and/or classical conditioning, while habituation and sensitisation are forms of non-associative learning. As a form of training, habituation takes the form of exposing a horse to a disconcerting stimulus until they become so used to it as to tolerate it easily. An example of such habituation would be where a horse becomes used to what they would normally regard as frightening, for instance, the noise of a motorbike. Trainers rely on habituation to desensitise horses to such ostensibly threatening stimuli, especially in the early part of their training. There are also trainers who resort to restraints and compulsion to forcibly habituate horses to an overwhelming abundance of certain stimuli that they would normally perceive as threatening. This is known as 'flooding'.

As a form of training, sensitisation occurs where a horse is exposed to a phenomenon so frequently that they become more sensitive to it. This is the theory and it is used to explain why horses become more 'sensitive' to the aids in classical riding, the aids including the use of leather and metal restraints, and other instruments of coercion, such as bridles, bits, spurs and whips. Of course this 'explanation' is nonsense, as the horse is more likely to simply learn to be very wary of the threat of force represented by them. Alternatively what may become sensitive is the communication which finally occurs between the rider and the horse when the former eventually learns to use their body and energy to communicate with the horse rather than rely on the instruments of coercion. Such sensitivity occurs despite the aids (rather than because of them).

Classical conditioning involves a human teaching a horse a secondary form of reinforcement (of the desired behaviour) through association. An experiment conducted by the well-known researcher, Ivan Pavlov (1849-1936), into the relationship of salivation and the movements of the stomach in dogs best illustrates this type of training. As part of this experiment a bell was rung at the same time as Pavlov fed his dog, who salivated when they saw the food. With repetition the dog came to associate the food with the bell and salivated as soon as they heard it, irrespective of whether or not they were offered any. This Pavlov referred to as a 'conditioned reflex' and called the process of acquiring it 'conditioning'. Clicker training is partly based on this approach, the clicker serving as the secondary reinforcement. The primary reinforcement on which any secondary reinforcement occurs normally takes the form of operant conditioning, which some trainers view as amongst the most important forms of training.

Operant conditioning involves the horse learning that, if they behave in a certain way, they will be rewarded or punished. The reward may take the form of a pleasant experience on its own to encourage the replication of the behaviour rewarded, such as a treat, or one which involves relief from an unpleasant experience, for example, the application of pressure followed by relief from that pressure when the desired behaviour is exhibited. In the former case we refer to positive reinforcement and in the latter negative reinforcement. The aim in both cases is to encourage the replication of the behaviour rewarded.

Punishment, and positive and negative reinforcement are not mutually exclusive and may be used together and in conjunction with classical conditioning with or without further refinements which extend beyond the scope of this discussion. Essentially, punishment involves forcing the horse to undergo an unpleasant experience. Such an experience may take the form of the application of an unpleasant stimulus, such as a shock (referred to as 'positive punishment', an oxymoron to many) or the withdrawal of a pleasant stimulus, such as food ('negative punishment'), in order to punish unwanted behaviour. What should also be noted with regard to negative reinforcement, timing is everything. If the unpleasant stimulus is not removed at exactly the right moment, some form of behaviour may be reinforced other than that which the trainer deems to be desirable. Taken to the extreme, negative reinforcement coupled with the psychological manipulation which is so typical of the 'natural horsemanship' approach to training can actually produce learned helplessness in the horse. At the very least it results in stress, very often severe. Yet I have also even seen such stress exhibited in horses trained with the aid of positive reinforcement.

Where training occurs with the aid of positive reinforcement, the reward which is provided to reinforce desired behaviour often takes the form of a treat. Probably the most well-known form of positive reinforcement is clicker training, which combines this form of operant conditioning, usually involving the use of treats, with classical conditioning in its use of a secondary reinforcement (the clicker) ultimately as a replacement for the primary reinforcement (the treat). A further refinement may involve the substitution of the clicker with a more subtle trigger to elicit the conditioned behaviour. As in the case of negative reinforcement, timing is crucial if positive reinforcement is to serve as an effective approach to horse training. It also involves the risk of training undesirable behaviour where the trainer's timing is off.

Anecdotal evidence suggests that the use of treats as a means of positive reinforcement may backfire depending on the horse's response. Anaïs, one of our mares, may serve as an example in this respect. She is highly food-focused, something which anecdotal evidence suggests she has in common with other orphan foals. Even when the timing was spot on, she became so obsessed with food rewards that she started to beg for treats. It was not that she mugged Vicki (my partner and wife) or myself for food. On the contrary, she made a point of avoiding physical contact while inching as close to the source of treats (she has a superb sense of smell) as possible. Of greater concern though was Anaïs' tendency to reproduce conditioned behaviour of her own volition and to follow this up with a nose in our direction to solicit a reward. Clearly, she is not a horse we were keen on continuing to train using rewards, even though she is a very quick learner. Clicker training was therefore abandoned.

It is said in defence of positive reinforcement that the horse is always at liberty to walk away. But is this really true? Is not the appeal of the reward so great, that freedom of choice is effectively removed and replaced with control albeit a vastly more benign form than in the case of negative reinforcement? Yet I have also even seen stress exhibited in horses trained with the aid of positive rein-forcement both while being trained and when called up to reproduce conditioned behaviour. Having said this, I am equally quick to insist – on the basis of what I have seen others do – that there can be a role for positive reinforcement to facilitate initial communication with a traumatised horse, which might otherwise be too difficult or impossible. This may be beneficial until sufficient trust develops between horse and human to permit genuinely voluntary, spon-taneous communication between the species.

At this stage it may seem to be very tempting to argue the merits and shortcomings of positive and negative reinforcement. Let us resist the temptation for there is nothing to gain in terms of insight by pursuing that avenue. Instead let us consider behaviourist training as a whole and contemplate its implications. Whether it is positive or negative reinforcement or punishment, habituation and so forth, what we are dealing with here is behaviour modification using a mechanical means employed in a mechanistic fashion and the behaviour which is produced is conditioned rather than the spontaneous expression of the horse's free will. As such, neither the training nor the outcomes which it achieves call upon the horse to utilise much or any of their essential characteristics as outlined above. Trust is rendered absolutely superfluous where acquiescence or obedience is achieved through conditioned behaviour. So too is cognition, or largely so, for little or nothing resembling knowledge or understanding is acquired where behaviour is modified through the mechanistic use of mechanical means. And all that is required in the way of sentience is sensitivity to the demands of negative reinforcement or the promises of positive reinforcement, and the demands of the one and the promises of the other necessitate little in the way of any meaningful communication in any form whatsoever, especially any that could be remotely construed as voluntary and spontaneous.

In short, behaviourist horse training as it is usually practised ignores the full spectrum of the horse's potential for the sociable interaction of which they are capable and for which they have a natural proclivity. As such, while behaviourist training actually occurs, we render it absolutely impossible for the horse to interact with us using more than a mere fraction of what they not only have to offer as sociable beings but what they would naturally seek to share with us were they invited to do so. Their natural curiosity and capacity to seek solutions are snuffed out, their enormous sensitivity is dulled and in the vast majority of cases they are also denied the *joie de vivre* on which they thrive. Indeed, we even deny them the ability to communicate with us as fellow sentient beings and then use this inability as an excuse to justify more of the same behaviourist training. If there has ever been anything that has the effect of dumbing down the horse, this is it: behaviourist training.

What is perhaps as sad to note is what behaviourist training has come to mean to so many of us humans. Because relatively few of us have had the opportunity to experience genuinely voluntary, spontaneous communication with horses, many if not most of us assume that such communication is impossible. We then look for alternative means of communication and assume that this can only occur through horse training. And as the vast bulk of such training is of a behavioural and behaviourist nature, we then assume that it represents the only means available to communicate with horses. Indeed, many humans seem to be incapable of conceiving that any alternative form of interaction could bridge the communication gap between horses and humans. Is this simply because we just do not know the horse?

Use

The vast majority of the horses that are held in captivity are used and we humans are the ones that use them. More often than not we use them as beasts of burden, the burden being ourselves or anything else we insist that horses bear, carry, pull or drag. Sometimes we require that they perform particular physical movements while they do so, whether it be jumping, rearing, Spanish pass, *haute ecole* or other tricks, or that they simply accept being pulled into a frame and ridden against the bit or noseband (to create the semblance of natural collection) in mindless, boring figures for up to an hour or more at a time. Alternatively, we may prefer to compel them to move without a burden, while we chase them around in endless, soul-deadening circles in circular enclosure with its never-ending fence line. Our use of horses varies enormously. But strip away the specific circumstances to bare the essence of our use of horses and it becomes a relatively simple matter to note the implications of such use.

Why we choose to use the horse is utterly irrelevant to the horse, be it in the name of gain, fame or love, unless the horse actually knows that it is to help them, for instance when implementing a convalescence rehabilitation exercise regime while recovering from an injury. Yes, horses can feel and understand the energy of genuine concern for and commitment to their well-being, and they respond accordingly. Our horses actually seek our assistance when they need help, for instance, when they want us to swat a horse fly on their neck or to scratch the rear section of their belly. They will stand still to let us flush out the fistula left after removing a molar and open their mouth to allow us to syringe the cavity clean. Such behaviour also extends to activities which could be interpreted as 'use' of the horse. For example, when I was helping Pip recover from a severe tendon injury in her right foreleg, I needed to implement a daily exercise regime which increased in increments of effort and challenge over time. This I coupled with Equine Touch bodywork and red-light therapy. Over the course of four months Pip was conscious of my concern and commitment to the extent that she cooperated fully either at liberty or with nothing more than a soft, lined webbing halter attached to a lead rope which always had a 'smile' of slack in it, even when we walked and ran through the forest.

'Yes, but he has his ears forward, so it can't be too bad.' You may have heard this or something similar mentioned to justify the involvement of a horse in some or other activity. And true, the horse may have their ears forward. Yet horses may also hold their ears forward when they flee either physically or psychologically. My Pip used to be a great one for the latter. If you wanted her to trot around in circles, she would. Faster? Fine. No matter that her saddle dug into her right shoulder at one end and extended over her lumbar region at the other. She would put her ears forward and simply escape from the pain and discomfort by withdrawing into herself and travelling on autopilot. Pressed hard enough, horses are survivors and in order to survive, they need to mask weakness one way or another. Let us not be fooled by one small body part. Rather, let us view the entire horse and above all feel the energy in the moment. It is only then that we will truly have some sense of what the horse is feeling.

This experience with Pip is also what I refer to as the willing victim syndrome. Take a sect, for instance. The members of a sect, more often than not women, place themselves at the mercy of its leader, all too often a man, in that they surrender personal control to the latter to some or other extent. There is a potential for abuse, which frequently materialises. The sect leader attempts to excuse their abuse by claiming that the victim allowed it to happen and that it is therefore not abuse. In some cases the victim may acknowledge this and blame themself. Should this be the end of it? Absolutely not! This line of reasoning is premised on the assumption that someone else should be held accountable for the sect leader's failure to accept responsibility for their own actions, namely, their refusal to live up to the trust which their victim has placed in them. And instead of accepting their responsibility in this respect, they lay the blame for their failure to do so on the very person who suffers as a result of their refusal to live up to the latter's trust. Ultimately, all of us are responsible for our own acts and omissions independently of anyone else, so too a sect leader. In the absence of any condition or circumstance which can excuse such responsibility, we may safely assume that a sect leader is aware that certain acts or omissions on their part would amount to abuse irrespective of whether or not their victim acquiesced in them, and that they are capable of refraining from such abuse. After all, acquiescence is not the same as conscious, considered consent.

So what does this have to do with horses? The willing victim syndrome normally (actually it is abnormal) occurs in grossly dysfunctional relationships of inequality where the party with more power knowingly abuses the other, weaker party. I have mentioned the relationship between a sect leader and a member as an example. A similar type of relationship may be found between a rock music celebrity (more often than not male) and a groupie (usually female). The violently dysfunctional relationship between an aggressive husband and a battered wife is another example, albeit an extreme one. And so too is the relationship between a human who abuses a horse and the horse that they abuse. The use of horses for racing from the tender age of two or three, when their bones are far from formed and they are consequently vulnerable to severe physical harm in addition to the mental and emotional stress to which they are subjected may be viewed as a viciously vivid example of such a grossly dysfunctional relationship.

Yet such an unequal relationship between horse and human can also occur at what might seem to be a more mundane and seemingly innocent level. I recall reading an interview with a very famous dressage rider who claimed that her horse did not like to be turned out all day but actually preferred to return to the stable in the middle of the day. Intrigued by such utterly uncharacteristic behaviour on the part of a horse, I continued reading in the hope of stumbling upon an explanation. Lo and behold, there was one. Not too far further on in the same interview I learned the reason for this anomaly. Apparently, the horse got fed in their stable at the same time each day. When? In the middle of the day. Small wonder that the horse wanted to cut short their turnout at that time of the day to return to their stable. As such, the horse was a willing victim of their owner's decision to curtail their freedom every single day of their life. This is but one small example of a horse acting as a willing victim in the service of a human who wittingly abuses or unwittingly misuses them. Countless more, many with more horrendous consequences for the horse, occur every single day. But because the horse is a willing victim in cases such as this, we often fail to see most of them.

In the absence of any knowledge of such concern and commitment on the part of their human, the horse simply experiences their use by humans as an exercise in control, domination and/or hostility, and they respond accordingly, more often than not simply tolerating what occurs while displaying signs of pain, anxiety or fear. Sadly, research indicates that a very significant majority of 'horse people', even professionals, cannot recognise such signs and are more likely than not to involve their own horses in activities which give rise to pain, anxiety or fear in those sensitive animals. In such a situation, the horse is a willing victim while being unwittingly misused rather than wittingly abused. Of course, such a distinction is effectively academic to horses. As they experience them, the effects are identical, differing only in degree.

Pressed hard enough, horses are survivors and in order to survive, they need to mask weakness one way or another. Let us not be fooled by one small body part and what we think that it may be communicating. Rather, let us view the entire horse and above all *feel* the energy in the moment. It is only then that we will truly have some sense of what the horse is feeling.

Do those of us humans who keep, use or train horses not have a duty to do all that we reasonably can to understand the intrinsic nature of the horse, so as to be able to recognise when they are in physical, mental or emotional pain or discomfort with a view to alleviating it? And where our horses are willing victims of our abuse or misuse, are we not called upon to acknowledge that responsibility for our actions is not contingent on what they allow us to do to or refrain from doing for them but is entirely independent of them and ours alone? So where do we start?

Our starting point with the horse

The knowledge that humans have of horses is impressively extensive, if the number of books, magazines, research papers, websites, audio-visual documentaries and films is anything to go by, not to mention the reflection of humans' understanding and imagination of the horse in our culture and the arts. It is testimony to the hugely important role which the horse has played and continues to play in human history, arguably more so than in the case of any other animal. Personally, I am astounded by the extensive knowledge that even ordinary horse carers have about so many different aspects of horse husbandry and training, everything from breeding and feeding through to medical treatments and the disposal of an equine corpse.

And yet, if we humans are utterly honest with ourselves, when we examine the way in which we keep, use, relate to and interact with horses, we must confess that the bulk of the available evidence reveals a profound ignorance on our part of the intrinsic nature of the horse. In almost all of the ways in which we keep, use, interact with and relate to horses we exhibit an extensive, detailed knowledge about horses but very little understanding of the horse.

We have become so alienated from horses, creatures that have played such a major role in individual human lives and the development of human society in general, that we are unable to relate to them as fellow sentient beings and we fail to see that the way we generally keep and train horses is so completely unnatural and bizarre that it generates a huge amount of stress in them and inhibits their natural predisposition for the highly sociable interaction and capacity for learning that they exhibit in the wild, if equine ethologists are to be believed. More often than not, this is our starting point with horses in captivity: highly stressed and traumatised creatures exhibiting stressful, if not violent or evasive, behaviour, with the result that chaos is just around the corner. This is not the natural condition of the horse but one that we humans – and no one else – have created.

With few exceptions, if any, we humans have also become so alienated from our essential nature that we have to all intents and purposes lost our humanity. We no longer know how to live consciously and joyfully. Instead, our lives are controlled by the need to fit in with other people's agendas, priorities and deadlines, be it as an employee, self-employed or unemployed individual or in any other capacity. *Joie de vivre* has been replaced with either the daily struggle to survive or the pursuit of achievements, objects, the latest gizmos, gadgets, various forms of self-pampering and so forth. And when we are not doing that, our minds draw us away from life in an endless contemplation of what-if scenarios, fears and regrets. On top of this many, if not most, of us are still working through past traumas. More often than not, this is the baggage we take with us to the horse and we are astounded when the horse shows us that they want nothing to do with it. (Of course, this should not be confused with those times when a horse approaches a human with personal issues and does so of their own accord.)

And how many of us have really taken the time and made the effort to discover ourselves and to develop our potential to live a conscious, joyful life? How many of us have discovered how horses respond to joy? I am not talking about raucous laughter but calm contentment and the ability to turn frustration into a smile. Our mare, Anaïs, has a pretty direct way of communicating her displeasure or disagreement. She resists and rears majestically. In the past we used to insist and she used to resist. Now, we simply back off and turn the situation into a game of sorts as part of which she gets to choose. She picks up the energy of joy and immediately softens like butter and everything becomes possible. Nothing would have changed, however, if we had not done so as well.

INSIGHT

The intrinsic nature of the horse makes it possible for us to approach them on the basis of choice rather than control, connection instead of coercion, and communication as opposed to conditioning.

So why should we change? The reason is simple and it starts with the horse. An understanding of the intrinsic nature of the horse points to the opportunity to employ a completely new paradigm in our approach to the horse, one based on choice rather than control, connection instead of coercion, and communication as opposed to conditioning. It is an approach which appeals to the growing tide of humans around the world who are searching for a new way of being with horses, one that is more in tune with their needs and require-ments as equines, which also contributes to their psychological and emotional well-being, and which facilitates understanding and trust between the species. This is not some pie-in-the-sky, air-fairy fantasy. Rather, it is a reality that I now experience with my own horses without tools of restraint, instruments of coercion and conscious training. And it is a dream that any human can live if they are really committed to doing so. Yet it is also in this that the horse lays down a challenge for us and it is the challenge of choice.

THE CHALLENGE

Put another way, the challenge which the horse lays down for the human is this: How can I become the kind of human a horse seeks to be with? How can I become the type of being a horse chooses to follow or to spend time with doing either something or nothing?

The very first thing to notice about this challenge is that it does not concern the horse but the human. It is not the horse that we need to train and change. It is the human. You, me or any other human who wishes to become the kind of being whom a horse enjoys being and interacting with, we need to change, not the horse. Without a commitment to such change on our part we will not be able to rise to this challenge.

———

INSIGHT

It is not the horse that we need to train and change. It is the human. It is me!

———

What? Not the horse? The horse does not need to change? What about that aggressive horse that nearly tried to kill me last week? And the one that is so traumatised that they have shut down completely? And that other one…? Yes, there are horses that, on the face of it, do need to change or so it would seem. Generally speaking though, horses exhibiting such systems are traumatised and in many, if not most cases, humans are responsible for their trauma. Unless and until such humans commit to change and start to become the kind of human a horse enjoys being and interacting with, they will always have to rely on control to do anything resembling 'meaningful' with such a horse. In my experience, once a horse carer commits to becoming a human for horses, they start to create the conditions in which such a traumatised horse reconnects with themself and the healing process commences. Within weeks, if not days, the horse's behaviour starts to change as they settle down in the absence of threats and start to trust again. Within months the healing is profound. I have also seen this work with traumatised dogs that have become part of our family.

The second thing that we may wish to note about the challenge of choice is that it is about followership and, contrary to current popular human mythology of the horse, not about leadership as we know it. In the absence of the coercive or bought leadership which is so typical of human society, are we to assume though that a community of horses has no leaders. What if they were to have some other form of leadership? If you were to ask a fairly enlightened human to provide you with the definition of a 'leader', it would differ radically from our everyday experience of 'leaders' and, as such, you may be presented with something of this nature: a leader is someone who is capable of exhibiting empathy, who is empowering, who sets an example, who is charismatic, and who inspires, motivates, encourages, and ultimately liberates. Let us assume for a moment that you actually manage to become someone who fits this description. Would this make you a leader? And if it does, would you not have followers? After all, you can only be a leader by definition if someone follows you, surely?

But what if no one knows that you are this kind of person? What if no one has heard about you, that you are capable of being all of these things? You would not have any followers, would you? Which means you would not be a leader by definition even if you do have all of these qualities, surely? And is this not in turn another way of saying that, even if you possess all of these qualities, which would make you probably the most enlightened leader the world has ever seen, would you not ultimately depend on someone first learning about you and then, based on acknowledge, choosing to follow you before you can become such a leader? So, if having these qualities would not necessarily make you a leader, what would they make you? A friend perhaps? And your horse, would they choose to follow you if they experienced all of these qualities in you? The chances are that your horse would not choose to follow you, even if you possessed all of the qualities that would make you the most enlightened leader the world has ever seen. Why not? Quite simply because none of these qualities correspond to those which draw a horse to choose to follow or be with another creature.

Yet let us assume that we are committed to undertaking the personal transformation that will enable us to accept the horse's challenge of choice and get on with it. This leads us to the first of two questions begged by this challenge and it is this: What sort of human do I need to become, if a horse is to enjoy being and interacting with me? To answer this question we need to return to our discussion of the intrinsic nature of the horse and to re-examine what it is in one horse that will hold enough appeal for another horse to choose to be with or follow them. In short, and this is the second question, why does a horse choose to be with or follow another horse?

As we have already noted in our review of the sociable horse, equine ethological studies reveal the existence of at least four identifiable roles amongst horses which hold appeal to other members of the species. Horses choose to follow or spend time with a friend, partner or a trusted horse that serves as a guardian or provider. Distilling this conclusion into a guideline for humans, we could say that, ideally, a human who is committed to becoming the kind of being that a horse would choose to be with or follow would first of all need to have the general qualities of a horse that is trusted as a guardian or a provider and such a human would also need to be a partner and friend to that horse.

So what do these roles entail in terms of the qualities which a human would need to develop? To answer this question we must again turn to the horses and what it is which draws them to choose to follow or be with a guardian, provider, partner and friend. In the form of the stallion a guardian offers safety, security and protection. In doing so, a guardian is reliable, dependable and trustworthy. This means that a guardian will not only protect the horse from external threats but will also refrain from any action or inaction which could hurt the horse or threaten to do so, except where necessary to protect the horse or safeguard their ability to do so. This is the role of the stallion in the wild and these are the qualities of the guardian which we need to develop and nurture in our dealings with the horse.

The same qualities of reliability, dependability and trustworthiness are found in the providers in harem bands in the wild. The members of a band, including the stallion are willing to follow any of the more senior mares who have exhibited that they are capable of finding feed and water when required. This is because they have shown that they can be relied and depended on to do so and that they can therefore be trusted to do precisely this.

The partnership exhibited by the members of a band of horses in the wild also implies trust to the extent that all of them have some stake in ensuring that they play their role in this capacity. In this case social involvement commitment predominate. The horses that comprise the band not only help each other to some or other extent, for example, by helping to educate juveniles, but they also take pleasure in socialising. Foraging and grazing together, mutual grooming and play are all examples of this. Conviviality and affability are the qualities that spring to mind in this respect.

The role of friend in the domain of the horse is a very special one, as we have already discovered. The qualities which it entails include those of the guardian and provider, albeit probably for different reasons. Reliability, dependability and trustworthiness are qualities which are exhibited in a friend that is worthy of the title. Yet so too are those of the partner, conviviality and affability. To these qualities we may add commitment, loyalty and joy.

Yet if a horse were to possess all of the qualities encompassed by these four roles, would they be enough to cause another horse to choose to follow or be with them? After all, how would the latter know that the former possesses those qualities? In the stallion's case the answer may be self-evident. After all, the stallion rounds up his band. But would this necessarily hold sufficient appeal to the other horses in his band? Not necessarily so, if one considers that up to 30% or more mares in the wild forsake their stallion for another. And what about a provider who had not yet proved through experience that she is reliable and dependable? What would induce the rest of the band to follow her?

Before we even get to the qualities that are associated with the roles of guardian, provider, partner and friend, there is a point where a horse 'decides' to trust another one in the absence of any evidence suggesting that they should do so. This is particularly true in the case of an untried provider. There is something in the approach and attitude of a horse which draws others to them and encourages them to take that first step. As already noted, we find this in humans as well. Although we may hear the same argument in favour of a course of action from different people, there may be one human who will receive our support, not because of the strength of their reasoning but rather the power of their being. We call it presence. But just what do we mean by 'presence'? In this context the word is often defined as impressive due to behaviour or appearance but possibly both. Presence, of course, goes much further than behaviour or appearance. It includes a huge dollop of corresponding energy. To describe such energetical presence we may resort to words such as 'authoritative', 'composed', 'commanding', 'majestic', 'strong'. What these words have in common is that they imply that a horse with presence is one whom other members of the species would in all likelihood choose to defer to, that is, to elect to yield to their path or to follow or be with them. At the same time there is nothing hostile or self-seeking about them, with the result that other horses do not experience them as threatening.

In the absence of any evidence that we can take to the horse to prove our good faith and experience, it is precisely this type of presence which a human first needs to develop as part of a new way of being, one which is commensurate with that of the horse.

A new way of being

It sounds like a very tall order, the development of this new way of being, a challenge that seems to be almost insurmountable if not entirely so. Perhaps it will not help you very much if I were to tell you that it has taken me a decade to reach this point and my development still continues. Ten years, you groan, that is a long time. Yes it is but put it into perspective. Look around you and note all the horse people who are and have been trying to achieve a synergetic relationship with their horse as a willing partner. The trainers, the methods, the gizmos and the gadgets may have changed but essentially they are still trying to take the same shortcuts after ten, fifteen, twenty years or more and have still failed to achieve what they set out to do based on choice. All they can manage after such a long time is to settle for control, which may or may not be accompanied by a controlled, choreographed semblance of 'closeness'.

By way of comparison, it is actually possible to start acquiring a new way of being from the very outset and you have a guide that is constantly at your side in the form of your horse, able to provide immediate feedback as to whether you are on the right track or not. But come, let us not confine this to theory. Why not start putting it into practice right here and now? Or at the very least, why not try and sense a little of what it feels like, this power of a new way of being? In the next minute you may take an initial step towards the intoxicating power of being by simply following these simple directions. And I would strongly urge you not to skip this section. Instead, I would encourage you to follow the few simple steps below to experience just a very small part of the power of being, for it is only then that you will really begin to understand the words on these pages. Without *feeling* what they mean, they are only words.

The ground position

The first step towards acquiring this new way of being lies in aligning our being with that of the horse. Unlike us humans, whose thoughts more often than not dictate our perception of life rather than the other way round, horses live consciously, constantly alive and alert to themselves and their immediate surroundings. If we are to make contact with and connect with a horse – a prerequisite for any meaningful interaction with them based on choice – we need to be able to enter into such a form of being as well. We have to enter the realm of the horse and, like them, become so intensely conscious and aware of ourselves, our horse and our immediate surroundings, which may include other creatures as well, with every fibre of our being, that there is no space for thought, doubt, fear or anything else. Such a process is sometimes referred to as 'centring' or 'grounding'.

PRACTICAL EXERCISE

The process of grounding starts by assuming the ground position. It is designed to help us relax our body while simultaneously focusing our energy as we connect with our body, the earth beneath our feet and our immediate surroundings. To assume the ground position:
1. stand upright with your knees slightly bent;
2. spread your legs until your feet are roughly as far apart as the breadth of your shoulders and tilt your body slightly forward if you need to in order to ensure that it is straight. The reason why you need to tilt you body slightly forward is because, most people who feel that they are standing straight actually tilt their torso slightly backwards;
3. shift your contact with the ground more emphatically to the balls of your feet but without raising your heels. If possible and necessary, stand sideways before a mirror to check that your body is straight;

4. now place your hands on your hips and swivel the base of your pelvis forward and upward while gazing straight ahead at the horizon to ensure that your head is straight;
5. relax your upper body entirely and focus on the energy in your belly (breathing in and out through your core if you have already learned to do this).

———

In purely physical terms your centre of gravity will have dropped to your belly, giving you better balance, and your body is now capable of moving in any direction at the drop of a hat, much like a horse. You can sense this by rocking your hips slightly backwards and forwards and to the sides. Your belly or core, as it is sometimes called, becomes the centre of your being. In time you will also learn to direct your energy accordingly, so as to be alert and responsive to every demand for movement, even more like a horse.

Being in the moment

To experience the power of being, even if ever so briefly, we also need to enter the moment in which living creatures, such as the horse, truly live their lives: the here and now. Some humans spend their lives trying to live like this all of the time. Conscious, they strive to be spontaneously aware of themselves and their immediate surroundings continuously, just like the horse. Most of us have huge difficulties doing this for any length of time. No wonder other living creatures have difficulties understanding us. What follows is a quick and dirty way of moving into the moment at the drop of a hat. Let us try it before seeking to understand how it works. Just follow the steps. If you do this exercise properly, you will be fully in the moment by the end of it.

———

Steps to enter into the present moment:
1. assume the ground position;
2. breathe slowly and consciously and, as you do, try and lower the location of your breathing from your chest to your belly. Try to relax your abdomen when you do this;
3. once you manage to do this, focus your awareness on your head. Is it relaxed? Is there any area of tension within it? If there is, focus on that area and consciously seek to relax it before moving on to your neck and doing the same. Once your neck is relaxed, move on to your shoulders and repeat the process. Then go to the next part of your body and do the same, and so on until you reach your feet. You should now be aware of your entire body and you should be relaxed;
4. now focus your attention on your connection to the earth. Your body is an extension of the earth. You are rooted to it, grounded;
5. while retaining this awareness of your body and its connection to the earth, extend it to include your immediate surroundings, using all of your senses where possible. Can you feel the breeze tugging at your clothes, smell the scent of flowers, taste the cold light of morning on your lips, see the bird swooping down in the distance from the corner of your eye, hear the nicker of a horse greeting their friend?
6. now, as you sense yourself and your surroundings, try and feel into what you are sensing, so that you *become* what you are aware of. Do not try to analyse it but simply accept and appreciate it for what it is, for this is your authentic, spontaneously conscious energy.

If you have done this correctly, you should end up in a position which resembles how you would sit on a horse with all your energy focused in your core (in your abdomen about a hand's width below your belly button) and your upper body entirely relaxed. More importantly, you will be aware of nothing but your body and your immediate surroundings so acutely that to all intents and purposes you *are* what you are aware of. You will be entirely relaxed and whenever anything occurs, either inside your body or in your immediate surroundings, it will immediately register its presence as a phenomenon of which you are aware and which you can feel. Yet it will do so not as a stimulus that seems to come from afar but rather as a sense that is part and parcel of the awareness that you have become. And once you are conscious of it, you may choose to focus on it or not.

What this means is that you will be so immersed in the immediacy of every moment, that your mind will not have an opportunity to wonder, for it will not merely be entirely engaged in supporting your awareness of yourself and your surroundings, it will also be part of the consciousness that you have become. You will not have any capacity available for irrelevant thought. And because it is thought, and only thought, which has the ability to generate doubt, fear, regret and all other adverse feelings in the absence of any immediate catastrophe, annoyance or other negative influence, you will find yourself free of those sensations thanks to the banishment of thought. All that you are capable of experiencing in the form of the consciousness which you have become is an overwhelming sense of well-being and calm contentment. It is now that other living creatures, such as the horse, will feel free to come to you. How do I know this? Because this is what our horses have shown me and continue to do so every single day.

In the unlikely event that you have not experienced this sense of well-being and calm contentment after performing this exercise and you do not feel capable of putting any negative influence aside for the brief period of time involved, why not try it again? But this time try and focus all of your energy as you go, from the top of your head to the tips of your toes and then including your immediate surroundings. If it still does not work, there is clearly something that is really bothering you. This is probably as good a reason as any to read the rest of what I have written, for I have been where you are along the path from there to here and, as I have moved forward, I have drawn many lessons from the horses.

The power of being

Assuming that the exercise has worked for you and you have arrived at the cusp of being and an intense awareness of it, consider for a moment just what this condition of spontaneously conscious being involves. Every single part of us, including our often wayward mind, is involved in being and in being aware of being. As such we are alert and attentive to ourselves, our immediate surroundings and other creatures that we notice within them. This means that we are capable of responding and initiating in an instant. And because our mind is so involved in a supporting role, it has little or no capacity available for a rational assessment of any stimulus followed by the process of devising a response and then implementing it. Instead we are more likely to respond intuitively in the moment, spontaneously drawing on all the physical and other resources that we have at our disposal. And this likelihood is heightened by the fact that the mind is so preoccupied with this supporting role that it has no capacity available for doubt, fear or a considered assessment of eventualities (what-if scenarios, if you like). Instead, the only constant is being.

And so we have had a brief but practical taste of the power of being. If nothing else, we now know that the power of being is not some pie-in-the-sky fantasy but a real-life experience which we can live whenever and wherever we want to. It requires no props, gadgets, gizmos, methodologies or trainers, merely a desire to do just that. Of course, there is much more to it than this, as is revealed in this book. But before we explore the power of being in greater detail, it is perhaps worthwhile to experience it with horses, if only because our interaction with them is the second of the two components of the process of becoming the kind of human whom a horse enjoys being and interacting with.

With horses

Interacting with a horse once you have set out on the path towards achieving the power of being can become a completely different experience for us humans from what we have been accustomed to. A horse is likely to respond very differently to a human who is fully in the moment with them and even more so, when the two species share energy with each other during such moments. Your horse will probably be more open to contact with you when you are fully present and is even likely to initiate such contact.

———————

PRACTICAL EXERCISE

But don't take my word for it. Why not try it out for yourself? Just follow these steps:

1. take your horse into a large or largish enclosure, such as a field or arena (NOT a round pen because it is a tool of control) and ensure that they have access to something to eat, for example, grass or hay. Leave your horse to their food for a few minutes;
2. now enter the enclosure and make your way to the middle of it. If your horse shows that they have noted your entry, you will probably have a better chance of this exercise working well, than if your horse is indifferent to your presence, although you may still experience a favourable outcome should that be the case;
3. once you reach the middle of the enclosure, stop and prepare to do the grounding exercise described above. It is important that you ignore your horse completely and that you do not expect them to join you, not even for a moment;
4. as soon as you are ready, assume the ground position and then go through the steps set out above to enter into the moment;
5. when you are so fully conscious of yourself and your immediate surroundings that you have no particular thought in your mind, try and remain in this condition by focusing more closely on a particular thing close to you, such as a blade of grass, the scent

of a flower, the kiss of the breeze on your skin or something similar, but without losing your awareness of self and your surroundings in general. If necessary, switch your focus from one object to another and feel free to move from one place to the next in order to do so but with intervals in between during which you are stationary. Whatever you do, though, do not approach your horse;

6. the chances are that, if you manage to enter into and remain in the here and now, your horse will approach you at some stage, perhaps initially out of curiosity. Should your horse do so, shift your focus to them and try and sense their energy;

7. if you manage to sense their energy, try and align yours with theirs. I usually find that it is much easier to sense a horse's energy if I observe them out of the corner of my eye rather than directly. Sometimes the immediacy of eye contact can block out other sensory channels of communication, although it may also enhance them in some instances. There is usually a calm moment when you can feel that your horse is sensing your energy as well. If you feel this, enjoy the moment;

8. now share something with your horse that they usually appreciate. It may be a gentle nuzzling of their muzzle, a caress at the base of an ear, a scratch in a favourite place or even a tiny snack. I am deliberately avoiding any reference to a 'treat', because this is normally given as a reward during training and this is definitely not what you are doing. You may even speak softly if you like.

Apart from the energetical connection that you may make with your horse at a moment such as this, there are two absolutely crucial points to be aware of in this situation. The first is that your horse has chosen to come to you. This is hugely important. Why? Because, if it is your horse's choice to approach you, the two of you have a far better chance of establishing a close energetical connection with each other than if you were to walk up to your horse directly. And such an energetical connection is essential if you want your horse to have a choice as to whether to be and interact with you or not.

Secondly, it is absolutely vital that this be a pleasant experience for your horse because, as in the case of any developing friendship, it is shared joy which makes it possible for creatures to befriend each other and they do so on the basis of free choice. From now on, whenever you go to your horse, you will no longer walk right up to them or rather, it would be preferable for you not to do so. Instead, you may wish to stop some way away from your horse, even if it is only an arm's length away in the beginning, to allow your horse to choose to come to you or not. And your horse will come to you sooner or later if they know that doing so is always a pleasant experience, a bit like friends greeting each other.

And so we have, firstly, the power of being and, secondly, the experience of this power with horses. Without the power of being it is impossible to become the kind of human a horse enjoys being and interacting with, that is, doing so by choice, the horse's choice and not the human's. They are two essential and inseparable components of the ongoing condition of the human that makes such choice possible in the horse. In the course of what follows we will take a closer look at the nature of these components and what they entail. And in doing so we will need to call upon the very thing that we will seek to do without when we actually live the power of being with horses, namely, the rational capacity of the mind. We will try to understand what such living involves, so that it will eventually be possible to experience it intuitively instead of as merely a product of intellectual understanding. For only then is it possible for us to become the kind of human a horse enjoys being and interacting with.

PART 1: THE POWER OF BEING

If we are to understand what the power of being entails and how we can live it, we first need to examine the nature of being itself, what it is, what it involves and what it implies. As human beings, we may already have a rudimentary perception or – more unlikely – perhaps even an in-depth understanding of what it entails to be such a being. This may read like a paradoxical statement. After all, as human beings, are we not aware of this merely by virtue of our status as human beings? The hard truth is that in all likelihood we do not have such an awareness, because the vast majority of us are far from being fully alive to ourselves and the surroundings in which we find ourselves. This is to say that we are not fully present in the situation in which we find ourselves, no matter what it is, in that our mind is usually or more often than not preoccupied with thoughts that have nothing to do with that situation as time unfolds. Instead, our mind wanders elsewhere, rehashing the past, speculating on the future or considering everything other than what is happening in front of our very nose, if not simply deserting the present for some or other fantasy. It is such thoughts, which more often than not, have little or nothing to do with our current situation, that dictate our impression of life rather than our mind being at the service of living and helping us to fully perceive and experience life as we find it. This is a bit like permitting the tail to wag the dog, is it not? After all, should we not put our mind at our service rather than ourselves at the service of our mind?

Inherent in our discussion of this anomaly is a dichotomy between life and our experience of it. It would seem that there are two essential aspects of living, which are two sides of the same coin. There is an objective side to being, which exists irrespective of whether we are alive or not, and a subjective experience of such being, which depends on our awareness of being and our interaction as part of such being. Because the objective aspect of being exists independently of us, I refer to it as the essence of being. Without it there can be no subjective experience of being, which we can refer to as 'you' or 'I', a human being that has the potential to be fully present in the ongoing moment that is always now, and to interact with other beings, human and otherwise, that are also present to some or other extent in that moment. These two subjective aspects of being I refer to as the presence and dynamics of being.

Understanding these three aspects of the power of being – the essence of being, its presence and its dynamics – is the first step towards *knowing* and living the power of being intuitively.

THE ESSENCE OF BEING

Human beings arc as varied as the number who have inhabited the earth to date and who may yet do so in the future. Yet, in that we are beings, we have some very basic things in common with each other. In the first place, we exist as complex forms of life and, secondly, we do so within a domain which we share with each other, what some might refer to as the 'universe'. There may of course be more features and characteristics that many or most of us share with each other but, ultimately, it is these two basic things that are common to all of us and which, as such, define us as beings. And common to both our existence and the domain within which we exist are motion, change and energy, all of them constant, which is to say that they are continuous and, as such, never stop. Indeed, the only constants of life as we know it are motion, change and energy. Given their variable nature, they may be constants but they are anything but constant.

Constant motion

The term, 'being', is a grammatical form which has the linguistic function of a thing, what grammar would call a noun, yet its structure is derived from a verb (an 'action word'), namely 'be', but not just any form of it. 'Being' is the form which we associate with the present continuous, a grammatical structure which denotes an ongoing action, such as 'living', 'beating' and 'breathing'. And it is in this notion of ongoing action that we can begin to discover the secret of 'being'.

Stop for a moment and consider yourself. You are sitting still, doing nothing. Motionless, you may think you are but you are not, not if you are alive but even if you are not. If you are alive, every single part of you is in motion, however minutely it may occur. Your heart is pumping, your blood is flowing, your lungs are bellowing, your cells are replenishing, and so the list goes on. Everything within you is in motion, even those parts of you which you may be tempted to feel are not, such as your individual cells and bones. It is only the speed of that motion which varies.

Look around you. Perhaps this constant motion is only inside you. After all, you are seated and, as such, you certainly cannot be moving around. Really? Consider for a moment just where you really are while busy being you. All around you there are signs of motion. For instance, as I write this I can hear voices of people coming and going accompanied by the sound of a car door closing followed by a gate opening. In the distance I spy clouds swirling over hazy mountains, while the tantalising smell of lunch cooking wafts in from the kitchen. Simultaneously a breeze tugs at my hair and caresses my skin. Pause for a moment and sense the motion around you as you take a break from reading this. What can you hear, see, smell, touch, taste? You are influenced by this motion and perhaps influence it in turn.

Now let me help you extend your awareness of your ostensibly fixed position. You find yourself in a particular location on our planet. Although it may seem as though you are not moving, the Earth is spinning around on its axis at an average speed of approximately 1,674.4 kph (1,040.4 mph), taking us with it and allowing us to experience day and night. Simultaneously, we are hurtling through space in a rotating orbit around the sun at a velocity of 107,200 kph (66,600 mph) to give us the seasons as our planet's axis rotates at a tilt at the same time. As if that is not enough, our solar system, which we share with other planets, such as Mercury, Venus, Mars, Saturn, Jupiter and Pluto, is part of a galaxy of stars, planets and other celestial phenomena – the Milky Way – which in turn gravitates with other galaxies, which in turn.... And this is where it gets mind-boggling.

Suffice it to say that from its tiniest to its most gigantic part, the universe's normal state is one of motion. In this sense one aspect of the objective nature of 'being', human or otherwise, is constant motion. It occurs before we exist as human beings, in the process of human conception, gestation, birth, life, death and decomposition, after we cease to exist, and both within and without our bodies while we exist.

Constant change

There is another aspect of this motion which makes it truly dynamic and it is this. None of the various movements I refer to is exactly the same. Each cycle differs from that preceding it, even if the difference is relatively small or even minute. What this means is that everything internal and external to us is constantly changing, with the result that change is another constant aspect of being.

Consider the implications by thinking of the 'here and now'. It is often said that horses live in the moment or 'here and now', as though *now* is a state of being that is static, one that is constantly replaced by another static moment of now at such a rapid pace that it seems to be in constant motion. The metaphor is that of a film, which is made up of a series of static images that are projected continuously onto a display at such a speed that we see movement rather than a series of static images.

In reality though there is no 'now' which exists for a brief moment before it is replaced, even though a photograph may suggest that there is. Rather, our reality is the dynamic motion of constant change and this has enormous implications for us humans and our horses, indeed, for everything and every being. It means that every single creature and situation is unique. In the case of complex life forms, such as horses and humans, change is also something that we experience with ourselves over time. With very few exceptions, almost all of the cells comprising our bodies are constantly growing, dying or being regenerated. The physical being that we were a decade ago is no longer alive. To this extent, we are the walking proof of life after death. Constant change is even in our genes.

Constant energy

Where there is constant motion and constant change, there is constant energy. The acknowledgement of energy and its role in the universe was quite possibly the single most important advance made in Western science in the twentieth century through the work of people such as Albert Einstein, he of the well-know equation inferred from his work, $E=mc^2$, where 'E' stands for energy, 'm' for mass and 'c' for the speed of light. What this equation implies is that every physical body which has mass also contains energy and that the smaller the body, the larger its energy content is likely to be relative to its mass. Expressed in layman's terms, this is a bit like saying, 'Dynamite comes in small packages and the smaller the package, the larger the potential explosion relative to its size'.

Although Einstein is widely misquoted and quotes are imputed to him for which there is no evidential basis, especially in 'New Age' social media, his discoveries and theories have gone a long way towards helping Western science understand the universe of which we are part. As such, there is an objective scientific basis for the concept of energy and its existence in every single life form, including ours. Put another way, in that Einstein and others recognised the essential nature of energy in material phenomena, Western science finally came to acknowledge what has been the accepted wisdom of Chinese teachings for thousands of years. What it is yet to do is comprehensively understand and explain the fundamental role played by energy in living creatures especially in their interaction with each other. This is particularly relevant in the case of our own species, and the importance of learning how to interpret, control and channel energy.

It is this vacuum which has led many humans in the West to discover and study energy-based approaches towards personal development and interpersonal interaction sourced largely from ancient Chinese roots. This is particularly evident in relation to martial arts and the more intuitive approaches towards personal energy control and use evident in the martial art of Tai Chi Chuan (Taijiquan) and the holistic practice of body movement known as Chi Gong (Qi Gong) along with the teachings that accompany them.

Perhaps the most striking property of energy lies in its physical absence in that we are largely unable to sense it with our physical senses, which are only capable of detecting the manifestation of energy at work. This they can do when energy reveals its existence in the form of a physical presence, such as movement, heating, lighting and so forth. To the extent that manifested energy at work is detectable using our physical senses, it can be measured, and as such its existence is objectively verifiable. Science is also capable of using mathematics to measure non-manifested forms of energy, such as the potential or 'rest' energy of an object but then only based on its manifested forms of energy.

Yet, as we will see when we discuss intuition further on, there are forms of energy for which science has yet to find an explanation, if only because it has still not acknowledged them as such. Yes, there is sufficient evidence of their existence to date to support such an acknowledgement but, because it is largely anecdotal and science insists on an almost fetishist application of empiricism focusing on quantitative at the expense of qualitative analysis, the validity of such evidence is more often than not disputed and we are compelled to rely on a highly personalised variant of experiential assessment.

In spite of these limitations, however, it is clear that we can no longer deny the essential role played by energy in all aspects of our lives and all that makes up the universe.

And so we have identified the essence of being, which may be summed up in three words: motion, change and energy. In that all are constant, these three components constitute the basis of the vibrancy of life and, as such, the objective essence of being. This essence exists irrespective of our presence in or absence from it. Being though, is also a highly subjective affair. In the same way that the objective essence of being is essential if either you or I are to really *be*, so too is our unique presence required. What defines our identity as human beings and hence the degree to which we are alive is the extent to which we are influenced by the constant motion, change and energy of life, and to mould and direct them with and through the presence of our being.

THE PRESENCE OF BEING

Of course you and I are or were present in the here and now, otherwise we would not be communicating this way. If you were not present, you would not be able to read this. And I would not have been able to write it, if I had not been present when I did. But does this mean that you are *fully* present as you read this or that I was when I wrote it? Put another way, is it possible to be partly present and absent simultaneously? If you find it difficult to answer this question readily, why not try and experience a practical exercise of this right now?

PRACTICAL EXERCISE

Just follow these simple steps to experience what it feels like to be partially present and absent simultaneously:
1. go to your horse and spend some time observing them closely while they are doing whatever it is that they are involved in at the time;
2. while doing that, simultaneously focus your attention on your own body and what your senses are picking up in your immediate surroundings;
3. now while doing Steps 1 and 2, continue to focus mainly on your horse, until you catch your mind beginning to wander (and it will unless you are very used to living consciously);
4. try and describe to yourself the extent to which your mind wandered and the extent to which it did not.

If you managed to stop your mind from wandering very soon after it began to do so, the chances are that you were partly present and absent simultaneously when that occurred. This is at best how most of us live, hijacked from the immediate presence of living by a mind which seems to have a will of its own rather than submit to that of its owner. Indeed, this mind of ours can frequently drag us so entirely away from the daily business of living that we are tempted to confuse the thoughts it presents to us as our experience of life, instead of actual day-to-day living moulding our ideas and our mind serving as an experiential mediator between action and reflection or a support mechanism when we are spontaneously conscious.

Rather, our mind seems to wonder all too frequently to a rehash of occurrences that have claimed our attention more readily and comprehensively than others. More often than not they are events that have occurred in the recent past, although our subconscious review may also draw on more remote experiences. As a result we often find ourselves mentally 'reliving' our experience of such occurrences but each time we do so the emotions that they evoke seem to grow stronger. Far more often than not, unfortunately, those occurrences claim our attention more readily and comprehensively than others because they arouse strong emotions which are associated with harmful rather than beneficial energy. This is not to say that we are incapable of mentally 'reliving' an inspirational experience. We are and we do. It may have been a splendid sunset over a remote cove with a loved one, a moving rendition of a favourite song or some other source of inspiration or contentment. Yet when measured against the frequency with which we relive a challenging moment with the boss at work, a frustrating time with our horse trainer or even with a family member at home, such uplifting or soothing relived experiences are all too often far and few between, in part also because of the daily circumstances which largely dictate and circumscribe our lives.

So what happens to us if we almost constantly allow our mind to dictate the experiences which we relive when most of them are a source of disappointment, frustration, helplessness and the like, giving rise to ever stronger emotions which seem to engulf our waking moments in waves of sadness, indignation, rage and a host of other destructive emotions? What becomes of our sense of living, our nature of being? In short, what kind of beings do we humans become? The kind of human a horse enjoys being and interacting with?

Little imagination is required to conclude that the frequent occurrence of such destructive emotions has the potential to wreak havoc in our lives. Such emotions can cause us to become architects of our own suffering and simultaneously victims of it. Our sense of self becomes the first casualty, followed not long after by our relations with others, a situation that is often compounded by the fact that some within our circle of friends and acquaintances may be experiencing something similar. The outcome is almost inevitably a downward spiral into ever darkening, thickening fogs of trauma which, in their most extreme form, have the potential to render us suicidal, homicidal or both.

Yet it is possible for us to head this off or, where it is too late to do so, to break out of that spiral and take the first step towards discovering the power of the human being that we were born to wield by becoming present in the situation in which we find ourselves. And this initial step towards the power of being lies in doing something so simple that most humans find it difficult to accept. Rather than urge you to be mindful, to seek awareness, to live consciously or to strive to achieve any of the other challenging goals that are also the subject of a growing number of well-intentioned albeit seriously pocket-lightening courses and retreats for human horse lovers seeking an alternative, what if I were to ask you to do what horses do and start with yourself right here, right now with nothing more than your own innate but largely untapped potential for no other reason than that the journey that will take you on your path to the horse actually starts within yourself and it is precisely there that you may find and realise that potential. Put another way, the guru whom you may be seeking is waiting to be discovered and released within you!

Grounded and balanced

So what do horses do that is so simple that you may find it difficult to accept? You have seen it yourself, haven't you? And you have been impressed by it too surely? When a horse notices something out of the ordinary – whether they hear, see, smell or otherwise sense it – they respond immediately. They raise their body, lift their head and neck, prick their ears, strain their eyes and poise to spring into action at the slightest hint of danger. And all this they do in a split second, as though they constantly carry themselves alert and balanced at all times. There is a simple reason for this. Being alert and balanced is their natural condition for, unlike us humans, they live spontaneously, being intuitively aware and present to the constant motion, change and energy of life. Put another way, their natural condition is to be grounded and balanced.

It is precisely there, at the cutting edge of the presence of being, that we are called to meet and interact with a horse that is free to choose to do so or not. Whether the horse decides to interact with us of their own volition or not will first of all depend on whether we are able to meet them there and, secondly, whether we have become the kind of human whom a horse would like to be and interact with if we are. Here we are concerned with the first part of this equation: achieving the presence of being. And in its simplest form, this requires that we start by mastering the art of standing and of breathing.

Oh, we already know how to stand and breathe, don't we? Aren't these the skills we began to acquire when we stopped crawling in our infancy and took our first tottering, tentative steps towards standing on our own two feet both literally and figuratively? So we have acquired them, haven't we? Really? Have we? Well, there is an easy way to test whether we have. Simply try it yourself.

PRACTICAL EXERCISE

The following works best if you have someone to help you by videoing you when you carry out the following steps:

1. stand up as you would normally do close to a doorway or corner without focusing consciously on how you are standing;
2. quickly turn your entire body, including your feet to the left;
3. now quickly turn your entire body, including your feet, to the centre;
4. repeat steps 2 and 3 but this time to the right.
5. now ask yourself the following questions and note down the answers:
   a) Was I standing straight at the beginning?
   b) Was my upper body tense or relaxed while standing straight?
   c) Were my knees locked while I was standing straight?
   d) Was I breathing through my chest, stomach or belly while I was standing straight?
   e) Was I intuitively aware of my body and my immediate surroundings while I was standing straight?
   f) When I turned my body, was it very easy to do so?
   g) Could it have been easier to turn my body?
   h) If so, what would I have needed to do to turn my body more easily?
6. now watch the video that your partner has made and review your answers.

————————

Unless you have already made some progress towards addressing your posture, presence and breathing as part of your self-development, I am willing to bet that you will have noticed some or all of the following:

1. you were not standing straight (check the alignment of your body against that of the doorway or corner in the video) but were probably leaning slightly backwards and your chin may have been raised above the horizontal;
2. your upper body was tense while standing 'straight';
3. your knees were locked while standing;
4. you were breathing through your chest while standing;
5. you were not intuitively aware of your body and immediate surroundings;
6. you would definitely have found it easier to turn your body if you had been aware of what I am about to mention before our next practical exercise.

If we are ruthlessly honest with ourselves when carrying out these practical tests, we very soon realise that, unlike horses, on the whole we humans are neither grounded nor balanced. I would suggest that the primary reason for this is that we have become so utterly divorced from nature and our part in it, that any imperative to be fully present within our immediate surroundings, which we probably would have been intuitively had we been living in nature as our forefathers did, has been completely or largely lost. The initial challenge then, if we wish to achieve the presence of being in our lives, is to learn how to become grounded and balanced. The gateway to this lies in relearning how to stand and breathe.

The art of standing

Taking the horse as our example, we are going to relearn how to stand in such a way that we are so fully grounded and balanced that, when coupled with the art of breathing and awareness, we will be able to respond to anything in our immediate surroundings promptly, supply, smoothly and appropriately, while simultaneously being still until we do so. What I suggest you do in this and the following section is meant to be so utterly practical and simple, devoid of all major intellectual effort and completely straightforward, that even a child would easily be capable of doing it.

First we are going to learn the art of standing, which goes like this and, because it is a highly practical affair, we can do this in the form of a practical exercise. It is an exercise which we have done before and one which we will repeat until we can do it without thinking. So important is it. I am repeating the steps here for your convenience.

———

PRACTICAL EXERCISE

Simply carry out the following steps to achieve the physical aspects of the ground position:

1. stand upright in front of a mirror that is large enough to view the position of your body with your knees slightly bent. If necessary, stand side on to the mirror to check whether you are indeed standing straight;
2. spread your legs until your feet are roughly as far apart as the breadth of your shoulders and tilt your body slightly forward if you need to in order to ensure that it is straight. The reason why you need to tilt you body slightly forward is because, most people who feel that they are standing straight actually tilt their torso slightly backwards;
3. shift your contact with the ground more emphatically to the balls of your feet without raising your heels. If possible and necessary, stand sideways before a mirror to check that your body is straight;
4. now place your hands on your hips and swivel the base of your pelvis forward and upward while gazing straight ahead at the horizon to ensure that your head is straight;
5. relax your upper body entirely.

———

Feeling stupid doing this? Don't! This is because standing in this position offers you some immediate benefits, which will help you not only in your ability to interact with your horse but also in general. These benefits may be summed up as follows in no specific order of importance:

- you are far more stable if you stand like this than if you were to stand otherwise;
- you are far more balanced if you stand like this than if you were to stand otherwise;
- you are able to move and respond more readily without compromising your balance should you need to do so;
- you are well on the way to becoming fully grounded in the present;
- you will find that you are standing in much the same position as you would sit on a horse.

You may want to learn how to stand with unlocked knees automatically wherever you are, because this will enable you to respond to what you are aware of more readily and easily.

Simply make a point of consciously checking how you are standing whenever you can. It took me about a year of doing this regularly before I automatically began to stand with my knees slightly bent whenever I stood still rather than lock them straight. Then again, I am a slow learner. You will probably master this a lot sooner.

There is one final thing that I should mention about the art of standing and it may be the answer to the question or questions that the entire concept of the art of standing begs. Why standing, why not sitting or lying down? Why not kneeling? Why not...? Essentially, any manifestation of our physical presence would suffice and to this extent standing is a metaphor for such presence and may represent all of the other forms in which we might be physically present. Yet the choice of standing is not quite as arbitrary as this explanation may suggest, for there is another important reason why I focus on standing rather than any other form. It is because standing is the form of physical presence which most closely expresses our potential readiness to do anything else and assume any other pose at the drop of a hat as it were. If we truly stand, then like the horse, we are capable of a prompt, energetical, focused response.

The art of breathing

Yes, it is something all of us humans do all of the time, which is simultaneously the reason why we need to rediscover breathing as an art. It is precisely because we do it all of the time that we tend to take breathing very much for granted. We breathe to live and die if we do not, and that is all there is to it, isn't it? Far from it!

The art of breathing has become the subject of books, videos, workshops, retreats and courses. Many of those workshops, retreats and courses present breathing as an art which has an enormous potential to become a highly complex activity eminently capable of utterly changing our experience and understanding of this basic component of being and they command prices that reflect this. Although we may benefit from those that do, we do not really require them for our purpose, which is nothing less nor more than to utilise the art of breathing to help us achieve the presence of being.

There are a number of ways in which mastering the art of breathing can help us do this. In the first place, breathing can help us drastically improve our balance and thereby facilitate our mastery of the art of standing and of moving. In addition, it can serve as a highly effective means of regulating and directing energy, ours and that of other creatures who also rely on breathing to exist. For the moment we will confine ourselves to its role in helping us master the art of standing.

By default we humans usually breathe through our chest. After all, this is where our lungs are located, so it is entirely logical to do so. There are two major shortcomings to breathing through our chest. First of all, it raises our centre of gravity with the result that, when we move, it is quite likely that we will do so from the chest. The great emphasis we place on the literal and figurative role of the heart in our interaction with other creatures and objects exacerbates this or has the potential to do so. It is a singularly sobering feature of physics that the higher the centre of gravity in an object, the more prone it is to becoming unstable and unbalanced when any force is applied to it either from within or without. Conversely, the lower an object's centre of gravity is, the more readily it is able to withstand internal and external forces which threaten to destabilise or unbalance it. As such, lowering the centre of gravity of an object will improve its balance and make it more stable, even when it moves or even more so. This applies to our body as well.

Once we have mastered the art of standing, we can also improve our stability and balance by lowering our centre of gravity. In order to do this we need to relocate our centre of breathing, that is to say, to move the focus of our breathing to another part of our body. Because we are seeking to ensure that our body is more balanced and stable, we need to lower that focus and hence our centre of gravity from our chest. But to which part of our body should we lower it? The most logical one obviously. Yet which part of our body becomes the most logical one once we have mastered the art of standing?

Recall the ground position, which we adopt when we learn to stand for the purposes of achieving the presence of being. Our entire upper body is relaxed and, as such, no part of it would be suitable to host the focus of our breathing and centre of gravity, both of which require some effort. At the same time our legs are spread somewhat and are already doing a good deal of work in that they are supporting our trunk. Adding to their workload might therefore not be such a good idea. Resting immediately on top of them is our pelvis and its base is cocked forward. Presumably, the opposite can also occur, with the base moving backwards. The way in which we are standing also makes it a relatively easy matter to move our body in any direction. When this occurs, it is also our pelvis that is the first part of our trunk to move with our legs, but it can do so without any effort on its part. It would seem therefore that the lowest part of our body which is not engaged in any major effort either supporting or moving our trunk is our pelvis. Would this not be an appropriate location for our focus of breathing and hence our centre of gravity?

Yet how, you may ask yourself, would it be possible to relocate our focus of breathing to our pelvis, if the apparatus that we use to breathe – our lungs – is located in our chest? I could launch into a lengthy explanation but the easiest way to answer this question lies in actually trying it in practice. So let us do so by way of an exercise.

PRACTICAL EXERCISE

Carry out the following steps:
1. stand upright and spread your legs until your feet are roughly as far apart as the breadth of your shoulders and tilt your body slightly forward if you need to in order to ensure that it is straight;
2. shift your contact with the ground more emphatically to the balls of your feet without raising your heels;
3. now place your hands on your hips and swivel the base of your pelvis forward and upward while gazing straight ahead at the horizon to ensure that your head is straight;
4. relax your upper body entirely;
5. now focus on the rhythm of your breathing and consciously breathe in and out;
6. while doing that start focusing on drawing your breath more deeply into your body and there is only one way to do this more deeply and that is to draw in your breath from below your lungs, your stomach for instance. Please note that this is not the same as drawing more air into your lungs. Rather, it is about switching

the part of your body that you use to consciously regulate your breathing, going lower each time;

7. once you are able to regulate your breathing through your stomach rather than your lungs, focus on going even lower to your belly until you are regulating your breathing through your core;

8. while standing in the ground position and regulating your breathing through your belly, try and sense how you feel in relation to the earth and your surroundings. You can help yourself do this quite effectively by shifting your weight from one leg to another, tilting the base of your pelvis forward and backward and also swivelling your upper body from one side to the other, while keeping it utterly relaxed (the movement is guided by your pelvis).

Once you have completed this exercise, note down any conclusions that you may have drawn from your awareness of how you were standing and breathing during this practical exercise. If you have done it correctly, you have probably noted all or some of the following benefits of standing and breathing consciously:

- you feel far more stable than when you stand in the ground position without regulating your breathing from your core;

- you are able to move your body far more forcefully even if the actual movements appear to be ridiculously small when measured over time and space;

- you are able to focus your body more emphatically in the direction in which you move;

- you are far more stable when you move than when you do so in the ground position without regulating your breathing from your core.

The question that we have not yet answered though is whether dropping the regulation of your breathing to your core has actually lowered your centre of gravity. Although the fact that you do feel more stable while regulating your breathing from your core in the ground position suggests that this is the case, the proof of the proverbial putting is actually in the eating. In this case we can actually test it with a practical exercise.

PRACTICAL EXERCISE

First we are going to check what it feels like to do a fairly simple physical exercise while regulating our breathing through our lungs. Then we are going to repeat it but this time while regulating our breathing through our core. The steps involved are as follows:

1. assume the ground position as explained in the previous practical exercise and regulate your breathing through your lungs;
2. slowly raise your right leg while keeping it bent until your knee reaches the height of your chest;
3. now slowly extend your leg in front of you until it is fully extended in a horizontal position;
4. slowly retract your leg until it is again bent with your knee in line with your chest;
5. lower your leg slowly until your foot reaches the floor and you return to your original position;
6. now regulate your breathing through your core and, while doing so, repeat Steps 2 to 5;
7. note whether you experienced any difficulties while doing these two exercises and decide for yourself which one was easier and consider why.

So which exercise did you find it easier to do? The first while regulating your breathing through your lungs or the second while doing so through your core ? If you are reasonably fit and have passable coordination, you may have completed the first exercise without interruption while regulating your breathing through your lungs. If not, the chances are that you may have found it difficult to do so without holding on to something or lowering your right foot to the floor. You probably found the second exercise easier to do and the explanation for this lies in exactly what we expected, namely, that you managed to lower your centre of gravity and were more stable as a result, because you were regulating your breathing through your core.

This then is the secret of the art of breathing in relation to how we stand. Regulating our breathing through our core can make us more balanced and more stable. And because it does so, it can help us be more grounded than merely by assuming the ground position. Learning how to regulate one's breathing through one's core all of the time is a bit more difficult. I must confess that I have not truly mastered this. At least, I feel as though I have not. Yet, when I consciously pay attention to how I am regulating my breathing, I find that I am doing so through my core. Still, I cannot account for how I am regulating my breathing when I am not consciously doing so.

Although they are but two small steps in themselves, Standing and breathing have the potential to serve as the gateway towards us becoming fully present and aware. All we have to do is master the art of doing both. The result is in the moment, in other words, being. All we need to do is to acquire the art of doing both properly whenever we stand and breathe. And in order to do so, we may need to make a conscious effort initially.

Consciousness

We may use the word, 'aware', fairly frequently. For instance, a friend may tell us something that we already know. In response we might say, 'I am aware of it.' This type of awareness is not what we are referring to here. This is because, often when we say, 'I am aware of it', what we actually mean is that we *know* it. In this context 'awareness' means knowledge, which is a product of the mind, and this is precisely what we do not mean here.

So what do we mean when we refer to 'awareness'? For the purposes of achieving the power of being 'awareness' means being rationally or spontaneously aware. Bear in mind though that these are not two different terms used to refer to one and the same thing. I use the term, 'spontaneous awareness', to describe a situation in which the individual is so intuitively aware of their immediate surroundings, that they have no capacity available for the rational mind to entertain any thoughts. On the other hand, 'rational awareness' indicates that the rational mind is decidedly active, albeit that, when it is, its entire focus seeks to enable the individual to be aware of more than just their immediate surroundings, so as to be able to assess and reflect on their situation and to devise a course of action. It is self-evident that awareness implies a subjective experience. Our awareness is not just anyone's. It is ours and it may differ from someone else's. This applies to both types of awareness.

Before proceeding to discuss rational and spontaneous awareness, it may be helpful to clarify some of the terms and concepts which we will use when discussing both types of awareness. Chief amongst these is the relationship between rational and spontaneous consciousness, and the difference between conducive and disruptive action or behaviour.

Rational and spontaneous consciousness

All too often the term, 'consciousness', is bandied about as though it always denotes the same state of being, namely, that of being conscious or aware, as in sensing and feeling, but also knowing as in having knowledge of or about something. Stop for a moment though and consider the state of your consciousness as you contemplate the meaning of the term. Is the state of your consciousness while doing this the same as when you are up close and personal with a horse at liberty, completely absorbed with their presence and movement within an arm's length of you and responding to them from the gut. Yes, you are also conscious then but is it the same? Are these two states of conscious being identical or is there an essential difference between the them? And if there is, what is it?

When we contemplate the meaning of the term, 'rational consciousness', or anything else for that matter, we are referring to the use of the rational mind for the purposes of rational awareness and our rational response to what we are aware of. Our intellect is fully engaged and in control while we are aware and respond to what we are aware of. All awareness and responses are routed through the brain. As such, this type of consciousness is rational and wilful in that we can use our mind to deliberately direct and focus our awareness and responses, study and reflect on them as well as anything which may be conducive to doing so, and devise a course of action accordingly based on what we rationally deem to be intuitive. This is what I call rational consciousness and it can be hugely beneficial to us as explained below.

However, the consciousness which we depend on while interacting actively with our horse is of a very different nature. Our awareness and responses occur too rapidly to involve the brain at the forefront. Rather we depend on all our senses and instincts to be aware of and respond to what we are aware of from the gut as it were, with our mind serving almost as a subconscious reservoir of resources on which we can draw. In this sense our awareness is spontaneous and our responses are spontaneously intuitive. I call this spontaneous consciousness. Our reflexes are a good example of this type of consciousness. Our sixth sense is another.

When we are conscious, there is a constant interplay of rational and spontaneous consciousness, and the implications of this are little short of extraordinary. What this means is that when we are rationally conscious, we are able to initiate spontaneous consciousness at will. When we do so, our rational mind relinquishes control of our senses and our mind is placed at the service of our spontaneous, intuitive awareness and responses, allowing us to control, influence, regulate and direct them as we *feel* the need to do so.

There are various ways in which we can rationally influence our spontaneous awareness directly or indirectly. For instance, we may opt for active or passive awareness. Being passive while aware simply means that, although we can sense and feel stimuli in ourselves and our immediate surroundings, we do not actively try to influence that awareness. Instead, we simply sense whatever spontaneously presents itself to us. This is not to suggest that passive awareness is constant in its selection of stimuli to sense and the intensity with which this occurs. On the contrary, our awareness may become more specific to one or additional stimuli because of fluctuations in their motion, changes and energy. For instance, a lamp at the periphery of our field of awareness may start to flicker. Consequently, our attention may automatically be drawn to that change and the movement and energy with which it pulses. The intensity with which we are aware of the flickering lamp is also likely to increase accordingly.

When we are actively aware, we can choose to influence our awareness in various ways. The most obvious way of doing this is to be selective in our awareness. For instance, while in a state of awareness we might sense a particular fragrance. If it holds any appeal for us, we may decide to focus our awareness on it in an attempt to identify its source. By focusing our awareness on the fragrance we would almost inevitably intensify our awareness of it and consequently diminish the degree to which we are capable of sensing other stimuli within ourselves or our immediate surroundings. Once we identify the source of the fragrance, we might decide to extend our awareness to include it. And if the source is a beautiful flower, we may even consciously boost the intensity with which we sense its shape and colour by focusing our awareness on it, thereby diminishing our awareness of its fragrance.

Yet it is possible to go even one step further than merely influencing our awareness directly. We can proactively influence our receptors of stimuli before we actually sense anything with them, thereby altering the nature of that awareness when it occurs. This we can do on either a short or long-term basis. On a short-term basis it is possible to influence one or more of our stimuli receptors directly and consciously for the purposes of deliberately changing the nature of our awareness of one or more stimuli and, by doing so, indirectly affect our response to those stimuli. It is also possible to do something similar on a long-term basis, although the effects are likely to be of a more general, lasting nature. So how does this work?

The fact that consciousness is an experiential affair also implies that there is both a subjective and an objective element at play. The stimuli, which encompass all that we are capable of experiencing within the confines of our field of experience and which may be as varied as the universe itself depending on where we find ourselves, represent the objective element to the individual experiencing them. This is because they can exist independently of that individual and, as such, may be experienced by other creatures as well. Yet how we experience them represents the subjective element, for there is a certain degree of personal interpretation at play. How we experience a particular objective stimulus is influenced by what we are feeling at the time. And the nature of that feeling is in turn determined by our subjective response to our experience of other objective stimuli within our immediate environment and perhaps also the subjective actions of any other human whom we encounter immediately prior to that (which would be subjective to that person in that they are their actions but objective to us in that they are not our actions).

For instance, something as simple as our sense of taste may be strongly influenced by our subjective response to tasting something else immediately beforehand, such as savouring a roast potato, which would ordinarily have an appealing, somewhat pronounced flavour of its own, immediately after downing a hot curry, an experience that could potentially reduce the distinctive flavour of the roast potato to a slightly milder variant of the curry. This is an example of our experience of an objective stimulus (the roast potato) being influenced by our subjective sense of taste at the time as a result of experiencing another stimulus immediately prior to that (the curry). Another example would be a bite of strong cheese utterly undermining the taste of what in more neutral tasting circumstances would be an excellent red wine. By the same token of course, it is possible for us to influence our awareness of the roast potato or the wine by exercising our subjective preferences so as to decide whether or not to become aware of both by tasting them, with what intensity we will do this and what we will taste immediately beforehand.

Similarly, our enjoyment of a bright, beautiful day on the beach with our horse could be impacted quite adversely, if we were suddenly to receive a call from a close friend expressing their grief in response to a sudden death in their family. While the objective elements of that day and our horse would not change, the appalling sense of loss articulated by our friend might be enough to cast a veil of gloom on our surroundings, significantly changing our experience of them. Because that sense of loss is an expression of our friend's feelings, this would be an example of someone else's subjective response acting as an objective influence on our experience of other objective elements, namely, the bright, beautiful day on the beach with our horse. Of course, we might also exercise a subjective preference in advance so as not to allow this to occur by deciding to leave our mobile phone at home. This would be an example of us consciously influencing awareness indirectly.

Normally, we humans slip into spontaneous awareness when our attention is drawn to its source. This may occur while we are rationally conscious or when our mind has been hijacked away from the present into some or other distraction from where we find ourselves at that particular time. Very often though, we need to make an effort to become rationally conscious when we need to use our rational mind, for instance, when we need to study, make a decision or anything else that requires rational consideration. Learning to live consciously as far as possible enables us to reduce the hijacking to a minimum and to move into rational or spontaneous consciousness as and when required.

Conducive and disruptive behaviour

There is no right or wrong except in the realm of morality but ultimately the true test of the appropriacy of morality is the same as for anything else: whether an act or omission is disruptive or conducive to the current flow of the motion, change and energy of the universe as exhibited within the specific confines within which we experience that flow. Such a flow may sometimes be referred to as destiny or fate and to the extent that it seems to point in a specific direction, it may appear to be something which we passively experience and over which we can exercise no control. This is far from being the case.

The fact that there is a subjective aspect to awareness has implications which are potentially quite radical. The reason for this lies first of all in the potential for our awareness to be so strongly influenced by other stimuli, both objective and subjective, that our intuitive responses to them and any interaction which we initiate in a particular situation may be similarly strongly affected as a result along with their energy and impact, and as importantly, our ability to consciously exploit that potential at will. This means that we are able to influence our awareness and consequently also those responses and actions along with their energy and impact to some or other degree not merely by consciously choosing many or most, if not all, of the stimuli we wish to become aware of and how intensely we wish to do so but also the very basis for and hence the nature of our awareness and consequently also the way in which we respond to them. And the extent to which we can do this may be quite considerable.

This in turn means that we have the power to alter our spontaneous experience of life by consciously choosing the creatures and other stimuli with whom and which we wish to associate and interact, and where, when and how we do so. True, this largely occurs within the constraints of the overall circumstances within which we find ourselves but those constraints are frequently (albeit not always) generous enough to offer us some degree of choice. We can choose to associate with creatures and other stimuli that embody or elicit tension, conflict, depression, criticism, indignation or any other jarring qualities which interrupt the harmonious flow of motion, change and energy. Similarly, we can decide not to do so but instead to opt for interaction with creatures and stimuli that embody or elicit qualities which complement or facilitate the harmonious flow of motion, change and energy, such as flexibility, tranquillity, joy, praise, empathy and other facilitative qualities. For want of more appropriate terms, I refer to qualities such as tension, conflict, depression, criticism, indignation or any other jarring ones as *disruptive* qualities in that they have the effect of disrupting the harmonious flow of motion, change and energy. In a similar vein, I consider qualities such as flexibility, tranquillity, joy, praise, empathy and other facilitative ones to be *conducive* to the harmonious flow of motion, change and energy. As such, any behaviour which is not conducive would be disruptive by definition and vice versa. As importantly, the degree to which we choose to associate with disruptive or conducive qualities will dictate our overall awareness of the present and our intuitive approach to it, which may similarly be either disruptive or conducive to the harmony of motion, change and energy which is the default in the universe.

In practical terms, the more we associate with humans, other beings and objects which embody or elicit conducive qualities the more in tune we will be with the harmonious flow of the motion, change and energy of life. And the more we are in tune with that flow, the more harmonious our awareness is likely to be and so too our responses to other beings and stimuli, and the actions that we initiate, along with their impact. It is for this reason that we can resort to the clichéd but so utterly appropriate exhortations to pursue a conducive rather than a disruptive choice of company, activities and other stimuli: *Be the change you seek!*. If we associate with humans and other creatures that embody or elicit conducive qualities, we will be more likely to embody or exhibit such qualities ourselves intuitively.

Of course, this is a long-term process and it will take some time before we are capable of pursuing such an intuitive approach. So is there anything that we can do in the meantime to influence our awareness in such a way that we are more open to receiving and capable of producing conducive rather than disruptive stimuli? Fortunately, the answer to this question is not only a resounding 'Yes' but also an emphatic 'Easy'! And it all has to do with consciousness.

As we have seen, it is possible for us to consciously influence our awareness directly or indirectly and we have a choice when doing so in that we can opt for either conducive or disruptive influences. It is consciousness which enables us to do this. We can harness our rational mind to make decisions in the service of spontaneous consciousness. As mentioned, we are also capable of initiating spontaneous, intuitive awareness by making a rational decision to do so and then immediately implementing it. The grounding exercise which you have already been introduced to is a prime example of this. With sufficient concentration and focus, it is possible to use this exercise to initiate such awareness at will. Done frequently enough, over time this grounding exercise can be whittled down to an almost instantaneous spontaneous consciousness, whenever you opt to immerse yourself in it.

Yet this use of rational mind can extend much further than merely initiating spontaneous consciousness. By choosing where, when and how to do the grounding exercise, we can also ensure that the type of spontaneous consciousness which we generate and hence also to a large degree our intuitive response to such awareness is conducive rather than disruptive. For instance, we may decide to perform the grounding exercise outdoors as close to the influences of nature as possible. Reconnecting with nature is more often than not a conducive experience in itself for ultimately we are a product of nature and not the forces that destroy it (in spite of the growing evidence which suggests the opposite). As such, reaffirming our ties with nature usually has a soothing, comforting, nurturing and calming effect, with the result that our experience of such connection is capable of reflecting itself in intuitive interaction which embodies many, if not all, of those qualities.

Spontaneous consciousness

What spontaneous consciousness refers to is simply nothing more nor less than a saturation of our senses with stimuli drawn from ourselves, our immediate environment and any other creature inhabiting it at a specific point in time to the extent that we are so preoccupied with what we are aware of that our rational mind cannot wander because it is completely at the service of such awareness, and we are therefore also capable of responding to what we are aware of as spontaneously. Here I am referring not only to our physical senses but also those we employ when we sense a change in energy (our energetical sensor as it were) or any other stimuli which are not perceptible to our physical senses, including our elusive 'sixth sense'. As such, awareness is experienced as sensing and feeling rather than knowledge. We can sense our body, we can sense our immediate surroundings and we can sense any creature whose presence we detect in those surroundings. This is spontaneous awareness and, as such, it is an experiential affair rather than an entirely rational one.

In that spontaneous awareness is a saturation of our senses, it has the potential to transform the human experience of life, most notably in reassigning the role of the mind to its rightful place thereby denying it the ability to undermine or compromise the innate feeling of spontaneous awareness. Imagine for a moment that we are so immersed in our ongoing experience of the present that we have absolutely no capacity available for our mind to do anything other than participate in this activity. What implications would this have for our experience of the way in which we are living then? Put another way, how would we feel if we were spontaneously aware, not partially but entirely so? If we find this question difficult to answer, it is in all likelihood because we have not yet experienced anything like this or because we find it difficult to access such an experience of living. Fortunately, as we have already seen, this is a situation which is relatively easy to remedy, because it is possible for us to draw on rational consciousness to initiate spontaneous awareness whenever we want to, provided that we know how to do so. So let us do so now and try to answer this question at the same time.

PRACTICAL EXERCISE

What we are going to do is use the techniques that we have employed so far to become spontaneously aware in the present within minutes. Then we will deliberately interrupt this process and try to define how we are feeling when we do so. To do this we will carry out the following steps:

1. place a pen and paper next to you;
2. set an alarm to go off in five minutes' time;
3. assume the ground position;
4. regulate your breathing from your core;

5. consciously focus on your body to relax it, moving from your head to your feet anchored in the ground;
6. while retaining this awareness of yourself, extend it to include your immediate surroundings;
7. if there is a living creature close by, try and feel into or sense their energy;
8. shift the focus of your awareness to different objects or creatures within your immediate surroundings if you have time to do so;
9. when the alarm goes off, try and determine what you are feeling there and then and immediately write it down using the pen and paper that you placed next to you at the start of this exercise.

———————

If you now think about how you felt while engaged in this exercise and, in particular, what you were feeling by the time that you were spontaneously aware of yourself and your immediate surroundings, how would you describe it? Did you feel uneasy, concerned or fearful? Did you experience any hesitation or doubts? Did you feel happy and chirpy? Invincible perhaps? Or would you describe what you felt as more a sense of soothing tranquillity and contentment? The latter is an accurate description of my own sense of spontaneous awareness and others have described theirs in similar terms. Perhaps this is the innate feeling of awareness when the mind is placed fully at the service of awareness with the result that it has no capacity available to prevent us from being spontaneously aware either by replaying past disappointments or hinting at future ones in the form of doubts, fears and the like. Our sense of spontaneous awareness simply enables us to be aware of ourselves, our immediate surroundings and any creatures within them to the extent that we are capable of experiencing them without judgement or opinion. All are simply as we feel they are.

Bear in mind though that my sense of awareness and that of the other humans whom I refer to here have been strongly influenced by the nature of our surroundings and some of the creatures found within them. As far as possible I choose to initiate spontaneous awareness in or close to nature, or in the presence of creatures whom I appreciate. This is in all likelihood why my experience of spontaneous awareness leaves me with a sense of soothing tranquillity and contentment. Initiating spontaneous awareness in surroundings containing disruptive influences is likely to leave one with a very different sense, one that is more in line with one's experience of those influences. Put another way, if the circumstances in which you experience spontaneous awareness are disruptive, your sense of that awareness and intuitive response to it may also be less conducive.

Spontaneous consciousness: conducive or disruptive?

This of course begs the question as to why our spontaneous awareness of and intuitive response to disruptive circumstances may merely be less conducive rather than downright disruptive. Most, if not all of what I have read and heard on the subject of spontaneous awareness suggests that it is an unquestionably benign and beneficial experience. Yet is it really? If we achieve spontaneous awareness, is it not possible for it to serve as a double-edged sword at the service of either conducive or disruptive interaction? What guarantee is there that awareness cannot be placed under the control of those dark forces which are intent on disrupting the conducive flow of motion, change and energy to cause mayhem and chaos in the service of self-interest? After all, if we are able not only to use our rational mind to initiate but also to influence awareness and we are committed to serving the demands of our ego even if this involves disruptive behaviour, what is to prevent us from controlling and guiding our spontaneous awareness and experience along with our responses to them in the service of such self-interest?

To answer these questions we need to return to the nature of spontaneous consciousness and examine its implications. We have defined spontaneous consciousness as a 'saturation of our senses with stimuli drawn from ourselves, our immediate environment and any other creature inhabiting it at a specific point in time to the extent that we are so preoccupied with what we are aware of that our rational mind cannot wander because it is completely at the service of such awareness, and we are therefore also capable of responding to what we are aware of as spontaneously'. Here we speak of the rational mind at the service of spontaneous awareness, yet we have already noted that the rational mind may be employed to initiate and influence such awareness. Is this not a contradiction in terms?

So it would seem but perhaps there is none if we view the role of the rational mind in relation to awareness as part of the interactive, sequential process which it is rather than a static affair. By way of an example, let us consider the grounding process again. Before we initiate this process, it is our rational mind that sets the scene in that it is what we use to choose the venue where, time when and manner in which it occurs. When we do so it is also our rational mind which determines this and, as we immerse ourselves into our spontaneous awareness and experience of the situation in which we find ourselves, so too it is our rational mind which initially influences the focus and intensity of this awareness. The object of the exercise though is to become so intuitively aware that there is no capacity available within us for our rational mind to play any consciously controlling or influencing role. We are so preoccupied with what we are aware of that our rational mind cannot even wander because it is completely at the service of such awareness, which is as a result spontaneous.

But what does this entail? How can our rational mind be completely at the service of our spontaneous awareness without controlling, directing or influencing that awareness? The answer is so resoundingly straightforward yet so at odds with the way most of us live with our rational mind in control – either as the director of our actions or a wayward distraction from them – that it is difficult if not impossible for many of us to understand it readily. In order to do so, we need to experience spontaneous awareness, such that we are so involved in being aware of our immediate surroundings that we have no capacity to think but only to feel. If you have been reading this book from the start, you will have already done this on a number of occasions. Nevertheless, it may help to do it again but this time with a different focus and purpose. Now we will try to assess just what it means to be so aware that our rational mind is no longer in control of our actions but instead serves our awareness and our intuitive responses to what we are aware of.

PRACTICAL EXERCISE

Now we are again going to employ the techniques that we have used so far to become spontaneously aware in the present within minutes. Then we will deliberately interrupt this process but this time we will try to determine whether we are thinking about anything in particular when we interrupt it and, if so, what. To do this we will carry out the following steps:
1. place a pen and paper next to you;
2. set an alarm to go off in five minutes' time;
3. assume the ground position;
4. regulate your breathing from your core;
5. consciously focus on your body to relax it, moving from your head to your feet anchored in the ground;
6. while retaining this awareness of yourself, extend it to include your immediate surroundings with the aid of your senses;
7. if there is a living creature close by, try and feel into or sense their energy;
8. shift the focus of your awareness to different objects or creatures within your immediate surroundings if you have time to do so;
9. when the alarm goes off, try and ascertain what you are thinking and immediately write it down using the pen and paper that you placed next to you at the start of this exercise.

If you are able to identify any thought that you had when the alarm went off as opposed to what you were aware of, then you may safely conclude that you were not spontaneously conscious when the alarm went off or at least not entirely so. In this case you may wish to repeat the exercise with a greater focus on yourself and your immediate surroundings. Alternatively, if you simply cannot identify a particular thought that you had when the alarm went off, try and describe exactly what you were aware of when it did. In the event that you were indeed spontaneously and intuitively aware when the alarm went off, you will have noticed that you simply have no mental capacity left for the rational mind to direct your behaviour or constitute a mental distraction from it in the form of a preoccupation with an idea, memory, concern or anything else that is unrelated to your immediate surroundings. In such a situation the only role left to the mind is to support awareness and whatever intuitive response is elicited by what you are aware of. When the rational mind is placed at the service of awareness and our responses to the latter, I refer to this condition as spontaneous consciousness. It is so because our awareness and responses to it are spontaneous and it is a condition in which we can spontaneously rather than rationally draw on what the rational mind has previously learned and retained in the way of knowledge and expertise during past conscious learning and mental development, including the mind's interpretive and other mental faculties. When we are spontaneously aware we operate on feeling and senses, on gut as it were, and not on reason. This is an important part of an experiential rather than a rational approach.

And to the extent that the rational mind is not directing or influencing our awareness, it is unable to impose its ideas, opinions or values on our awareness and our intuitive response to it. As such, morality and amorality become redundant, as do good and evil. Fear and bravado disappear, hesitation and compulsiveness vanish, and so too do all the weaknesses, false strengths and any other manife-stations of ideas, opinions or values. All that remains is what unfolds in the moment, our experience of and our intuitive response to it, pure and untainted but entirely supported by the rational mind, whose role becomes that of a vast collection of resources comprising the learning and skills that we have previously acquired, which are 'in our fingers' as it were and which we can intuitively draw upon while spontaneously aware. Instead of controlling our actions or distracting us from them, our rational mind has been fully placed at the service of awareness and the intuitive responses which it elicits. The tail no longer wags the dog.

Now we are ready to answer the question that we initially raised. Can spontaneous awareness lead to either conducive or disruptive behaviour? It is clear that, when and while we are intuitively aware, we are no longer capable of using our rational mind to dictate the nature of our awareness and hence our responses to it. This would suggest that we would only be capable of default behaviour while intuitively aware. So what would be our default behaviour if our rational mind were not in control because we are fully absorbed in our awareness of the unfolding present? Would it be conducive or disruptive?

And what about the circumstances which are capable of influencing our awareness? Would they not also play a role in determining whether our default behaviour when spontaneously aware would be conducive or disruptive? As we have already noted, even – if not *particularly* – where we choose to become spontaneously aware within minutes, it is possible for us or circumstances to influence the nature of our awareness indirectly beforehand in the short, medium and/or long term and hence also the nature of our intuitive response to it. We have also considered some of the ways in which this could occur. Yet we have also noted that the circumstances within which we become spontaneously aware and the process of doing so may also affect the nature of our awareness and hence also the nature of our intuitive response to it. By way of example, easing rapidly into spontaneous awareness by grounding oneself while standing on a hill overlooking a forest-clad valley across to snow-capped mountain peaks would evoke a very different experience and response than the intense concentration required to do so while standing in a courtyard surrounded by towering concrete buildings and breathing in exhaust fumes amidst the clamour and bustle of a busy city. It is readily understandable that the latter situation could have at least a slightly dulling effect, a bit like viewing the movements of the day through dark glasses. The same would probably apply in the case of an individual who receives bad news shortly before grounding themselves to enter into spontaneous awareness, where emotion may have a similarly dulling impact.

Ultimately though, spontaneous awareness is just that. Every part of us is so involved in the process of experiencing the motion, change and energy of the never-ending moment that all else is blocked out. Why? Simply because, if all else is not blocked out, then by definition we are not spontaneously aware or not entirely so. As we have also noted, full spontaneous awareness entails a total involvement in sensing and feeling. Nothing exists within our immediate awareness beyond what we sense and feel. We *are* what we sense and feel while entirely spontaneously aware, and not what we think. *Cogito ergo sum* (I think, therefore I am) is reduced to the rationalistic fantasy that it is. And it is in this sensory form of being that we respond to what we are aware of, employing the same senses and feelings while drawing on the latent potential of our mind in support. In short, while spontaneously aware we can only act intuitively. And if all that is left to guide our actions when we are spontaneously aware is intuition, then it is only in intuition that the answers must lie to the question as to whether our default behaviour at the time will be conducive or disruptive.

Spontaneous consciousness and intuition

So what is intuition? In its most basic form intuition is the ability to know or understand something based on a feeling rather than a rational assessment of the relevant circumstances. In this context 'feeling' bears the meaning of sense as in using one's senses. The ability to sense is the predominant, if not the only way in which we can perceive and experience the cutting face of living that is spontaneous consciousness. It goes without saying that we employ our physical senses for the purposes of sensing. We use our eyes to see, our ears to hear, our nose to smell, our tongue to taste and the entire interface between what is internal and external to us to touch, which is predominantly but not only the skin. It is also these five senses that serve as our primary physical interface with the external world. However, they are not the only ones.

When we discussed the essence of being and identified it as a combination of constant motion, energy and change, we also observed Western science's twentieth century acknowledgement of the importance of energy in understanding the universe, thereby confirming what some Eastern cultures have known for thousands of years. We also noted that not only is Western science capable of measuring manifested forms of energy, it is also capable of using mathematics to measure non-manifested forms of energy, such as the potential or 'rest' energy of an object based on manifested forms of energy.

As yet though, science is incapable (as yet) of explaining those forms of energy which do not reveal themselves to our physical senses and cannot be computed based on the manifestation of energy at work. Yet we know intuitively that such forms of energy exist, because we feel them at times. If at this stage you are beginning to wonder whether I am not edging too far towards the mystical realm of the fairies, stop and consider your own experience and perhaps what you may have even encountered in popular media reports on scientific research. Who, for instance, has not heard of communication between humans being largely non-verbal? We may listen to someone speaking but how we respond is predominantly determined by our *sense* of them and how they communicate, and not so much what they say. Alternatively, you may find yourself in a situation in which your mind suggests a logical response but your *gut* prompts you to do the opposite. What about the times when you have instinctively *known* (as opposed to having information about) that a close friend is about to arrive or call and they do? Or when you sense the presence of someone well before your physical senses confirm this?

All of these are examples of heightened awareness which seem to be inexplicable coincidences. Yet they occur so often that it beggars belief to consider them as mere examples of chance occurrences. Indeed, they occur so frequently that we have also invented a term to describe the faculty within us which is capable of experiencing such heightened awareness. We half-jokingly refer to it as our 'sixth sense'. Yet what if it is not a joke or even half of one? What if we do have a sixth sense? What if it is one which we can explore, and even develop, nurture and use?

The good news is that we do, we can and it is not a joke. What our sixth sense detects is energy in some form or another, yes the very thing which Einstein claims is found in everything that has mass. But do not believe me. Consider your own experiences of this sixth sense. Speak to others and listen to theirs. Awareness of this type of energy is spontaneous, experiential and intuitive: we sense and recognise it with our gut, as it were, not rationally with our rational mind first and foremost. And as we will see when we discuss intent, such a gut-level experience and acknowledgement of energy in another living being can in turn prompt a spontaneous, intuitive or instinctive response which, when coupled with intent, can place us firmly and creatively at the interface of interpersonal and interspecies interaction, conferring on us a strength of presence which we may never have imagined we could ever be capable of possessing.

In that spontaneous awareness is a saturation of our senses with stimuli in our immediate surroundings and intuition is the ability to know or understand something based on feeling, any particular act which we undertake in such circumstances in response to our awareness is by its very nature intuitive, that is, based on feeling rather than a rational assessment of information. Although such action relies for support on what the rational mind can offer in the form of learning, skills and the like, it is by definition not controlled or guided by the rational mind. The essence of the dynamics of any action that we take is not only a response to our awareness but also a reflection of it. So again we may conclude that, as such, morality and amorality become redundant, as do good and evil. Fear and bravado disappear, hesitation and compulsiveness vanish, and so too do all the weaknesses, false strengths and any other manifestations of ideas, opinions or values. All that remains is our spontaneous, intuitive response to what unfolds in the moment, pure and untainted but entirely supported by the mind. And it is such intuitive responses which constitute our default behaviour.

But is such behaviour conducive or disruptive? To answer this question we now need to return to spontaneous awareness. When we are consciously aware of our immediate surroundings, we experience motion, change and energy as they flow in the situation in which we sense them. The question as to whether our intuitive response to what we are aware of is conducive or disruptive refers to that flow. As such, the question is this: does our intuitive response amount to behaviour which is conducive or disruptive to the flow of motion, change and energy of which we are spontaneously aware? With what we know now about spontaneous awareness and intuition, little imagination is required to answer this question decisively. If the essence of our response is as charged with sense and feeling as our awareness, then essentially it can only be conducive to the flow of motion, change and energy which we are spontaneously aware of in the immediate surroundings in which our awareness and response to it occur. As such, within the context of spontaneous awareness intuitive behaviour is by definition conducive and not disruptive.

Conducive behaviour while spontaneously conscious

It is within this context too that we may note several features of conducive behaviour while we are spontaneously conscious which are so essential to the nature of spontaneous consciousness that, in the absence of any of them, behaviour which is truly conducive cannot occur. They are discussed below in the following order:

* intuitive;
* the joy imperative;
* congruence and authenticity;
* acknowledgement and acceptance;

- no judgement;
- no expectation.

Intuitive

As we have already noted, anything that we do while entirely spontaneously aware is intuitive by definition. This is because it is prompted by and grounded in feeling rather than a deliberate determination by a rational mind. While we are spontaneously aware, we are only capable of sensing and feeling what we are aware of and our rational mind is only present in the service of spontaneous awareness. As such, it is incapable of directing activities while we are entirely spontaneously aware, yielding that role to intuition.

The joy imperative

The term that I have coined to refer to what I am about to describe is probably a misnomer, as the word, 'imperative', is peremptory by nature, suggesting a command, as in 'Be joyful!', which is a contradiction in terms. Why I have nevertheless opted for this term though, is because it emphasises the acknowledgement of joy as both an essential feature of conducive behaviour while spontaneously conscious and, in that it is precisely that, as a prerequisite for such conducive behaviour. Here I refer to joy, not as an abundance of pleasure or raucous exuberance, with which it is often confused, but in its most pared down form of *joie de vivre*, the joy of living. Please note that this is not merely about being alive (existing) but about living. This is to say that we are talking about a life of awareness and intuition involving conducive action that is part of the overall flow of motion, change and energy.

This *joie de vivre* is what we experience when we achieve spontaneous consciousness, especially if we do so in surroundings which are complementary to our innate character as creations of the earth, such as the countryside. Where we can breathe fresh air, taste the sea on our lips, hear the rustle of the wind through the leaves, see vast tracts of untouched wilderness and feel the breeze fan our body, that is where we can best experience the joy of living. This is not to say that it is impossible to do so in less complementary environments. It is, albeit somewhat more challenging.

And it is this *joie de vivre* that horses respond to so readily. They do not want our baggage (unless they *choose* to do so), preferring instead to celebrate the dance of life (which may nevertheless include our baggage, provided that they have opted in favour or this). The joy of living in a human is a stimulus to a horse. Why not see it in action for yourself?

Congruence and authenticity

If we are open to an approach to life which is predicated on the need for consciousness with horses, we are more likely to be aware of the call for congruence and authenticity. They are terms that are bandied about with relative abandon by those who seek or preach a more horse-friendly way of being with horses but just what exactly do they mean?

Let us examine each in turn. 'Congruence' is the quality of being in agreement or harmony, or fitting in well. For instance, something may be said to be in agreement or harmony with something else or fit in with it, if the two coincide with, are identical to or are commensurate with each other. Conversely, if they are not or do not fit in well with each other, we would describe them as being incongruent with each other. A similar match or mismatch may occur in relation to a human's actual presence and the image which that human has of themselves and seeks to project. As we will see when we discuss congruence within the context of energetical communication with a horse, whether a human is congruent or incongruent will have a major impact on the two species' ability to communicate with each other. If a horse and a human are to communicate meaningfully with each other, the human will need to be congruent.

So what about authenticity and the need for a human to be authentic when with a horse, as we so often hear from fellow humans who are presumably in the know? Used in this context, 'authentic' is similar in meaning to 'congruent' in that there is no discrepancy between the human as they are present and their image of themself. What you see is what you get. An authentic human is someone who is genuinely themself and does not pretend to be other than who they are at a particular point in time. We might also describe such a person as 'genuine'. The term, 'authenticity' simply refers to the capacity to be, or the state of being, 'authentic' in much the same way as 'congruence' does in relation to 'congruent'.

So how can we become congruent and authentic? In that I have presented congruence and authenticity as essential aspects of conducive action while spontaneously aware, you will probably already have arrived at one answer to this question, and it is this. Become spontaneously conscious. Not only is this one of two ways in which we can achieve congruence and authenticity, it is the faster of the two by a long shot. If you have done the practical exercises presented up until now, you will already know how to use your rational mind to initiate spontaneous consciousness. It all starts with assuming the ground position. There is no better way of clarifying this, than to go through the exercise again using an alarm clock to bring us out of spontaneous awareness abruptly enough to make it possible to focus on our congruence and authenticity.

PRACTICAL EXERCISE

Essentially, this is the same exercise as the one we did when I introduced spontaneous awareness. All that differs is our focus. Instead of noting our feelings when the alarm goes off, we are going to ascertain whether we could detect any discrepancy between our actual and preferred presence while we were spontaneously aware. To do this we will carry out the following steps:
1. set an alarm to go off in five minutes' time;
2. assume the ground position;
3. regulate your breathing from your core;

4. consciously focus on your body to relax it, moving from your head to your feet anchored in the ground;
5. while retaining this awareness of yourself, extend it to include your immediate surroundings with the aid of your senses;
6. if there is a living creature close by, try and feel into or sense their energy;
7. shift the focus of your awareness to different objects or creatures within your immediate surroundings if you have time to do so;
8. when the alarm goes off, immediately try and determine whether you can detect a difference between who you know yourself to be and what you are feeling there and then.

If you have done this exercise properly and have consequently attained full spontaneous awareness by the time the alarm goes off, you will simply find it impossible to detect a discrepancy between your actual and your preferred presence. The reason for this is simple. When you are entirely spontaneously aware, it is impossible for such a discrepancy to exist. The only way it can exist is in the condition in which you find yourself while reading this or doing anything else which requires the presence of the rational mind. This is because it is only the rational mind that is capable of such self-duplicity.

By doing this exercise and using your rational mind to become entirely spontaneously aware being within moments, you will hopefully also realise just how easy it is to become congruent and authentic. All it takes is becoming fully and spontaneously aware.

Beware the argument though which claims that, if an individual is more inclined towards disruptive behaviour for one reason or another, then this is essentially the type of conduct which we may expect of them when they are authentic. As we will see further on, this may indeed be the case when we achieve awareness and hence authenticity in the presence of the rational mind. However, it is utterly impossible for this to occur if we become authentic while entering full spontaneous awareness. As we have already noted, when this occurs, the rational mind, which is responsible for creating the discrepancy between our actual and preferred awareness is no longer in control when we are fully and spontaneously aware. Instead it is placed entirely at the service of spontaneous consciousness. It is this spontaneous consciousness which dictates how we sense and feel and influences our intuitive behaviour, which is the only type of conduct available to us while spontaneously aware. And as we have not only discussed but also felt in the course of our practical exercises, what we sense and feel while in a condition of full, spontaneous awareness is a sense of wellbeing or joy.

Acknowledgement and acceptance

When we acknowledge and accept a situation in which we find ourselves, we can refer to our acknowledgement and acceptance of that situation. Taken at face value, acknowledgement and acceptance would therefore appear to be activities of the rationally conscious mind and they can be. For this reason they are dealt with in greater depth in the section on rational consciousness. Suffice it to say for the moment that, when we are spontaneously conscious, we implicitly acknowledge and accept the situation in which we find ourselves. Such implicit acknowledgement and acceptance is inherent in the nature of full, spontaneous consciousness. Put another way, when we are spontaneously conscious, our acknowledgement and acceptance of our situation is automatic.

There are two key aspects of such acknowledgement and acceptance which can have a major impact on how we interact with horses when we are fully and spontaneously conscious. In the first place, they imply an absolute absence of judgement about the creature before us. In the same way that we implicitly acknowledge and accept our situation when we are fully and spontaneously conscious, so too are we implicitly incapable of judgement when we acknowledge and accept that situation. The creature before us, in this case a horse, is simply as they present, nothing more and nothing less.

Similarly, our acknowledgement and acceptance of our situation implies the absence of any expectation on our part in relation to the horse before us. This is because such absence of expectation is inherent in our acknowledgement and acceptance of our situation. And it is precisely the absence of expectation, which will go a long way to enabling a horse to choose to be with us for no other reason than that the horse will not feel any pressure to do so. Instead, the horse will have the option to be with us and, if we can ensure that it is one which holds appeal for them, there is no reason why they should not be drawn by it.

Rational consciousness

Rational consciousness occurs when our rational mind is fully present in the currently unfolding moment and we are actively using it to monitor and respond to it. What we experience and do is guided by our rational mind while fully conscious of our surroundings. Whereas it is relatively easy to achieve and maintain full spontaneous consciousness, it is far more difficult for an untrained and undisciplined human to do the same in relation to rational consciousness. Once our rational mind is in control, it is very easy for it to stray from our control. What we seek to achieve when we are rationally conscious is not only to have our mind in control of what we experience and do but also to ensure that we are in control of our mind, not allowing it to rule us with distracting but potentially harmful preoccupations with past regrets, future fears or the like. Of course, this immediately begs the question as to the purpose of such conscious control. What should such rational consciousness and the consciously intuitive responses which it elicits entail, what should they involve, in what direction should they take us and what should we seek to achieve through them?

When we are rationally conscious and in control, there are five primary types of activities in which we may wish to be involved.

These activities require the presence of the rational mind and are as follows:
1. sensing;
2. reflection;
3. learning;
4. planning;
5. doing.

Each of these categories is dealt with briefly below. When considering them, it is important to realise that, although they generally occur in the order listed in respect of a particular experience, living involves such a rich collection of experiences unfolding at different times that we never really find ourselves in the same stage of the cycle in relation to every experience at the same time. What we may choose to do however, is to consciously implement this cycle in a general fashion as a means of securing the structured incorporation of rational and spontaneous consciousness in our way of living.

Sensing

Sensing or feeling within the context of rational consciousness is the same as what we experience in the case of full spontaneous consciousness but with two exceptions. In the first place, it cannot be an all-absorbing experience, as spontaneous awareness can. The reason for this lies in the second exception, namely, sensing within the context of rational consciousness occurs as a secondary activity subordinate to the rational mind, which controls rather than serves it as in the case of spontaneous consciousness. We rationally determine what we are going to sense, how long we are going to do this, how it should occur and with what intensity.

Reflection

Assuming that our rational mind is in control but under our guidance, reflection represents the essence of rational consciousness. We focus our mind on identifying what it is that we sense. This we do not only by intuitively sensing our immediate surroundings in the unfolding present but also by consciously identifying the overall context and conditions within which we are active, whether spontaneously or rationally so. Reflection is usually the second step in an experiential approach to life. We experience something and then reflect on it preparatory to any learning that we may indulge in before planning our next step. When we reflect on our experience, we actually review what we have been aware of and how we have responded to it, intuitively or otherwise. As such, this reflection also takes the form of an assessment. Again though, the criteria for such an assessment are not based on a particular moral code. Instead, our criterion is simply whether our actions have been conducive or disruptive both in the immediacy of the moment and the overall situation in which the present unfolds.

This would suggest that sensing within the context of spontaneous and rational consciousness may have the same outcomes even though the rational mind may play a subordinate role in the case of the former and a dominant one in the latter. More often than not, though, this is unlikely to be the case. This is because our spontaneous consciousness is confined to the immediacy of our surroundings and the present, and does not extend beyond either. Within such a narrow context at the cutting edge of the flow of motion, change and energy, where all that we experience is what we sense and our responses can only be intuitive, it is self-evident that our actions will inevitably be conducive to that flow throughout each such experience. It is intuition which makes this possible on the one hand and the brevity of each span of spontaneous awareness on the other.

The dynamics change though when we engage our rational mind to consider particular spans of spontaneous consciousness in similar circumstances over a period of time on their own and in relation to other relevant developments in the light of what we have intuitively and consciously learned over time as part of reflection. It is while we reflect on our experiences that we are able to identify relationships between various forms of motion, change and energy, interpret their significance and draw conclusions as to whether our experiences and those of others are disruptive or conducive to the natural flow of motion, change and energy. In this way it becomes possible to identify patterns and trends of such natural flow of motion, change and energy both in what we observe in general and what we experience specifically in our own life. Such patterns and trends are what some view as signs of our fate or destiny. Some may be so confronting that we initially resist them, which may often result in some or other degree of hardship. Others we may embrace because they seem so logical and easy.

Reflection can also help us to situate experiences that appear to be conducive in themselves within a context which may reveal that, taken together with other experiences, as well as relevant developments and circumstances, are actually highly disruptive. Here is an example taken from my own life. In April 2011 my partner, Vicki, and I sold up everything and left Australia to return to Europe with a mare and an elderly dog to attend a year-long course with a well-known 'horseman'. We had recently moved to Bellingen, a picturesque town in the hinterland of the subtropical coast of New South Wales. There we met others who were on a similar journey to ours with horses and who were also strongly influenced by the written and audio-visual publications of this horseman, whom I refer to as 'Guru' below for want of a better name and because any mention of his real name would probably be a distraction from the point that I am trying to make.

There were two aspects of Guru's teachings which had come to have a great influence on my approach to life at the time. The first was his focus on the need for change, if horse and human were ever to do anything meaningful with each other, this need being situated in the human rather than the horse. It is the human who needs to change and Guru introduced us to a highly practical way in which this could occur through body and what he termed 'spiritual' awareness. What he promised and revealed was not pie in the sky though. Guru's body awareness programme involved a series of sophisticated physical and energetical exercises drawn from and inspired by ancient Eastern teachings and martial and related arts, such as Tai Chi and Chi Gong. Especially when performed in natural surroundings, these exercises had the effect of bringing one into full spontaneous consciousness within minutes. As such, they effectively occurred as a form of meditation in motion, giving intuition free rein in the process. This constituted the 'spiritual' dimension and came to be an invaluable tool in my interaction with horses, for it is there – and only there – at the cutting edge of living, where the constantly unfolding objective present intersects with our spontaneous consciousness of it that we finally have the opportunity to connect with the horse.

The second aspect of Guru's teachings which was beginning to insinuate itself in my approach to life was his insistence on a human's need to identify their destiny through ongoing reflection on what is conducive and disruptive to the flow of life, theirs in particular. And it seemed to me upon reflection on developments preceding and immediately following our decision to sell up and leave Australia in order to attend Guru's course, that this was indeed where our destiny lay. Fate appeared to be pointing us in this direction.

First we proceeded to organise two weekend courses over several months for humans who were interested in learning the body awareness techniques which Guru taught as a prerequisite for doing anything meaningful with horses. Indeed, we were fortunate enough not only to engage what was then Guru's most senior international body awareness instructor to give the body awareness component of the courses but also to arrange for Guru to address the trainees via a phone link during the second course. The turnout was beyond our expectations, with students from other parts of the country also attending. And it was while we had Guru on the speaker phone on the Saturday night that he announced his year-long course with horses. By the time our guests and fellow students left our home late Sunday afternoon both Vicki and I instinctively knew that we were about to commence preparations for a return to Europe to attend that course. Of the humans that had just spent the weekend together studying Guru's teachings, we were two of five who decided to attend Guru's year-long course. And from there everything that we did by way of preparation to sell up, move to Europe and attend that course just seemed to fall into place. We sold most of our belongings and all of our farm equipment, even a fairly esoteric horse manure vacuum cleaner and mulcher, which we had given up earning anything on but which yielded a welcome financial contribution to what turned out to be a rather expensive removal to the other side of the world. What took our breath away, however, was the news that our mare, Anaïs, would be able to fly to Europe far sooner than expected. We had been warned that it could take some time to place a single horse in a transport bay, as at least three horses needed to share a horse transport container. Yet, as we were driving down to Melbourne, we received a call that the horse needed to enter quarantine the day after we were scheduled to arrive. And within days of our arrival we also managed to arrange the sale of our four-wheel drive vehicle, a prospect that we had viewed with apprehension, as we had so little time at our disposal before we were scheduled to fly out of the country. More of these 'happy coincidences' occurred and each time they did, we counted ourselves blessed with 'good luck' and told each other that this was 'meant to be'. Reflecting on our experiences as we made our way across the world, it seemed to me that the flow of motion, change and energy which appeared to map out our destiny was leading us not only to return to Europe but also to a year-long course with the horse guru on his Danish island.

The trend continued after we arrived in Europe but with one major exception. Everything that had anything to do with the course began to fall apart within the first week following our arrival. As the weeks and months passed, it seemed as though the more time and effort we channelled into attempts to attend the course in the face of mounting obstacles, the worse the situation became over time to the point that we found ourselves travelling with our elderly dog to Denmark for a meeting with Guru, his promise of a final settlement and entry into his course ringing loudly in our ears. But it was not to be. I finally met Guru, the horse saviour whom I had created in my imagination, and found that I had discovered the wizard of Oz. Little reflection was required to know that the yellow brick road represented a highly disruptive flow. What followed confirmed this. The experiences which ensued during the years that we subsequently spent in Europe taught me more about horses and my role as a human in relation to them than I could ever have hoped to have learned during the year-long course (based on discussions and experiences with a number of the students who attended it both while the course unfolded and after it entered the realm of memory). I have never regretted missing it. In fact, I count myself very fortunate that I did not attend that course.

This example also illustrates that there are two sides to this coin. On the one hand, those of our actions directed at returning to Europe with our dog and horse must clearly have been conducive in that they appeared to become part of the natural flow of motion, change and energy. On the other hand, reflection revealed that our attempts to attend the course, which initially appeared to represent part of that same conducive flow of event, became so disruptive as to amount to a metaphor for running up a treadmill set up to ascend a slope only to descend it even faster and to do so repeatedly. Not only were we not making any headway, it seemed that we were actually being dragged further away from the prospect of ever reaching the summit. With hindsight, it probably was not a summit after all or, if it was, not one of consequence.

Learning

The notion that the rational mind is in charge when learning occurs is one which readily holds appeal for it seems so true. We can study facts and concepts ranging from the exceedingly simple to the highly complex, understanding and memorising them, so as to be able to draw upon them at will or spontaneously at some or other stage in the future. This type of learning demands the presence and engagement of the rational mind as its primary arbiter and perpetrator. It requires our rational awareness of what is available to learn, what we decide to learn, what we actually learn and how we do so. This is rational consciousness at work as part of the process of learning.

Yet there is a another type of learning available to us and it occurs intuitively. This is the type of learning which is involved when we acquire a skill. Once we have drawn on the rational mind to select the skill we wish to learn, to understand any facts and concepts involved, to opt for a specific approach or method and/or to decide on the time to devote to the process, we start to move from rational to spontaneous awareness and our responses to what we are aware of change accordingly. This is where we move from understanding the skill to feeling what it entails. The more readily we acquire that skill, the further we move from knowing what it involves to feeling what it is at work. We move from understanding it to having it 'in our fingers'. Simultaneously, the less rationally conscious we are of it, the more spontaneously aware we become of it. And as we know from our understanding of spontaneous aware-ness, the less our rational mind is in control of our consciousness and the more it is placed at the service of that awareness, the more intuitive our responses to that awareness are likely to be. The upshot is a growing likelihood that our actions will be conducive to the flow of motion, change and energy.

In as much as both types of learning are available to us in everyday life, so too can we avail ourselves of them in our inter-action with horses. Here is a very practical example of precisely what I mean.

PRACTICAL EXERCISE

Suppose that we are walking with our horse. We all know how to stop a horse, right? Or do we? It is a simple as coming to a stop yourself. The horse will simply pick up on our energy and do the same. If you already know how to do this, please feel free to give this exercise a miss. What we are going to do is first use our rational mind to learn how to stop in such a way that our change in energy will induce the horse to do the same. Once we have mastered this skill, we will involve the horse. To do this, we will carry out the following steps:

1. Ensure that you are on your own in a safe environment in which you have ample space to walk, that you are aware of where you are and that your rational mind is in control;

2. start walking and keep going until you feel that you would like to stop but instead of thinking about it, try and *feel* what 'stop' entails throughout your body;

3. repeat this a number of times until you actually stop because you feel it rather than because you think it. If you are doing this properly, you should feel your energy sink, your entire body relax, and your legs slow to a halt within one to two strides;

4. now walk side-by-side with your horse either at liberty if you are accustomed to doing this but on a loose lead if you are not;

5. when you are ready to stop, do nothing other than *feel* it and note how your horse responds;

6. initially your horse may respond a bit late and stop slightly ahead of you. There is a reason for this, namely, that your horse may not be accustomed to you communicating through nothing other than your own personal energy;

7. repeat this a number of times and note how your horse quickly learns to respond to the change in your energy;

8. if you are feeling particularly confident, you can repeat this exercise at the trot.

Planning

In addition, to reflection and learning, planning is an activity which relies on the rational mind playing a leading role. And as in the case of those two other activities, it is a role for which the rational mind is not only required but is also one in which it excels. Nevertheless, as in the case of reflection and learning, planning also has a pronounced intuitive aspect to it. In the same way that we can employ our rational mind to detect and identify the natural flow of motion, change and energy in all that we experience and do when reflecting, so too can we use it to try and draw up plans that are conducive to this flow. And if our plans are really conducive to it, we should encounter little difficulty when trying to implement them. This we do rationally at the outset. Yet, if our plans are truly conducive, we should soon find ourselves acting spontaneously in accordance with them following that rational start.

Still, not every plan turns out to be conducive to the natural flow of motion, change and energy. If it is not and is consequently disruptive to that flow instead, we will soon know. The signs are usually very obvious. We encounter difficulties when we start to implement a disruptive plan. And if we simply press ahead, those difficulties mount. It is possible to knuckle down and simply try to overcome such difficulties and impose our will. In many cases we may succeed in doing so. There is a question though that we may wish to ask ourselves before trying to force through a plan in the face of mounting difficulties and it is this. At what cost will we succeed? This question in turn begs another. Is it a cost that we are willing to pay? And this question in turn begs another. Why?

Of course we can find a justification for pursuing a disruptive plan. Human ingenuity is notorious in this respect. History is littered with examples of humans riding roughshod against the natural flow of motion, change and energy in the pursuit of plans guided by little more in the way of principle than an unfailing commitment to self-gain and a complete disregard for the true cost involved. Of course, there is a limit as to how far we can go before that cost begins to reveal itself and we are presented with a huge bill and an ultimatum to pay and reform or risk massive self-destruction. Within a few hundred years of our abandonment of intuition and our embrace of rationalism coupled with its application of the material advantages of the industrial revolution to this dubious principle of self-gain we have brought the planet to its knees along with all who know it as their only home, including our own species. We humans may be as intelligent as we claim and prove ourselves to be but we are anything but as smart. Indeed, if the condition of and prospects for the earth and its inhabitants are anything to go by, we must conclude that our intelligence is devastating. If this is what the planet's most superior species is capable of even when it is trying to curb the destruction that it is wreaking every single day, then it is in sore need of salvation.

Perhaps horses can serve as a guide in this respect, for in their natural element they are masters of conducive behaviour as we will discover further on. It is possible for us to go to our horse with a plan which, although seemingly conducive when we conceived it, turns out to be disruptive in the specific circumstances. We could press ahead regardless, as we humans often tend to do and we could indeed manufacture some or other justification for doing so, as we are so demonstrably capable of doing. But what would the cost be and are we really committed to paying it? Yes, it is highly likely that we could make our horse work according to plan and do or refrain from doing as we require. Yet, if we were to do so, would we really have the horse, that sensitive sentient being, with us as a willing partner? And what is worth more to us, having the horse interact with us fully present and of their own volition or simply as a docile shadow of themself? If the former, why not simply abandon the plan and allow our spontaneous consciousness to shape our actions as the horse does? After all, a plan is only a plan, is it not? And its value can simply not be compared to the true worth of our horse and our relationship with them. There will be another day and time for another plan, won't there?

Doing

As already noted, when we are rationally conscious our mind is fully engaged not merely in the service of that awareness but also in the active role of directing it with us in the driver's seat. And it is precisely because the mind is actively directing matters under our control, that we can also initiate and guide our actions in addition to our awareness. Essentially, this is what doing involves. As in the case of rational consciousness, we seek to align our actions with the natural flow of motion, change and energy by consciously feeling into the overall situation in which we act. To this extent, doing is an exercise in rationally conscious intuition, at least initially. And once we are comfortable with the fit of our actions in that situation, it is possible for us to relinquish rational control and yield to spontaneous intuition again. Of course, as an intuitive process, this is guided by feeling and is therefore not as mechanistic as my prosaic description suggests.

If our actions are to be rationally intuitive initially, they need to have their basis in an approach which is founded on the following indispensable characteristics:

1. acknowledgement and acceptance;
2. integrity and intent;
3. conscious and spontaneous intuition.

Acknowledgement and acceptance

Urging someone to acknowledge and accept their situation and condition at a particular point in time may almost seem to be little more than an unhelpful platitude to some of us. It may appear to imply little more than acquiescence, the reluctant acceptance of the situation without protest. To others, the concept of acknowledging and accepting one's situation may seem to go much further. Such an exhortation could be interpreted as a call to yield to that situation unquestioningly and to abandon any temptation to deal with it. Still others may respond to it as the proverbial bull to a red flag, rejecting and resisting it as firmly as it fails to budge in the face of such rejection and resistance.

Little imagination is required to understand that all such and similar responses are hopelessly inadequate and unhelpful. They may give rise to emotions and corresponding responses which may not be beneficial at best and utterly destructive at worst.

So what may the acknowledgement and acceptance of one's situation entail in the absence of such hopelessly inadequate and unhelpful responses and why do they represent such an important first step? In the first place, the acknowledgement of a situation requires that we be both rationally and intuitively aware of it and its implications. While such knowledge may be potentially depressing if not downright devastating, without it there can be no full acceptance. It is simply impossible to accept a situation as it is, until we are capable of identifying it and its potential consequences.

Fully accepting a situation as it is involves no more than a calm realisation on our part that we are in that situation, however alarming such awareness may be. This does not require us to yield to that situation and surrender ourselves to its consequences but only to be aware of them. However, this should not be confused with mere awareness because, if we are rationally and intuitively aware of our situation, it is impossible to be *merely* so. While such awareness may be hugely threatening, the flip side of the coin is that it is also enormously empowering. This is because it is only once we are rationally and intuitively aware of our situation that we are capable of dealing with it. Without such awareness we are powerless to do anything meaningful about the situation. This awareness of our position can also provide us with the calm required to step back and give ourselves the time and space that we need to produce a measured consciously intuitive response. While the measure may be influenced by our rational assessment and appraisal of the situation in the light of our knowledge and research, our response will primarily be the one that *feels* right.

In our discussion of spontaneous consciousness we noted that implicit in it is the acknowledgement and acceptance of our situation. We also noted that the absence of judgement and expectation in relation to a creature with whom we interact is implicit in such acknowledgement and acceptance. Obviously, this cannot apply when we are rationally conscious, because in this case such acknowledgement and acceptance are acts of the will, that is, rational decisions. As such, so too is the option of refraining from judgement or expectation, both of which are implicit in the acts of acknowledgement and acceptance. Nevertheless, when we are rationally conscious, judgement and expectation are also acts of the will. We can choose not to judge someone and not to expect anything of them. Conversely, we may decide to do so but, if we opt for this, we will by definition effectively fail to acknowledge and accept our situation completely.

Integrity and intent

As we have already established, *doing* involves rational intuition, at the very least initially. This is to say that during the initial stages of doing we use our rational mind to respond accordingly to our sense of the overall natural flow of motion, change and energy in the situation in which we find ourselves. As such, rational consciousness gives rise to rational intuition in action. However, in such a situation it is very easy to tempt ourselves away from any rationally intuitive action, especially if the latter appears to be particularly challenging for one reason or another. This is where integrity comes in.

The quality of being honest about what one feels is right and standing up for it: essentially, this what integrity is. In this context what we feel is right is what we rationally sense is an appropriate intuitive response to what we are aware of following reflection on it and aided by what we have learned and planned. And the criterion which we employ in order to rationally determine whether any potential action on our part is intuitive is whether such action would be in line with the natural flow of motion, change and energy in the overall situation in which we employ it. Exercising integrity would therefore require us to be brutally honest when assessing the situation and making such a determination.

When doing this, we are honest enough to acknowledge that such an assessment and determination will in all likelihood be coloured by our intent. It is for this reason that the nature of our intent is important. So what should it be? By now you will probably suspect that the answer does not lie in any commitment to a moral imperative. Indeed, you may suspect that it is more likely to be found in an undertaking to act in line with the natural flow of motion, change and energy in the overall situation in which we find ourselves. To this extent our intent would be to act in accordance with what we ourselves feel to be the most obvious direction in which we should be moving ahead based on our sense of any trend that is already evident, rather than trying to bulldoze our way through adversity.

This may seem to be a deterministic approach to living, in which we humans are reduced to the status of cogs in someone else's machine and are denied the possibility of being authors of our own lives. This is far from being the case. Ultimately, what presents itself as an obvious direction in which to move is something that may differ markedly from one individual to the next, for ultimately intent is highly personal, because the circumstances in which motion, change and energy flow differ from one person to the next, even if there is a significant overlap of shared experience due to the common denominators which define our species and the environment in which it lives. Added to this is the fact that we humans are capable of free choice and we exercise such choice, often even if this means running completely counter to the flow of motion, change and energy that is natural to our self-preservation. And to the extent that we have such choice and are capable of exercising it, we are at the very least co-authors of our destiny.

Rational and spontaneous intuition
As mentioned, rational intuition is what we may employ when responding to what we are aware of while in a condition of rational consciousness. It is however a temporary affair, because it is unsustainable for most humans. The effort required to remain rationally conscious and to respond intuitively while being so is simply beyond the capabilities of the vast majority, if not all, of us. Although some approaches to life advocate constant rational consciousness as a goal to aspire to, I seriously question whether we should. Why I do so has everything to with the fact that spontaneous consciousness and intuition are as, if not somewhat more, essential

to awareness as an indispensable part of the everyday power of being than their rational counterparts. Not only are spontaneous consciousness and intuition both easier to achieve and sustain than rational consciousness and intuition, they are ultimately also more effective when dealing with the day-to-day minutiae of life and in our interaction with other living beings.

As we have already experienced, rational consciousness and intuition are briefly required to enter into the experience of spontaneous consciousness and intuition. This is what occurs when we ground ourselves. In the course of grounding ourselves we abandon rational consciousness and intuition to immerse ourselves in their spontaneous counterparts. Our focus switches from what we are sensing to a total involvement in sensing. We become fully active within the domain of spontaneous consciousness and intuition. The more frequently we do this, the easier and faster it becomes for us to move from the rational to the spontaneous. Eventually we are able to do this at will within seconds. And it is now that the dynamics of being can become an everyday reality, utterly changing the way in which we interact with anyone and anything whenever we live them.

THE DYNAMICS OF BEING

Being is not a state or condition but a constant flow of motion, change and energy. As such, references to 'now' or 'present' – as in 'entering into the here and now' and 'being in the present' – are not pointers to entry into a static state or condition at a specific point in time or even a series of such points in time. Rather, they denote an interface with that constant flow of motion, change and energy, which may sooner be compared to immersing one's hand in a stream rather than watching an ongoing series of still pictures of the same stream, which is the nature of a film or movie. This is what I prefer to call the dynamics of being. Although our discussion of the power of being has largely resembled the description of such a state or condition, we need to be aware that it cannot exist independently of the dynamics which shape it. Put another way, the power of being lies in its dynamics of rational and spontaneous awareness of the natural flow of motion, change and energy, and our intuitive responses to such awareness, both rational and spontaneous.

The interplay of the rational and the spontaneous

Perhaps one of the most important aspects of the dynamics of being is to be found in the constant interplay between the rational and the spontaneous in our intuitive awareness and responses to what we are aware of. In those moments when our mind has not hijacked us away from the interface of living to dwell on past regrets or future doubts and the like, our intuitive awareness and responses are governed by our rational mind or spontaneous presence as and when our intuition predisposes us to one or the other. For instance, just before going to my horse, I might find it appropriate to ground myself, entering into an intuitive presence of spontaneous awareness and responses. Partway through interacting with my horse, I may feel a need to engage my rational mind to review and evaluate some of that interaction. This may induce me to adjust my approach, which I do by rationally seeking what I feel to be the most intuitive response. Still acting rationally, I then re-initiate interaction and a return to spontaneously intuitive awareness and responses while fully in the moment with my horse.

There are also times when I rationally yield to the spontaneous briefly in order to do or refrain from doing something, before returning to my fully conscious state again. This I do, because experience has shown me that I can achieve my rationally chosen action or inaction more effectively by withdrawing my rational focus and allowing myself to act as spontaneously and intuitively as possible for as long as that particular action or inaction lasts.

By way of a mundane example, when I feed our mares muesli at lunchtime, our Australian warmblood mare, Anaïs, who is as fixated on food and humans as any orphan horse can be, usually hovers close by while I prepare the feed for both her and her Dutch warmblood mate, Pip. To wet the feed down to facilitate the consumption of the few additives that go into it, I need to pass between Anaïs and the water while carrying both buckets of feed and while both mares are at liberty, and then enter Anaïs' enclosure to put down her feed before doing the same for Pip. (We need to feed the girls separately, otherwise Anaïs would devour both helpings.) In the past I would either have confined both mares to their separate enclosures before starting to feed or I would have used a whip to drive Anaïs out of my space. Now neither are required. When I emerge from the feed room with both buckets of feed in one hand, I simply slip into spontaneous consciousness mode, if necessary (usually not) raise my other hand with a relaxed elbow to approximately the same height as my head slightly ahead of me to give myself a somewhat larger physical presence, ignore Anaïs (while being intensely aware of where she is and what she is doing) and simply walk deliberately but unhurriedly to wherever I need to go. The mare, who is a big girl, simply backs off and gives me all the space I need. Pip is usually in her enclosure by the time I enter with her bucket of feed. Usually, I also need to motion her to step back to give me space to put it down and I employ the same spontaneous consciousness to do so.

So what is the secret? Fully intuitive spontaneous consciousness is certainly an important part of the equation but there is another which is as essential and it is intent.

Intent in action

As we have already concluded in our discussion of it as an integral part of rational consciousness, intent involves a commitment, not to some or other arbitrarily determined moral imperative, but rather to a specific rational or spontaneous form of intuitive action which is as closely aligned as possible to the natural flow of motion, change and energy. In action – much if not most of which is spontaneous if not initially at the outset – intent is not only what guides our actions but also, and more importantly, what our actions become.

This is probably one of those moments again when you may begin to doubt my sanity. 'Intent is ... what our actions become.' This is actually what the man is saying. How can this be? After all, is it not in the nature of intent, defined as intention or purpose, that I live independently of it and merely apply it when I am determined to do or to abstain from doing something? And does this not imply that there is always a duality involving a human, on the one hand, and their application of intent, on the other? Is it not the very existence of this duality that enables us to differentiate between human actions with and without intent. This is quite normal, isn't it. After all, it serves as one of the pillars of our Western criminal law system, determining what is and what is not a crime. And so we open up the possibility of actions or inaction occurring without true intent. There is a discrepancy between what we do or refrain from doing which marks action or inaction as inauthentic, not congruent. When this happens, this is where other species that are as sensitive as the horse begin to question our true intent, which has the effect of undermining all that we choose to do or not to do with them.

This duality between who we are and how we normally act is what we need to bridge to the extent that the possibility of there ever being a discrepancy between the two is completely abolished. The only way of doing this is to ensure that our actions or inaction become not merely an expression of our intent but the living epitome of it. We become whatever we do or do not do. In a word, we become our intent.

So how can we achieve this? Actually, it is a very simple, easy process. Think about what could possibly be the cause of this duality between who we are and our intent. There is really only one potential culprit and that is the actual one, our rational mind. As long as our rational mind is present, we tend to focus on who we are and what we are trying to do or not to do. Something as simple as raising one leg to stand solely on the other can become a veritable balancing act, because our rational mind focuses so closely on trying to maintain our balance that there is almost no chance of any authentic expression of our true intent, which is not to retain our balance but to stand on one leg. True, the latter depends on the former but retaining our balance is not our true intent. Indeed, by focusing on it, we undermine our true intent, namely, to stand on one leg, with the result that we find ourselves focused on balancing rather than merely standing on one leg. Now imagine that I am standing in the shower and my intent is extended beyond standing on one leg to washing the toes at the extremity of the other leg that I raise. What is likely to happen if I am still only focused on trying to retain my balance on one leg when my true intent is to wash the toes at the end of the other? In this case my intent may be undermined not only figuratively but also quite literally by the discrepancy inherent in the duality of me and my intent.

By now the solution to eliminating this duality and hence potential discrepancy between our true intent, on the one hand, and our actions or inaction, on the other, may be suggesting itself. We need to eliminate the rational mind from any direct control over our actions, so that it may serve as a support for our intuition. And we already know how to do this, for by now we have done it so often that we may be able to do it almost instantaneously. We need to ground ourselves to assume the role of spontaneous intuition in both our awareness and our response to what we are aware of. It is only when we are so present in the moment that we are spontaneously intuitive in all we do and do not do that there is no longer any scope for a duality and hence discrepancy between either and our true intent. Acting spontaneously and intuitively we become our intent. So when we move, we are that movement. And when we do not move, we are that absence of movement. As such, once we become our intent, we feel that intent.

Energy and how to influence it

Various types of energy may be found in creatures as complex as a human being and, taken together, they seem to represent an impressive amount. There are times when I look at myself and others around me and consider the huge amount and variety of energy that we are capable of producing, especially when we are emotional, and wonder how many times over we would be capable of illuminating the earth at night if we could only harness that energy. While this may be impossible, can you imagine what we humans might be capable of if we were able to mould and direct the energy within us when interacting with other creatures. The good news is that it is possible for us to so. The bad news is that very few of us have actually learned how to do so. If you have ever engaged in a martial art, you will probably have learned to channel your energy. I recall that, when I did karate during my student days, we were taught how to harness the energy in our body in the service of our movements, even when we were not fighting anyone but were only (not *merely*, performing a *kata* (a fairly lengthy series of formal offensive and defensive moves). Essentially, we were taught to move from the core and to direct all energy from there to the part of our body that was involved in striking or blocking a strike. Even where no combat was involved, the success with which one managed to incorporate energy into one's moves, lent to them a vibrancy and power which could not only be sensed immediately but which also directly differentiated the *karatekas* into those who had mastered their level of the art and those who had not. One learned not merely how to fight but how to be and move with purpose even when not involved in combat.

Much of the essence that I learned during my karate period went on to lie dormant until I discovered *tai chi* and *chi gong* much later in life when I was searching for a form of active meditation to help me achieve a presence with horses that – as I had come to learn – would open the door to meaningful interaction with them in general and ultimately also facilitate the development of a mutually trusting relationship with our own in particular. More refined and subtle than karate, tai chi and chi gong, in particular, have been especially helpful in doing just that, not in that they address such interaction or relationship directly but rather because of how instrumental they can be in helping a human acquire the power of being and the presence which accompanies it, which are the prerequisites for such interaction and relationship. It is for this reason that I would not hesitate to recommend both tai chi and chi gong to anyone seeking to do the same.

This is not to suggest that one should strive to become an expert in either. Rather, I would recommend that the focus be largely confined to acquiring proficiency in the basics. It is not so much the performance of the various routines that matter but the nature and quality of that performance. To this extent I found it useful to be selective in what I chose to learn and the aspects I elected to focus on. As such, it is perhaps useful here to list the skills on which I decided to concentrate and how they have help me influence the energy within me. They are as follows:

1.   being calm, stable and balanced;
2.   being relaxed and inviting;
3.   being capable of immediate movement and stillness;
4.   being aware and alert;
5.   being able to shape and focus such movement and stillness;
6.   being able to regulate and direct internal energy;
7.   being able to do this with intent;
8.   being able to do all of this intuitively.

Each of these points is dealt with below.

1. Being calm, stable and balanced

If there could ever be a starting point in the natural flow of motion, change and energy, it would surely be this, being calm, stable and balanced. It is a welcome condition to return to after exertion. Think halt and relax your upper body entirely, spread your legs at least shoulder-wide for maximum standing support, lower your breathing to your abdomen, dropping your centre of gravity to improve stability and slowing your breath rate to induce greater calm. This process of grounding or centring has the effect of lowering our energy, bringing us to rest, rooting us to the earth and allowing us to rediscover ourselves within our immediate experiential cocoon. We are balanced physically, mentally and emotionally.

2. Being relaxed and inviting

Relaxing our upper body along with slowing our breath intake and being intent on halting all activity and coming to rest are the key to inducing calmness. Such calmness does not only serve to create favourable conditions for other energy-dependent action within us. It also serves as a signal of invitation to other creatures revealing that we are open to contact, communication, connection and interaction. Yet this is an invitation which is not simply one of yielding to just any type of response to it. Rather, it is an invitation which offers acceptance without threat or expectation.

3. Being capable of immediate movement and stillness

Because we are stable and balanced, we create some of the conditions required for immediate, rapid, coordinated movement should the need arise. The prerequisites for such movement, however, are not confined to stability and balance. We also need to have the strength and energy that are needed for this purpose. This means that we also need to be healthy and fit enough to respond readily should the need arise for us to move promptly and appropriately. Let us not fool ourselves here for it is easy to do so. We cannot afford to be excessively overweight, underweight, weak and lacking in energy. The goal here is to be physically strong and fit, for these qualities serve as a prerequisite for the awareness and alertness which will ultimately confer on us the mental and emotional power that we require to achieve and maintain the power of being in our daily life and to be able to interact meaningfully with other creatures.

Taken together, our stability, balance, strength and fitness also enable us to be still. Here you may be tempted to confuse stillness with not doing anything. Resist it, for stillness involves doing nothing, actively so. Rationally or spontaneously, we create the capacity to be aware and alert.

4. Being aware and alert

It is precisely this condition which lends itself to a heightened awareness of our immediate surroundings and any creatures within them who reveal themselves to us. And it is this heightened awareness that dictates the nature, direction and intensity of our rational or spontaneous responses to what we become aware of, in either case intuitively. By now we should be quite familiar with the skill of employing our rational mind to switch from rational to spontaneous consciousness. We have learned to do this by grounding ourselves and we have done it so often that we can do it almost instantaneously. And when we have done this, we have moved fully from the rational to the spontaneous.

Where we sense and respond rationally, we may sometimes have difficulties achieving the appropriate focus and intensity. This is because the rational mind is more often than not less effective a guide of our immediate actions than spontaneous feeling. What I am referring to here is akin to the difference between how we employ a new skill that we are consciously studying and our use of it once it becomes second nature, when we can rightly say that we have a 'feel' for it. In essence, it is feeling, and as such, spontaneous awareness, which enables us to have this 'feel' and not our rational mind. And this 'feel' takes the form of largely spontaneous awareness and responses while using that skill but without surrendering overall rational control over our actions.

Acknowledging this should make it easier to understand that there may be moments while we are rationally conscious, when our rational response may take the form of deferring to spontaneous intuition in our awareness and our response to what we are aware of but only to a limited extent. The extent to which we do this is just enough to perform a specific action or series of actions while relying on spontaneous awareness and responses. Again though, we yield to such spontaneous intuition just long and far enough to perform the relevant action or series of actions. Here is a practical exercise to illustrate the use of this technique in practice.

PRACTICAL EXERCISE

Carrying a full open container of water without spilling any can be a challenge. This exercise demonstrates how it can become a relatively easy task. First we will do it the way most humans do and then we will try a different method. To do this we carry out the following steps:

1. find a shallow container with a relatively wide diameter. The base of a large plant pot will do just fine;
2. fill the container with water until just under the rim;
3. activate a timer and carry the container to a spot about ten to fifteen metres away and place it on the ground, while focusing on not spilling a single drop;
4. stop the timer when you have completed the task and note down the time it took;
5. repeat Steps 1 to 4 but instead of trying not to spill a drop, shift your focus to something else, such as the place to which you are moving and various items along the way.

If you managed to carry out this practical exercise, it is quite likely that you will either have spilt some water during the first part of it while concentrating on not spilling any. Alternatively, you may not have spilt any but you probably spent more time on the first part of the exercise compared with the second. There is a simple reason for this. When we use our rational mind to focus on not spilling any water, we actually make it easier for ourselves to do so than if our spontaneous consciousness were to be in control. This is because, when we are spontaneously conscious, we are able to respond more rapidly to minute shifts affecting us than when we are rationally conscious. By shifting the focus of our rational consciousness to something other than an attempt not to spill any water, we allow our spontaneous consciousness to take over this task, thereby achieving a more effective outcome. Usually the shift of our focus is to our intent.

5. Being able to shape and focus movement and stillness

Ideally, when we are as still as can be in a universe whose essence is constant motion, change and energy, we want to be as aware as possible of the part of that essence to which we are exposed. Simultaneously, we would like to be able to respond to what we are aware of as appropriately as possible. More often than not, this demands the ability to be able to move at the drop of a hat and to do so in as stable and balanced a manner as when we are standing still. The secret lies in mastering our core, so as to be able to move and find stillness through and from it.

In order to achieve this we need to ensure that we are breathing through our belly and that our entire upper body is relaxed. Not only does this have the effect of lowering our centre of gravity so as to make us more stable and balanced, it also concentrates the where-withal to engage our inert energy in our core. This concentration is crucial, for it is what enables us to use our core to regulate our energy and to direct it intuitively in response to what we become aware of.

6. Being able to regulate and direct internal energy

My introduction to the practice of regulating and directing my internal energy took the form of lessons in how to maximise my physical and psychological power for the purposes of and while throwing a karate punch and raising a block against one. In each case I recall being struck by the logic and economy of the exercise contrasted with the synergistic physical power it unleashed. Later on in life tai chi has also taught me to how to achieve relatively greater synergistic effects with even less physical power involved. Again, the explanation lies in the ability to use one's core to regulate and direct one's internal energy.

So how do we use our core in this manner? It is possible to break the process down into a number of elements, including the following:

- *adjusting one's breathing* – apart from lowering our breathing to our belly to become more balanced and stable, there are four main ways in which we can adjust our breathing to achieve a different effect. Our breathing may be shallow or deep or we may vary it in between. In addition, we can adjust the pace at which we breathe anywhere from slow to fast. Then we may also opt for a combination of the two. For instance, slow deep breathing can help us to relax after any excitement, shallow deep breathing can induce calm. This in turn can affect any creature with whom we are interacting at the time to help them achieve a similar outcome;

- ***deep pelvic tensing and relaxing*** – the ability to tense and relax the deep muscles of the pelvis is crucial if we are to harness the energy within us in order to direct it where required. It is important to realise though that this should not be confused with the conscious tightening and relaxation of the superficial abdominal muscles. Such tightening constricts the flow of energy and makes it more difficult for us to act intuitively. It also interferes with the flow of energy when we are interacting with another creature. Our internal energy can best be harnessed when the superficial muscles are relaxed and the deep pelvic muscles are intuitively engaged, especially when this is combined with appropriate breathing. This is particularly effective in movement together with another creature. Similarly, relaxing our deep pelvic muscles will allow us to come to rest, a process that is enhanced by simultaneously breathing more shallowly and slowly;

- ***varying the angle of the pelvis*** – if we tilt the base of our pelvis forward while harnessing our internal energy, it is possible for us to direct our internal energy outwards in the direction of any creature in line with our pelvis. It is possible to use this to particularly good effect when interacting with a horse. In the absence of any tilt to our pelvis, we are able to direct our energy either internally or indirectly towards an external target through another body part, a hand for example. This is illustrated in the practical exercise described below;

- ***opting for internal or external focus*** – we may choose to regulate and direct our energy with either an internal or external focus. The focus refers to the target of the energy which we seek to harness. By way of example, my most vivid experience of harnessing my energy with an internal focus while interacting with my mare, Pip, occurs when I am asking her to transition from walk to trot while walking next to her. It takes the form of having such intent on doing so that I actually feel the build-up of energy in my pelvis with such intensity before my legs start to move faster, that very often Pip breaks into a trot before I even begin to run. An example of harnessing energy with an external focus may be found in the practical exercise below;

- ***opting for direct or indirect external focus*** – when we choose to harness our energy with an external focus, this may occur directly or indirectly. A direct external focus refers to an external target that is directly affected by the energy build-up in our core and the projection of that energy directly from our core to the external target by tilting the base of our pelvis forward. This can be particularly effective during lateral interaction with a horse on the ground. The direct projection of energy may be used to communicate a request for lateral flexion, shoulder-in or some other form of lateral 'gymnasticisation'.

7. *Being able to do this with intent*

In essence intent refers to a rationally or spontaneously conscious or intuitive commitment to acting in accordance with the natural flow of motion, change and energy in the situation in which we find ourselves. As such, the substance of intent can vary from one situation to the next. What intent entails in any situation though is that, when it is fully present, it is imbued in all of our actions. And this occurs, as already mentioned, with such intensity that we are not merely humans doing something with intent. Rather, the intent is in the doing and the doing defines our being. This means that no part of being can exist outside our intent. We are entirely what we do even when we do 'nothing'. The implications are profound, for it also means that, when we are fully aware, either consciously or spontaneously, there is no room for hesitation, doubt or fear. It is through our core that we mainly give expression to our intent. As such, intent both guides the regulation and direction of our energy and is simultaneously the epitome of the quality of that energy. This cannot be achieved without feeling.

8. Being able to do all of this intuitively

All that we do while either rationally or spontaneously conscious, we seek to do intuitively. This includes regulating and directing our energy from our core. Although it is possible to do this with the rational mind in control, my experience is that spontaneous intuition works more effectively in the immediacy of the instantaneous movement which interaction involves. This is because spontaneous intuition involves gut feeling and effectively precludes the route to the brain, as the latter not only slows things down but may have the effect of distorting the response in the instantaneous nature of the moment. Increasingly, I find myself deliberately deferring to spontaneous intuition even when my rational mind is actively directing proceedings, a technique that has already been mentioned and which is also dealt with when we consider the art of moving below.

PRACTICAL EXERCISE

And here is a practical exercise of energy at work between the species, which illustrates some, if not all, of the aspects of regulating and directing our internal energy. This one you can try out with your horse. Simply carry out the following steps:

1. place some hay on the ground and allow your horse to eat it without any restraint on any part of their head or body;
2. casually approach your horse while their head is down and they are eating from the ground. Crouch down and place your hand palm up underneath your horse's jaw towards the rear and calmly

say, 'Lift', while exerting a bit of upward pressure. Note how your horse responds;

3. after waiting a little while until your horse is eating from the ground again, move around to the other side and prepare to do the same. This time though, calmly explain to your horse that you are going to ask them to lift their head just using your personal energy but without exerting any pressure through your hand. Place your hand palm up underneath your horse's jaw towards the rear;

4. if your horse does not raise their head in response to your words (some will), try and feel into what you are about to do, which is this. You are going to raise your body calmly but intently with every fibre in your being while leaving your hand resting (but NOT pushing) beneath your horse's jaw when it is raised. You are so intent on this that you do not for a moment doubt that your horse will raise their head. When you *feel* the impending rise of your horse's head, calmly but intently say, 'Lift' and raise your body with the same intent but *without* applying any pressure under your horse's jaw. Again, note how your horse responds.

———————

Unless you have trained your horse to raise their head when you say 'Lift', nine times out of ten the horse will not raise their head during Step 1 but will do so of their own accord during or shortly after Step 2. Why? Essentially, there are two reasons why this is likely to happen. Firstly, a horse is hardwired to resist pressure when it is exerted directly against them and not to yield to it. This is a reflex reaction. As such, your horse is likely to resist your attempt to raise their head during Step 1. Secondly, your energy will probably not have given the horse any indication that you were asking them to lift their head during that step. The opposite situation occurs during Step 2. No direct pressure is exerted against the horse's jaw, with the result that they do not resist. Simultaneously, the horse senses the energy of your impending or actual move and responds to it by lifting their head, in some cases before the human has even started to raise their body.

The art of moving

Moving is essentially an extension of stillness in the same way that stillness is an extension of movement with only the distance covered changing and the extent to which the legs are engaged varying. Dancing is the epitome of the art of moving in action. It encompasses both pulses of movement and hiatuses of stillness, both types of being an extension of the other. Although dancing is also a controlled flow of movement and stillness and the rational mind directs its overall shape and structure, it is spontaneous intuition which dictates its execution, especially where two individuals dance together in close contact with each other. It is within the minutiae and immediacy of such interaction that only spontaneous intuition can excel. Again, this is because such intuition allows responses which are as spontaneous as the awareness which elicits them and as instantaneous where they need to be so.

What we are looking to achieve when we endeavour to master the art of moving is actually very simple but simultaneously very powerful. With the exception of movement, it is identical to the art of standing as I have elaborated on so far and its source is identical in that both are rooted in the process of grounding. The spontaneous awareness and physical, mental and emotional realignment which we achieve when we ground ourselves, along with the intuitive ability to respond as spontaneously, is what we retain when we move. This means that we move from the core, to which our breathing has dropped to lower our centre of gravity and make us more stable and balanced while stationary or mobile. At the same time our upper body and superficial muscles remain relaxed, so as to avoid the occurrence of any tension, which could interfere with our movement or stillness.

When we combine the art of aware movement with the ability to regulate and direct energy while interacting intuitively with another creature, such as a horse, it becomes possible to communicate with them not merely with the aid of mechanical techniques, such as body language and positioning, but also energetically. And when you do, your horse will notice this immediately and respond accordingly. I have already mentioned that my mare, Pip, often responds to my energy build-up when encouraging her to transition from trot to walk, by breaking into a trot before I even start running next to her myself. Well, why not this with your horse and see what response you get?

Even though you may be accustomed to interacting with your horse at liberty, f you have little or no experience using nothing more than your personal energy to encourage them to move from walk into trot, it is advisable to perform this practical exercise with your horse on a lead. This is because the inexperienced use of personal energy may lead to unpredictable results if you cannot adjust the intensity and focus appropriately. The following steps are based on the assumption that you will interact with your horse on a lead which is long enough for you to move a safe distance away from them if necessary:

1. take your horse into a large arena or an area of similar size where it is safe to walk and trot;
2. spend a few minutes walking next to your horse, while ensuring that your upper body is entirely relaxed;
3. try and vary the pace of your walk by raising and lowering your personal energy while directing all movement through your core. The secret here is to *feel* the variation of energy within yourself. Do not expect anything of your horse, although you should find that your horse starts to vary their pace accordingly;
4. when you are ready, prepare for trot by beginning to *feel* trot in your core, pelvis and thighs but without tightening your abdomi-

nal muscles. You should be able to sense the build-up of energy in those parts;

5. quicken your pace as you prepare to run. If necessary, tilt the base of your pelvis forward. Resist the temptation to urge your horse forward. This is not about your horse but about you and your ability to feel and energise trot within you;

6. break into a slow run and increase the pace when your horse breaks into a trot;

7. if you feel confident enough, you may also try and vary the pace of your horse's trot by raising and lowering your personal energy while directing all movement through your core. Again, the secret here is to *feel* the variation of energy within yourself.

It is quite possible that your horse may start moving before you do. This is to be encouraged for it means that your horse is picking up on your energy. The aim is to render the use of everything other than your personal energy redundant. Try not to be discouraged if your horse does not respond initially. Remember, this is new to both of you. In addition, past training may have had the effect of diminishing your horse's sensitivity to variations in human energy.

Presence

Consider for a moment just what happens to us whenever we achieve the power of being. We are fully aware, alert and intuitively intent on acting in line with the natural flow of motion, change and energy in the situation in which we find ourselves to the extent that there is no scope for anything other than this. As such, there is no space for hesitation, doubt or fear not because of any arrogance on our part but for this reason alone. We have no internal resources left to devote to such concerns. Accordingly, they effectively do not exist. The flip side of the same coin is that the prerequisite for the absence of such concerns is full awareness at the cusp of being, the ever-flowing here and now.

As a result, we are fully congruent. This is to say that what we do and who we are when we do it are precisely the same as what they appear to be. There is and can be no discrepancy between substance and appearance. What any other creature sees in us is exactly what they get. This means that the being whom we have become is entirely authentic when we are fully aware and intuitively active with intent and that the quality of such authenticity is to be found in the calm, authoritative and dependable self-assurance which such congruence confers on us. And it is predominantly this quality of authenticity which gives us presence. As such, presence is the visible measure of the extent to which we have achieved the power of being in and at a particular situation and time respectively.

PART 2: THE POWER OF BEING WITH HORSES

Living the power of being on our own entails first and foremost that we are alive and alert to ourselves, our surroundings and the creatures within them to the fullest extent that we can be and that this awareness, imbued with integrity and intent, may be rational or spontaneous, switching from the one to the other as and when required or convenient. Living the power of being with horses enables us to do precisely the same but only now we are alive and alert not only to ourselves but also to the fellow sentient being known as horse. And it is here in the immediacy of being that we can truly meet and get to know the horse for, in the absence of a wayward mind unlike us, this is where they normally live, fully alive and fully alert.

CONNECTION AND RELATIONSHIP

When I look at the conditions in which we live and consider the extent to which so many of us are alienated from the earth, each other and even ourselves, it is difficult to conclude that we are truly content except perhaps at a material level. Of course, this is not the same as stressed or traumatised but, judging from the alarming figures for poverty (even amongst wage earners), family violence and other abuse in so very many countries around the world, it would seem that millions of humans are already stressed, if not traumatised, in their teens or by the time when they exit them. The growing number of equine aided, guided, facilitated or whatever therapeutic and other centres would also appear to be testimony to the extent to which stress and trauma have become almost inevitable aspects of human society and we as a species have come to live with the abnormal as normal. As such, there is a good chance that many of us are stressed or traumatised to some degree or another by the time when we contemplate interaction with our horses.

Now consider the likelihood that horses in captivity may almost always have to contend with stress or trauma. This then is our starting point when contemplating interaction between horses and humans. The two species may have to contend with stress or trauma, either in themselves or in both. The likelihood of neither being weighed down by stress or trauma is probably minimal. As the species that ultimately controls the parameters of interaction between horses and humans, it is therefore up to us to find the wherewithal to enable us to initiate and facilitate the dance between them. And I would respectfully insist that it is in presence within the present and all this implies and encompasses where we will find it.

Spontaneous awareness and response

As we already know, it is precisely in the present where we will find the horse. The assumption here is that the horse is at liberty to be the acutely aware, sensitive, sentient being that they are and, as such, is also capable of energetically experiencing and articulating presence. For it is only then that truly authentic – that is to say voluntary and spontaneous – unbridled interaction can occur between a horse and a human. It is in such a situation that we can and need to call on the capacity for spontaneous awareness and response which we have spent so much energy and time developing both on our own and in partnership with our horse. It is now that we can assert our control over our mind by placing it at the service of the similarly aware, sensitive, sentient beings that we are, authentically congruent in our energetical dance with the horse. And here we are referring to the genuine article, up to half a tonne or more of a supremely energetic collection of live tissue capable of the swiftest dashes and the gentlest caressing breaths, not some 'bomb-proof' shell of learned helplessness. Now you may legitimately ask whether it is possible for us to stay safe, if we abandon control and seek voluntary, spontaneous interaction with this magnificent creation of both elegance and power. How do we deal with fear? Should we become fearless? Or is there another way?

Fear is an emotion, the expression of being afraid. But are we afraid of what we are aware of or our idea of it? This may seem like splitting hairs but try and avoid the temptation to conclude that it is, because the difference between our awareness of an awe-inspiring horse and our idea of the same horse is as essential as that between 'awesome' and 'awful'. They are two totally different things. Understanding the difference is key to knowing that the question as to whether we should be fearless or not is utterly irrelevant. Our bodies have built-in defence mechanisms which enable us to respond to danger far more quickly than the time it would take to transmit a signal to the brain and receive a coherent conscious response. Reflexes are an example of this and so too is the proverbial adrenalin rush. When we are so fully present in the here and now that all which meaningfully exists for us is what we are spontaneously aware of, our responses are as spontaneous and rely on those defence mechanisms if the body senses that we are in danger, as well as any other skills which we may have acquired through past study and practice. During this process our rational mind serves as little more than a support but a very worthwhile one at that.

As such, while we are in this ongoing process of spontaneous awareness and response, we have no capacity available to be afraid. This is because fear relies on a rational rather than a spontaneous awareness of our situation. For it is only then than that the mind can consciously produce an image of that situation along with images of its potentially harmful effects so as to elicit associated feelings of fear. What we fear is not what we are spontaneously aware of but the collection of associated images of potential danger which our mind presents to us. It is through this that we experience fear but it is also in this that we can find the answer as to how to deal with this fear.

By now you would probably suspect that the solution lies in dismissing the mind from rationally active duty and you would be right to do so. Better still, we could ensure that the mind stays relegated to the provision of support for our spontaneous awareness and responses, which remain in the foreground, allowing those of our faculties which are best capable of dealing with a potentially scary situation to do so spontaneously. In this way it becomes possible to bypass fear, while simultaneously remaining safe and present with presence.

This is not an exercise in mere theory that I am presenting here. It is a strategy that I have used to great effect on the few occasions where I have unexpectedly found myself in potential danger with a horse. Perhaps the most frightening occasion (with hindsight, as I was too embroiled in being fully present at the time to contemplate the danger consciously and hence experience the fear) occurred when Anaïs came into season several years ago. All of the livery ('agistment' to my Antipodean friends) clients at our yard had been given their marching orders and we had found a temporary address for our mares while we looked for a replacement facility. The horses were stabled at night and during the day we turned them out into a large field adjacent to an even larger one which held a further five mares. They came into season soon after Pip and Anaïs arrived, which in turn prompted our mares to do the same. Always hormonal at the best of times, Anaïs could be very unpredictable when in season and sometimes behaved with the mindless aggression of a stallion on steroids. This particular time was the worst I have ever seen. She was besides herself. En route to the stables from the field one evening, Anaïs suddenly tried to dart off in the direction of the field serving as home to the other mares, who were careering around in it. Alert to the possibility of something such as this occurring, I had the lead rope attached to her softly lined webbing halter in my right hand and a dressage whip in my left. I immediately leapt into what I assumed would have been her path, dropped into a partial crouch and raised both hands while angling the whip to serve as a barrier crossing it. Fortunately she has sharp reflexes and came to an abrupt halt before me. I held my ground but remained completely motionless.

Again with hindsight, if there had been or more times during what occurred that evening when she would have reared as majestically as she had often done in the past, that would have been the first occasion. Calmness was my instinctive response. This is a mare that will return any aggression with considerable interest and my intuition cautioned against an exhibition of this truth. As time stood still we eyeballed each other until I noticed a flicker of acknowledgement. Slowly I straightened my knees to walking height and, while keeping the hand holding the lead rope raised between us, I lowered the one holding the whip but kept it angled across her intended path. Then I shifted my body back into the direction of the stables and waited for her to resume her walk towards them. For a moment she declined the invitation but I held my ground and just waited. Then we resumed our walk towards the stables. Every now and then she would vary her gait, searching for a break in my vigilance and looking for an unguarded path through me. In this respect she was very unlike Pip, who would have sought a way to slip past me. Anaïs was more intent on finding a way to overcome me full frontal. She found none.

There was going to be another challenge and it was going to be major. I felt it build up in her as we approached the entrance to her stable. This time I was ready for this gloriously powerful horse or so I hoped. The door to the stable was open. We halted before the entrance. Now I was to her right. I averted my eyes from hers. I needed to sense her energy. Anaïs had to go in of her own accord. I could not do it for her. It was then that I felt her go skyward. It was breathtaking to see her rear. She rose upright and erect, her balance disconcertingly superb. The clash of wills would start upon her descent but I was ready for her. There was no room for hesitation or doubt. When she descended, when her hooves touched the ground, then she would be ready to walk through the entrance into the stable. I was so intent to the point of being convinced of this that no alternative was left available to contemplate, not even to me. And so it came to pass.

Descending from her dizzying height, Anaïs inclined her nose slightly towards me as her hooves hit the concrete in front of the stable. This I noticed from the corner of my eye for I held my gaze firmly on the entrance. There was no doubt. Nothing else was possible. I sensed the mare trembling next to me. What to do? Then abruptly her energy softened and she calmly walked into the stable. As I quickly shut the door, she turned around towards me and started to lick and chew. I smiled, praised her, gave her some hay and invited her to eat. This subsequently turned out to be a watershed moment in my relationship with Anaïs. We have never experienced such a challenging incident again since.

Through this experience and my overall interaction with horses, our own and others, it has become very clear to me that it is impossible for a horse and a human to have any meaningful inter-action with each other outside the ties of control in the absence of a bond of connection between them. It is this connection which makes it possible to abandon the tools of restraint, the instruments of coercion and control in favour of voluntary, spontaneous contact and communication. Yet there is another absolutely important aspect of connection which I personally consider to be utterly essential to the horse-human equation and it is this: safety! In the past I used to do a variety of things with horses, including riding, relying solely on restraints, coercion and control, with absolutely no connection between them and myself. Now I shudder when I look back on this, for I would never dare do anything remotely risky with a horse in the absence of connection, for it is far more reliable for the safety of both horse and human than any mechanical device devised by man. And it is possible for a human to establish such a connection with a horse very quickly, provided that they have a knowledge of the essential nature of horses and have the presence which is achieved through being in harmony with the current flow of motion, change and energy in the situation in which they find themself.

As horse and human interact with such a connection over time, they are able to develop a relationship with each other. Such a relationship may become very close In that it does, it also serves to facilitate interaction between the species. Similarly, it also boosts safety in that communication improves on all fronts and mutual trust grows and is consolidated. As humans developing the power of being with our horses, we can learn how to establish and nurture true connection and a close relationship with them.

Connection

So what exactly is connection between a horse and a human, both of whom are sentient creatures? Essentially, connection occurs when there is a voluntary, spontaneous and energetical confluence of being between a horse and a human which each can sense in the other and which, as such, is intuitive and our overriding perception of it occurs through feeling. This is how onlookers may also experience it. There is a harmonious intuitive alignment of being between horse and human whose fullness during connection is greater than the sum of its parts. To achieve a connection between a horse and a human, neither species requires a small enclosure, such as a round pen, or any tool of restraint, such as a bridle or a halter, or an instrument of coercion, such as a whip or any surrogate in the form of a reed, stick or whatever. Connection is precisely that: horse and human *choose* to be and/or interact with each other. It is a two-way thing, like a dance involving a sensitive, loving couple. Where such a dance occurs, there is as much need to insist on boundaries as between close friends. And because connection is the result and expression of choice, it cannot be the product of behaviourist training by definition.

For such intuitive connection to occur between a horse and a human there are three prerequisites which need to be fulfilled. The first of these is self-evident. There must be *contact* between the horse and the human. Equally obvious is the second, namely, *communication* must occur between the horse and the human. Perhaps most 'horse people' would suffice with these two prerequisites. After all, if there is contact between a horse and a human, then there is a potential for communication between them. And if there is communication between them, then it should be possible to get things done. Indeed, so it is and things do get done. They usually get done using mechanical means in a mechanistic fashion involving human control of the horse with the aid of tools of restraint, instruments of coercion and/or rewards. As such, all of the horse's innate potential for voluntary creative interaction is denied, thereby creating difficulties between the species which could so easily be avoided if the third prerequisite for intuitive connection between horse and human were also to be fulfilled, namely, a voluntary, spontaneous, and energetical *confluence* of their respective beings.

Contact: presence and the horse

In all too many cases initiating contact with a horse in captivity involves a human entering their stable to place a restraint on their head with a lead attached to it preparatory to doing whatever the human has planned. If the horse has been turned out or lives outside, the human initiates contact with them by entering the field and proceeding to chase and catch the horse in order to do exactly the same. Alternatively, the horse may already be confined to the space or area in which a planned activity is scheduled to occur, when their human arrives.

If we find yourself in such a situation, the first question that we may want to ask ourselves is whether our horse actually notices us when we enter the space or area in which they are held? Does our horse acknowledge our presence, for instance, by inclining their head towards or approaching us? If our horse does not does not pay any attention to our entrance, then it is safe to conclude that, while we may be present, we have no presence, are of no interest to our horse and as such have not even touched first base with them. There is simply no contact between the horse and the human. And without contact there is nothing we can do with a horse. Indeed, there is not even the potential for anything, unless we are prepared to resort to control and imposition.

Fortunately, there is something we can do to remedy this. Essentially it is very straightforward because it is based on the essential characteristics of the horse, which we have already discussed. In the first place, we can commit ourselves to developing the presence of being as set out in the first part of this book. It is such presence which makes it possible for the horse, first of all, to acknowledge our entrance into their domain and, secondly, to choose to be with us. As we have already noted, horses are alert to the energetical presence of spontaneous awareness, are drawn to the authoritative presence through which empathy, reliability and dependability are expressed and are favourably disposed towards the energy of joy. When they encounter such a form of being, they usually acknowledge its presence and respond accordingly.

In very practical terms, horses note such presence in the way in which a human stands and moves. The upper body is relaxed and free of tension. The relaxed energy of controlled power is always evident. Any movement embodies congruent, intuitive awareness and balance. And contact is clear but gentle.

In addition, horses are highly curious creatures to the point of being downright inquisitive once their need for some assurance of their safety has been satisfied. This innate curiosity is something that you can draw on to introduce yourself to a strange horse or the new you to your own horse. The following tip should be of some service in this respect.

TIP

Ensure that your horse is in a fairly large enclosed space, such as field or jumping arena and has ready access to food and water. Enter this space but do not approach your horse. Instead, make your way over to some other part of this space and do the grounding exercise and any other body awareness routines with which you are familiar, such as Tai Chi, Chi Gong or yoga. As you become grounded and more aware of yourself and your surroundings, also ensure that you are aware of your horse but expect nothing of them.

It is very likely that your horse will approach you of their own accord while you are doing this. Initially, this may occur only out of curiosity. Depending on how stressed or traumatised your horse is, this may not happen during the first session and one or more additional ones may be required before your horse approaches you voluntarily. The fact that your horse comes to you rather than the other way round is hugely important, because it occurs through choice. Your horse *chooses* to come to you. You do not impose your will on your horse. The mere fact that your horse takes the initiative to seek contact rather than the other way round means that your horse is also open to any other interesting activity that you may wish to initiate.

Here the emphasis is on 'interesting'. As we know, horses are highly sociable creatures, almost obsessively so. We humans are also very sociable, although we may have much to learn from horses in this respect, especially when it comes to honesty in our interaction with each other. When considering how to maintain and build on contact with our horse on a daily or somewhat less frequent basis, we may want to reflect on what attracts us to other humans on a social level. Is it their bubbly spirit? Perhaps it is because they have something inspiring or challenging to show us? Maybe they enjoy sharing a drink or meal with us? Or could it be that we enjoy jogging with them every morning? Just hanging out together maybe? Any or all of the above? Anything else? Could I perhaps dare to suggest that what draws other humans to seek contact with us is first and foremost *joie de vivre* in the broadest sense of the term? And could I simultaneously suggest that the situation is essentially no different in the case of a horse?

You would be forgiven for concluding that what I seem to be implying is that if we wish to establish and maintain contact with the horse, we have a duty to be happy whenever we seek to do so. Of course, this is a tall, if not impossible order for any human? What then is the alternative? If you have been reading closely so far, you will know the answer to this question. Indeed, grounding ourselves to enter fully into the moment that is always now, that state of being in which we are spontaneously and intuitively aware of ourselves and our immediate surroundings to the exclusion of everything else.

It is as this type of being that we can achieve the type of presence in the presence of horses which brings us together with them in the present. For it is as this type of being that we can experience the feeling that such presence embodies, contentment. This the *joie de vivre* which horses find so inviting. Initially a significant amount of time and effort may be demanded of us to become this type of being, yet the more frequently we ground ourselves, the easier it becomes and the faster we succeed until at a certain point in time it becomes possible to do so at the drop of a hat, as it were.

In this case we may also place the emphasis on 'inviting'. We invite the horse to spend time with us and to interact with us. Yet we do so in the full knowledge that the horse may decline this invitation. This is where we called upon not to expect anything. This is not the same as 'expect nothing'. If you expect nothing, you are likely to get nothing. And this is already what most humans do in relation to the horse. It is precisely because they expect nothing of their horse, that they resort to control, the tools of restraint and the instruments of coercion. This expectation of nothing is based on the assumption that, if you give the horse a choice, they will choose not to spend time with us and most definitely not to interact with us. And we humans would be absolutely right to anticipate this but only if we are not prepared to change our approach and become an interesting, inspiring partner to our horse, inviting them to share our *joie de vivre*. rather than insisting that they do as and when we require.

One way of ensuring that we adopt an inviting rather an insisting approach lies in changing the way in which we go out to greet our horse when we wish to initiate interaction with them. Here is a tip that you may wish to employ.

TIP

Whenever you go to your horse, avoid the temptation to walk up to and touch them. Instead, ground yourself before you enter their enclosure. Once you are inside it and can see your horse, simply stand and enjoy their presence for about a minute or until they acknowledge your presence. If your horse does not acknowledge your presence, walk a bit closer and wait again. Should it be necessary to do so, repeat this until your horse acknowledges your presence, even if this only occurs when you are right next to them. Then and then only should you touch them.

Of course, it is entirely possible that your horse may not acknowledge your presence. Do not interpret this as a reproach. Instead, be thankful, for it is a lesson. Your horse is telling you that you need to work on your presence. In addition, spend more time with your horse doing nothing but being spontaneously conscious in the moment with them. You are hanging out with your horse. It is only a question of time before your horse also hangs out with you. Perhaps not this time. Why not come back later or the next day? It will take as long as it takes, because your horse is not in a rush. Neither should you be.

Constraints of time represent an factor which has the potential to make it difficult to establish and maintain contact with our horse. Because of the utterly unnatural way in which most of us humans live, we have pretty demanding schedules and agendas. Our horses have to fit in with this, so we allocate them time slots, which are usually not long enough to accommodate what we have in mind. Horses, on the other hand, do not have to contend with pressures of time. They may respond abruptly to a stimulus but there is no need for them to do so all of the time and in most cases they do not. It should therefore come as no surprise that there is often a conflict between horses and humans as a result of our different approaches to time. This is particularly true when we plan to do something specific with our horse.

By all means let us have a plan when we go to your horse but let us also remember that it is only a plan. It can be changed or even abandoned!

When our rational mind is in control, this advice may sound unacceptably frustrating. Yet, if we consider for a moment that, should we wish to do anything meaningful with our horse, we will need to draw on spontaneous consciousness in order to enter into the present with them, we will realise immediately that the flexibility of this approach is inherent in such consciousness. It also offers both horse and human greater potential for meaningful interaction, because we will be able to respond as spontaneously as our horse allows. It is also quite likely that instead of what we had planned, our horse may offer us something equally meaningful if not more refreshingly creative. Nevertheless, there is always the chance that our horse is not ready for us. Perhaps they would prefer to graze, spend time with their equine friend or not do anything at all. Respecting and accepting this will probably make it much easier to spend a far more enjoyable time with each other during our next visit, whenever that occurs.

Communication: body language and energy

Without contact there can be no communication between a horse and a human. Conversely, once there is contact between the species, they can also communicate with each other. So how can we communicate with horses? Increasingly, it is becoming quite difficult to find a human who would not answer this question by citing 'body language'. This is largely true but it is far from being the entire answer. But before explaining what I mean, it may be useful to clarify what is meant by 'body language'.

Essentially, the term, 'body language', is employed to refer to the use of the body, the horse's or our own, to convey meaning to the other species. This may occur through the movement (or lack of it) of one or more body parts on their own, or in relation to the horse, human or both, the position of the body as a whole on its own or in relation to the other species, or a combination of body part movement(s) and body position along with the speed and intensity with which this occurs. An example could take the form of a horse pinning back their ears or a human urging a horse to go forward by positioning themself behind their shoulder while facing the latter's head, extending the outer arm forward with the palm open to invite the horse to move forwards while urging them to do so simultaneously by lowering the inner arm towards the hindlegs with the palm open and facing forward.

This all sounds pretty mechanical and all that seems to be needed is a mechanistic technique to enable us to communicate our requirements to the horse, as it is self-evident that we will be able to gauge their response if we learn enough of their body language to do so. More often than not, we opt for the most obvious form of 'communication', behaviourist horse training, because no one appears to have discovered either the need or the potential for any other form of interaction with the horse. As we have already noted, this approach ignores most of what the horse is capable of in the realm of communication. In that it does this, behaviourist training also has the effect of dumbing down the horse and the level of communication with them. Clearly, if we are looking to achieve the most creative form of communication between horses and humans as fellow sentient, cognitive beings who are capable of understanding and influencing each other through spontaneous intuitive interaction, behaviourist training is definitely not what we seek.

Yet body language in itself is not enough on its own, not to horses anyway. As we have already noted in our observations about the way in which horses communicate, body language occurs as part of energetical communication. It is the energy with and through which the body moves which fully expresses and clarifies the meaning and intent of the movement. It is precisely for this reason that we need to learn how to harness and direct our own energy if we are to communicate meaningfully with a horse.

Communication may be channelled through conscious awareness and responses, although it does not stop there. As we have already noted, energy may be harnessed and directed not only rationally but also spontaneously. We are able to do this rationally when we place our rational mind in the driver's seat. This occurs when we use our rational mind to reflect on our situation, decide on a course of action and begin to implement it, for example. The initial stage of intention is a vivid example of this. We consciously intend to execute a course of action and rationally begin to do so. Yet once we get underway, we enter fully into the present to join the horse in the realm of spontaneous, intuitive awareness and responses and the mind reverts to its role of supporting the spontaneous intuitive interaction which occurs in that domain. In this situation communication now occurs spontaneously rather than rationally.

It is a simple fact of life that spontaneous consciousness cannot occur without energy. Yet we need to be aware that life imbued with energy does not in itself imply that a life form is also spontaneously aware. On the contrary where humans are concerned, or so it would seem in the case of the majority of us, our energy is utterly divorced from any form of awareness for much, if not most, of the time. As we have just noted, energy can be rationally or spontaneously harnessed and directed, with the result that it is in harmony with our actions. As such, there is congruence between what we do and the energy that embodies and imbues our actions. But what happens during those times when we are not rationally or spontaneously interacting with our horse while in their presence?

In this case our energy is not in harmony with our actions by definition. In fact, our energy and our actions are saying two different things. We are not congruent. To us it is not an issue because we are not aware when this happens. To the horse though, this is puzzling if not disconcerting. While we may think that we are only communicating with the horse when we choose to do so actively, the horse experiences this very differently. Because the horse is always alert and aware during their waking moments, we are always communicating with them when we are in their presence. Everything we do is communication to the horse, as is the energy which accompanies it. However, if we are incongruent, we will be communicating two different things. For this reason alone, we may want to ensure that we are always fully present when we are in our horse's presence. Only then will we be communicating fully and clearly with the horse.

Confluence: voluntary, spontaneous and energetical

Just as there can be no communication between a horse and a human without contact, so too can there be no confluence bringing them together in connection with each other without communication. As such, this confluence represents the third essential component for true connection between a horse and a human. The term, 'confluence', literally means flowing together and this is precisely what happens in the case of such connection. Synchronicity, the phenomenon of moving in unison spontaneously, is an essential aspect of this confluence but it is not confined to the physical. It occurs on all levels. Horse and human stand and move together physically, mentally, even emotionally and not least energetically. And they do so of their own volition, constantly reciprocating the connection which they experience from the other creature. Yet, except initially, it is not a rational act dictated by the mind. Rather, it is spontaneous and occurs as a constant response to a constant awareness of the other species in the circumstances in which they find themselves and each other. In a nutshell then, true connection between a horse and a human is a voluntary, spontaneous, intuitive confluence of the life forces of two sentient beings at multiple levels of experience which is synchronous and reciprocal, and which cannot be trained.

Or can it? There is an emerging trend on the part of horse and other animal trainers towards the presentation of connection between horse and human as a trainable technique. Books, videos and online courses are being offered to help humans achieve a connection with their horses through training, not just of the human but also the horse. While it is clear from what we have discussed so far that selective human training could indeed help a human learn to develop the essence of being which is required to facilitate connection between them and a horse, it is difficult to imagine that this could also be true for the horse if such training takes the form of conditioning behaviour, which is by far the most widespread form of horse training on offer and provided.

As already discussed, behavioural or behaviourist training is designed to modify horse behaviour by conditioning it. This is an approach which first and foremost denies the horse an opportunity to express themself spontaneously and of their own volition. Voluntary, spontaneous intuitive self-expression on the part of both the horse and the human is a prerequisite for authentic connection between them. Conditioned behaviour is by its very nature neither voluntary or spontaneous and it is definitely not intuitive. Behaviourists may respond to this by arguing that behaviour conditioning does not reduce the capacity of the horse for voluntary, spontaneous self-expression but merely redefines the parameters within which this can occur. True, but is this not sleight of hand, the kind of thing that we may expect of magicians and illusionists? For if we modify the horse's behaviour through conditioning, do we not only deprive them of significant scope for such self-expression but also do so permanently, especially where such conditioning occurs as effectively as it can through positive reinforcement, for instance?

In addition, trying to train connection in a horse represents not an abandonment of the paradigm of human control but the reinforcement of it, does it not? And is it really possible for the horse to express themself spontaneously of their own volition while their behaviour is subject to immediate human control? It is self-evident that the answer to both questions must be in the negative, especially where immediate human control takes the form of human interaction with a horse in a confined space with or without the use of tools of restraint and/or instruments of coercion.

Practitioners of positive reinforcement, such as clicker trainers may be tempted to beg exception for their behaviourist training techniques in that they do not rely on confined spaces or such tools and instruments. However, any claim on their part that the horse is free to walk away and decline to participate may rightly be viewed with some scepticism. After all, the rewards which positive reinforcement practitioners employ, especially during the initial stages of training, have been shown to be much more effective in controlling and conditioning the behaviour of horses than the tools of restraint and instruments of coercion used by their fellow behaviourist trainers who employ negative reinforcement. Given that this is the case, one may legitimately ask whether a horse that a capable positive reinforcement practitioner trains is indeed actually able to decline further participation in such training.

Of course, all of this begs the question as to whether connection is possible between a horse and a human where the human controls the horse. Bearing in mind that connection is a two-way affair, the answer to this question is both straightforward but potentially confusing: yes and no. Time and time again I have been amazed to see a horse connect to a human even where control is involved both in my own immediate experience and in some of the interaction that I have observed between other horses and humans. The only common denominator that I have been able to identify in all of these cases lies in the genuine care for and delight in the horse which is so manifestly evident in the energy of the human that it is almost tangible. Horses respond very favourably to such energy and are ready to connect to a human who embodies it. This connection on the part of the horse represents the 'yes' to the question. The horse has connected to the human. Yet they have done so – not because they have been trained to connect but rather – in spite of the human's attempts to train them and to curtail their scope for voluntary behaviour as a result.

However, the human has failed to connect to the horse and this is the 'no'. To the extent that even such a human still feels the need to rely on control, it would appear that they are only capable of partial connection. They can sense the potential of what the horse has to offer but are unable to embrace it for fear that it may not be forthcoming. As such, they are afraid to let go and expect absolutely nothing, because they suspect that absolutely nothing will be forthcoming if they do. The human does not trust their horse to give what the horse offers without control nor do they trust themself to be capable of eliciting what the horse offers. To this extent the human's control of the horse represents their current level of impotence.

This is a hard lesson to learn, because it requires an admission of inadequacy on the part of the human. The horse is effectively telling the human, 'You are not enough!' If a horse makes this very clear to us by reflecting our inadequacy, we can essentially respond in one of two ways. Either we can reject this damming reflection or we can accept it and start looking for a way to become enough to our horse. There is nothing in between. Most, if not all, of us probably reject such a telling reflection of our inadequacy, at least initially. This is not surprising, because an admission of impotence requires humility and humility does not come readily to a human, especially where the human is aware that their horse depends on them for every aspect of their existence, the quality of their life and the nature of their well-being if any.

Yet it is precisely in such dependence that we humans can find the strength to yield to such humility. If the horse is so very dependent on us that they cannot live without our care and commitment, then surely this is a telling indication of just how strong we are in relation to them. Knowing this, do we really have anything to prove to the horse? Do we really need to show them who is ultimately in charge? No, of course not. We already know the answer to that question. We are. So then what have we got to lose by being humble enough before the horse to acknowledge our impotence? Ultimately, nothing, for at the end of it all we will still be in charge and the horse will still depend on us for their life and the quality of it. And do we have anything to gain by doing so? If we did not know better after what we have discussed so far, would it really matter? Probably not, so why don't we just assume that we do not have anything to gain. That way we will also not have any expectations. This means that in theory at least we might be pleasantly surprised.

My experience and that of a growing number of humans is that we definitely are very pleasantly surprised. The reason that we are is precisely because we dare to be humble enough to learn from the horses just how to allow them to express themselves without any expectation on our part. This should not be interpreted as allowing the horse to do as they want whenever they wish. In any interaction between two creatures, there are two life forces at play and, if that interaction is to be a dynamic harmony between them, they will spontaneously and voluntarily seek the path of intuitive synchronicity and reciprocity. This dynamic also occurs within the framework of the horse's innate nature as a highly sociable being. Small wonder therefore that the growing number of humans who give the horse the freedom to be without expectation while being a reliable, affable and stabilising force are afforded an opportunity to revel in the creativity, sensitivity, playfulness and collaboration which the horse has to offer by their very nature. It is then that we discover that connection is a two-way thing and we can reaffirm what it is.

INSIGHT

True connection between a horse and a human is a voluntary, spontaneous, intuitive confluence of the life forces of two sentient beings at multiple levels of experience which is synchronous and reciprocal, and which cannot be trained.

Relationship

A true connection between a horse and a human is indispensable if the two species are to interact with each other in any meaningful, mutually beneficial way. It can also be achieved relatively quickly, often within minutes if not moments of a horse and a human encountering each other, depending on the individuals involved and the circumstances of their encounter. Connection between the two may end after this. Alternatively, it may improve and move towards the development of a trusting, caring relationship between horse and human. And it is precisely such a relationship which is both at the heart of and indispensable to the closest possible interconnection between the species. If this is what we seek, a true connection between horse and human is not the goal of our interaction with each other but merely the first meaningful step towards such a relationship.

Followership, partnership and friendship

So what does a trusting, caring relationship between a horse and a human look like? If we are to believe the bulk of the 'horse trainers' out there, such a relationship must be based on trust and respect. In both cases demands are made of the horse and not the human. It is the horse that must trust the human and not the other way round. Similarly, it is the horse that must respect the human and not vice versa. This is a one-way street. Knowing this, we should be on our guard immediately. After all, is a trusting, caring relationship between two creatures not one which is at the very least reciprocal, with voluntary commitments given on both sides?

To know the type of relationship that is possible with a horse, we have to know the horse, not only the particular one before us but also the species. As we have noted in our discussion of the essential features of the horse, theirs is a species which eschews leadership as we know it but is open to two main types of relationship, the very close friendship of which they are capable and the somewhat looser relationship of loyalty to other members of their band within a larger herd. In the latter case their social relationship also extends to a type of followership in some cases. The younger or more junior members of a band may choose to follow another member whom they deem to be reliable, dependable and trustworthy. Both friendship and followership would appear to readily suggest themselves as possible models for a long-term horse-human relationship.

Followership

This would appear to be confirmed if we view these variants in the light of the way in which humans not only keep and interact with horses but in which a growing number of us aspire to do so. In the first place, our horses depend on us for their physical safety, and also to a large extent their mental and emotional well-being. As such, we are their protector, a guardian on whom they rely for their very life. To this extent, we are also their provider.

Protector

The role of protector is that played by the stallion in a harem band. Contrary to popular human mythology of the horse, a stallion is not a leader. Rather, the stallion usually takes up the rear when his harem band is on the move. His task is to keep all of the members of the band together for their protection and ultimately to help him keep his mares safe from any creature that might want to attack or run off with them. This includes chasing up stragglers or any horse that may stray from the direction in which the band is heading. Part of this duty of protection includes chasing off predators or competitors.

Our horses may view us as protectors if they see us play a role which resembles the type of protection which they appreciate. Although this role may vary, what is perhaps the most essential feature of it is the presence which a genuine protector radiates. Such a protector exhibits reliability, dependability, trustworthiness, intent, decisiveness and calm. There is no need for a protector to prove themself to those they protect. They are simply what they are: a protector. This role, which is assigned to the stallion in the wild, is what we humans are called upon to play in captivity.

And we have already learned how to start developing such a presence. It will not happen overnight but it will materialise, provided that we persist in developing it until it becomes second nature. The key to being our horses' protector is to have a plan to protect and help them. Yet, when we enter completely into full, intuitive spontaneous awareness with them, we need to be able to respond to what we are aware of in our horses as intuitively and spontaneously even if this means abandoning that plan. Being fully in the present also means that we have no capacity available to entertain doubts or fears. As such, we will not be fearless. Instead, fear will simply not feature.

Being present as a protector in this way enables us to move amongst our horses without the need to set boundaries, as some trainers insist. Instead, we find that our horses set their own boundaries. They do not crowd us in or mug us and move out of the way if we show them that we require this. This occurs even if we are carrying a bucket of feed. And if there is a need to intervene quickly in order to protect them, for instance, to move them quickly out of harm's way or to discourage one from pilfering food from another (one of the drawbacks of captivity), they do not interpret this as an attack against which they need to defend themselves. The energy with which we do this differs completely from that of an attack. This they pick up on immediately. We are there to protect them and this is the energy that we radiate.

Provider
Just as they might have followed a reliable mare in the wild to pasture or a source of water, so too can our horses in captivity take their cue to obtain what they need from what we provide. Yet this is not simply a matter of putting down feed and water, after which we just walk away. It is about being fully present with our horses when we do so, intuitively and spontaneously aware and ready to respond in the same vein. As when we serve as a protector to our horses, so too when we act as their provider, we go about our business calmly but decisively without any doubts or fears. And similarly our horses recognise the energy of the provider within us. Neither do we need to set boundaries for them while assuming this role, as they define their

own, even when we carry a bucket of feed amongst them to take it to another horse and motion them to step aside and make way until we bring them theirs.

I know of at least one training method that utilises the role of the provider in an attempt to create a closer bond between horse and human. As we have already noted though, it is simply impossible to train a horse to connect with a human, for less will remain of the sentient horse for the human to connect to and, if the horse does connect to the human, this will occur in spite and not because of training. More importantly though, there is absolutely no need for such training. Horses are familiar with the role of provider. And if the provider is reliable, dependable, trustworthy and fully present with them, horses are ready to acknowledge this role and defer to it as in the case of that of protector.

Partnership

If we keep a horse on their own in the absence of any equine companions, as many humans do, we are their only source of companionship. As such, we are also called upon to be their partner. The horse stands to benefit from this. So too may the human. The role of partner corresponds to that of any member of a band of horses in the wild in relation to any other member of the same band. Thinking back to our discussion of the essential characteristics of horses, we may recall that sociability is arguably the most predominant of them in terms of the time, effort and energy involved. In the wild horses spend most of their time actively doing things as part of a close-knit group, a harem or other small band. They forage together, drink together, move from one place to another together, play with and groom each other.... The list is long. If horses are not actively doing things together, they spend their time doing 'nothing' together or at least this seems to be the case. Often they are simply dozing together, although they are still alert to the smallest sign of anything out of the ordinary, even the calm approach of an aware human. In some cases one or more members of a band may be enjoying the deep sleep of REM, while at least one of their number stands sentry. In all of these active and less active communal undertakings the horses making up a band are partners to each other.

The situation is obviously different in captivity. Ultimately our horses rely on us for partnership. We are called upon to become partners to them, choose partners for them or do both. If we wish to be a partner to our horses, we need to enjoy spending time with them either doing something or seemingly nothing, just as horses do with each other, and we need to make time available for such enjoyment. If it becomes a chore, we will not enjoy it. And if we simply use that time simply to do stuff of our invention, our horses may not enjoy it. At the end of the day partnership is all about enjoyment and socialising, and this could involve going out together, some type of sport, playing with each other, grooming, just hanging out together or whatever. This is much the same as we might do with another human. The substance might differ but the essence is very similar.

There are a couple of misconceptions which regularly do the rounds in human circles when we consider partnership with a horse and they revolve around quaint ideas of respect. At some stage or another you have probably heard a human claim that a horse needs to show the human respect by staying outside the human's 'personal bubble'. The human, it is claimed, needs to teach the horse to respect their personal boundaries to protect this bubble. A more enlightened approach might insist that both the horse and the human have a personal bubble and that, although the human needs to train the horse to respect the former's personal boundaries, the human should also respect those of the horse. Yet I must confess that I have never known any human who even insists on respect for mutual boundaries choosing to desist from the ultimate disrespect of a horse's boundaries, namely, riding.

Contrary to popular equine mythology, this insistence on re-specting boundaries is utterly alien to the horse. This is because adult horses do not feel a need to insist that their personal boundaries be respected in their natural surroundings. Instead, they maintain boun-daries of their own free will. They are alert to the presence (I use the term advisedly) of the other creature and respond accordingly. In part they do this because they have learned the social conventions of their band from its other members and the extent to which they do this is determined by the presence of the other horse as a partner, protector, provider and/or friend. A horse usually sets their boundaries more distant from a protector or provider but in greater proximity in the case of a partner. The closest two horses will allow themselves to venture towards each other occurs within a friendship. The existence of such a friendship is physically reflected in the form of head-to-head grazing and frequent mutual grooming, amongst other things. It is important to realise, firstly, that these roles are not mutually exclusive. All of the members of a band of horses are by definition partners to each other. Yet they could combine this role with that of protector or provider plus that of friend, although it is unlikely that a single horse would be both protector and provider. Secondly, these are observations and not hard and fast guidelines. There are obvious cases in which they will not apply, for instance, in the case of mating and the upbringing of juveniles. Nevertheless, these roles can serve to help us understand the dynamics of horses' interaction with other creatures, including ourselves, and why it is so important for us to develop presence.

There is however a growing tendency for some of us to suggest that horses and humans are equal partners. This may be the case during much of the interaction that we undertake with our horses as partners. Yet we should perhaps bear in mind that it is we and not our horses who determine the parameters of such interaction, including the time, venue, and tools or methods we choose to employ and any other factors which only we are able to determine. In this sense we are very unequal partners to our horses in many respects. This is also one of the reasons why horses do not acknowledge us as merely other members of their species. They are aware of the essential differences between horses and humans.

Nevertheless, if we factor in our roles as protector and provider, then it becomes readily apparent that our inequality as partners also entails special responsibilities on our part. These responsibilities are quite obviously those of a protector and a provider but they are not confined to them. They also include what we may expect of ourselves if we wish to be a genuine partner to our horses. Recall the willing victim syndrome which we have already discussed. Horses can sometimes seem to be the ultimate willing victims when we consider the amount of abuse that they accept from humans before they respond with resistance. As such, relying on our horse to define the boundaries of abuse for us is a bit like adding insult to injury, if not just more of the latter. If we wish to be an honest partner to our horse, we need to step up and define our own boundaries of what we feel is disrespectful to our horse. And if we are perfectly honest in the light of what we now know about horses, those boundaries will be a good deal more strictly defined than the horse's.

Friendship

As in the case of humans, a friendship is the closest form of relationship which a horse can have with another living creature and it may or may not be accompanied by courtship and sexual relations where the same species is involved. In the wild such friendships have been known to occur between two males and between a male and a female but not really between two females. Perhaps this is because most of the females that have been observed have been part of a harem band and the resulting frequency and intensity of contact between the mares in such a band may render close female friendships superfluous. Whatever the case, such friendships between horses may be very close and last a long time. The same may occur in captivity if given a chance. Our two geldings, Gulliver and Farinelli, became very close friends soon after we brought them together at the age of seven and four respectively. The bond between them grew stronger over time and they remained together as good friends for twenty-two years until the earth reclaimed Gulliver.

Although horses in the wild are partners to each other in their respective bands, this does not mean that they are friends. While a friend starts out as a partner, not every partner becomes a friend. So what is it that makes an equine friend? Observations of horses in the wild and in captivity reveal that equine friends spend as much time with each other as they can. They move, forage, graze, snooze and sleep close to each other and may even play together. They usually also groom, hang around with and call out to each other. And if they are separated, they fret and pine to the point where they may deprive themselves of food, sleep and safety. In extreme cases they may even die. In captivity, where the abnormal (to the horse) and stress become the new 'normal', such friendships may be particularly intense. More often than not, we humans do not realise what emotional pain and hardship we inflict on horses when we separate equine friends. I know that I did not when we separated Gulliver and Anaïs, a decision I now profoundly regret.

If we seek to have the closest possible relationship with our horses, the way forward is self-evident or it should be by now. Quite simply, we need to become a true friend to our horses. To do so, we need to learn from the horse what exactly true friendship means to them. We are not tasked to emulate them in precisely what equine friends do together, although broadly speaking, similar activities may occur between horse and human within the context of friendship as amongst horses on the one hand and amongst humans on the other. We may move together with our horse, often in synchrony, or simply hang out together. Alternatively, we may share food with them or groom them. Anaïs enjoys mutual grooming with me sometimes, as does Farinelli on occasion. They manoeuvre themselves into position under my hand until it is over the spot where they require attention. I knead the area which they indicate with strong rhythmic finger movements, while they nibble the palm of my other hand. When the spot is done, we switch sides to address the corresponding area on the other side of the horse. In a single mutual grooming session I might be asked to address several areas or only one. Some horses are not overly keen on this. Gulliver was one of them. Pip is quite happy to be groomed at times but is quite emphatic that she does not reciprocate on the human hand or any other body part for that matter. Play is something that males are quite happy to indulge in but mares do not seem to be overly pleased with the prospect.

Choice and trust

If we examine the roles of protector, provider, partner and friend in communities of horses in the wild and to a more limited extent in captivity, it is possible to identify two key elements which all of them have in common. These two elements are choice and trust. Essentially, they represent two sides of the same coin. In the same way that there can be no choice without trust so too can there be no trust without choice. The one not only implies the other but is also a requirement for it. As such, we may learn a great deal by examining both elements in greater detail.

Choice

As we have noted when discussing the essential features of horses, these fellow sentient beings do not impose their will on others of their kind. Even the stallion, the protector who herds his mares and their progeny together to protect them, does not insist that they follow him wherever he goes. On the contrary, many mares desert their stallion in favour of another and he expels his progeny from the band when they attain adulthood. Similarly, the mares who act as providers when they head off and are followed to a source of water or food, do not insist on any type of leadership as we humans understand it. The other members may choose to follow them or not and there are recorded incidents of them deciding not to do so.

As we might expect, equine partners and friends also relate to each other as an expression of choice. Unlike humans, who often approach relationships, even intimate ones with expectations, as though they involve emotional transactions based on a fair and equitable exchange of undertakings, horses have none. They choose to be sociable with one another and delight in doing so, expecting nothing in return. If there is any reward, it is in the doing and not the receiving. What they receive is a bonus, freely given without expectation. And what they receive is considerable, a highly sociable partner at the very least or that plus a caring, committed, loyal friend.

If we wish to relate to our horses in a way that is utterly natural to them and one which they feel to be appropriate, then we will have to face up to a rather inconvenient truth and it is this. To the horse choice is an essential aspect of all of the roles that we play with them, be it that of protector, provider, partner or friend and, as such, we are called upon not merely to take up the challenge of choice, not simply to dare to overcome it but rather to delight in doing so and to find joy in it without expecting anything in return. This in essence is the call of the horse. Can we find it within ourselves to answer this call?

———

INSIGHT

The call of the horse is essentially the challenge not merely to allow the horse to exercise choice but also for the human to find joy in doing so without expecting anything in return.

———

Many of us may feel that this call is very threatening and we may do so for two reasons. First of all, there is the question of choice and what it seems to imply in a live bundle of moving parts weighing up to as much as a car. Is this not a recipe for mayhem and chaos, if not downright life-threatening situations? It could be if we misinterpret the choice that we are dealing with here. Let us be very clear that choice should not be interpreted as laissez-faire. This is not about allowing a horse to do precisely what they like in the absence of any intervention on our part. Neither is it about a horse acting out of character. There are limitations on what horses can do just as there are on our potential actions. Part of these limitations are external to the horse in that they involve outside parameters, such as those just mentioned. Yet part of them are internal to the extent that they are dictated by what the nature of the horse permits and what it does not.

Even in the wild horses bump up against external limitations of choice, either natural or man-made. Round-ups and culling are examples of such man-made limitations. In captivity the external limitations are infinitely starker and more widespread depending on how we keep and interact with our horses. Far more often than not horses are denied choice in captivity, especially when interacting with us. This appears to be motivated largely by fear, ignorance or both. We may be afraid of the unfettered power of the horse, a fear which is predominantly based on our supposed 'knowledge' of the horse as a 'prey animal' rather than as the creature they really are when truly given a choice: highly sociable and predisposed to setting their own boundaries when interacting with a being of presence, especially where such a being is viewed as not merely a partner but also as a friend, protector and provider.

And this is where we encounter the horse's internal limitation of choice, which ironically is an expression of choice in itself. A prerequisite for being the obsessively sociable being we know as a horse is the exercise of restraint, enough to encourage any creature seeking to share such sociability to do just that. It is as though the horse is intuitively aware that, if they do not set their own boundaries in the course of social interaction they will discourage their interlocutor, perhaps even chase them away and, by doing so, kill the sociability on which they thrive. Of course, there is more at play where the other creature is a protector or provider. As we have already noted, the latter two roles are ones which other horses defer to. If a protector makes their way through the band, the other horses will normally step out of the way to allow them unimpeded passage. And in the case of a provider, although they have a choice, the other horses are more likely to follow them if they have proved themself in this role in the past.

When we note the restraint which horses exercise in their inter-action with creatures of presence and their voluntary imposition on their actions of their own boundaries. It should be clear that there are good grounds for concluding that choice does not lead to a free-for-all in the case of the horse. Knowing this should make it easier for us to actively acknowledge the horse's inherent ability to choose and express themself without fear of harm. Doing so initially however may require a leap of faith and this is where trust comes in.

The second reason why the call of choice may seem threatening lies in what it demands of us. Imagine for a moment that you have this creature called horse, strong, heavy, vigorous and bursting with the self-expression that is unbridled life. You have forsaken all tools of restraint, instruments of coercion and training methods of control. What is left to rely on in order to avoid being buried under the rubble occasioned by mayhem and chaos? Just you. And therein lies the ultimate challenge of choice for all of us. Somehow or other we need to dig deep within us to find the means not only to be fully present with the horse but also to convince the horse that what are asking of them is so good that they will not only want to do it but that the goodness in doing it will be rewarding in itself.

So where do we start? By now the answer should be second nature. We ground ourselves and enter the present moment with the horse and then.... This we will come to shortly. For the moment though we are again being asked to make that leap of faith, so it is perhaps an appropriate moment to consider trust.

Trust

When it comes to horses, 'trust' is a word that humans bandy about with growing frequency. Yet when we do this, it all too often becomes a one-way street. The horse, it is said, must learn to trust the human. If you look up 'trust' in a dictionary, you might find a definition such as this: 'Firm belief in the reliability, truth, or ability of someone or something' (the Oxford online dictionary at www. lexico.com, consulted 3 February 2020). Alternatively, you might find this definition: 'assured reliance on the character, ability, strength, or truth of someone or something' (the online version of Merriam-Webster at www.merriam-webster.com, consulted on 3 February 2020). In both cases we are presented with a conscious acknowledgement of a development that has actually occurred. We have learned to trust and we consciously acknowledge this.

What these definitions ignore is the process of learning to trust. When do we start learning to trust another creature? When does a horse? And how do we do this? Trust starts with a small step and it usually does so spontaneously and intuitively. When we meet other humans, for instance at a party or when we start a new study or job, we listen to what they have to say. The first human's talk may be highly articulate, well-reasoned and persuasive, more so than another's. Yet we may find ourselves swayed more by the second human, who is less convincing in what they say but more so in who they are. We may feel more apprehensive about the first, yet more accepting of the second, with the result that we may agree to meet for coffee with the latter but not the former. This could be the first small step towards a trusting relationship and it begins with a spontaneous, intuitive response to what you are spontaneously and intuitively aware of in that human. And this can happen within minutes of meeting them.

So too with a horse. In the same way that a human can decide to start trusting a horse spontaneously and intuitively from one moment to the next, a horse is capable of doing the very same in relation to a human. And this can happen within moments of a horse and a human meeting each other for the very first time. For this to occur though the human needs to have enough presence to be fully aware of the horse within their immediate surroundings and to respond to what they are aware of spontaneously and intuitively. For only then will horse and human establish contact, communication and a connection with each other. And it is that connection which marks the moment when horse and human spontaneously and intuitively move in the direction of trust.

Yet such connection and its initiation of trust is not an indication of one-way traffic. The spontaneous, intuitive move towards trust is one which occurs in both the horse and the human. Such is the nature of connection. If the horse and the human continue down this track both of them will learn to trust each other and not just the horse.

Increasingly, the human will notice grounds for growing trust. For instance, whereas the horse may have collided with the human's body when they swung their head in the past, now the horse will raise their head or find some other way to avoid bumping into the human. And at a certain point the horse may even go out of their way to avoid knocking over their human when they spook.

This is not to suggest that a human's trust in their horse is a passive exercise which depends on the horse creating favourable conditions for it to develop and flourish. When we enter into the present in the course of connection with our horse as partner, protector, provider and above all friend, we are effectively choosing to trust them. This is an active process and, in that it is, it presents the horse with something very tangible to rely and depend on, and to find joy in. And the more frequently and intensely this occurs, the more trust it elicits in the horse. This in turn encourages and nurtures a deeper trust on the part of the human. Trust in either species feeds off and reinforces it in the other if we let this happen. This continues until there is a reciprocity of trust which enables both horse and human to grow more self-assured in each other's presence. The resultant strength in both species enables them to relax their guard with each other to the point of being vulnerable without feeling weak. This is when it becomes possible to dispense with the tools of restraint, the instruments of coercion and the training methods of control.

Interestingly, this cannot occur in the absence of another aspect of trust on the part of the human. The development of trust in the horse is contingent on the human learning to trust themself. As such, trust between horses and humans is a three-way affair. It is simply impossible for us to trust our horse if we cannot trust ourselves to be the kind of human whose presence the horse experiences as that of a partner, protector, provider and friend. The only way in which we establish and develop such trust is to be a human with such presence. And the only way to do this is by harnessing the power of being in our interaction with horses.

Trust between horses and humans is a three-way affair: the horse learns to trust their human, the human lears to trust their horse and, as importantly, the human learns to trust themself ... to be the kind of human whose presence the horse experiences as that of a partner, protector, provider and friend.

Before learning how to harness the power of being, there is one very important aspect of trust that we need to be aware of and it is this. Trust is easy to abuse. There are two sides to this and they depend on the degree of trust that the horse has developed in the human. In the initial stages, while our horse's trust is still fragile, abusing their trust may destroy the relationship which we are developing with them. And it may be very difficult to re-establish such trust, if not impossible.

The other side of the coin is that a horse can learn to trust us to the extent that their bond with us is more secure than any tool of restraint could ever be. In fact, it is so secure that I personally would never engage in an activity with any of our horses which involves significant risk, such as walking or riding along a busy road or path, without such trust no matter how much tack I have at my disposal. It is the first line of protection for both my horse and myself. Yet, it is when trust has developed to this extent that it also becomes very easy to abuse with impunity. This is because the horse has become so accustomed to associating with a human who is fully present with them, who interacts with them energetically, who acts not only as their friend and partner but also as their protector and provider, that they seem almost no longer capable of comprehending that matters could be otherwise. This may be particularly true if you are someone like me, someone who still slips up now and then, albeit far more rarely than in the past, and wittingly or unwittingly abuses the horse's trust, for instance, through impatience, frustration or something else.

It is then that we need to recall the willing victim syndrome to which horses can sometimes seem so susceptible and assume responsibility for our own actions. Making mistakes is very human. Atoning for them can be equally human if we choose to let it be so. And fortunately, the horse is a hugely forgiving creature.

HARNESSING THE POWER OF BEING

So now that we understand the nature of the power of being within ourselves and in relation to the horse, how do we actually go about harnessing this power? By now you should be pretty clear on how to start and you may have some idea of the enormous potential which the power of being offers us in our attempts to become better humans to our horses. Because the process of becoming a better human is open-ended, what we are going to cover in our discussion of how to harness the power of being is inevitably going to be far from exhaustive. What we can do though is explore some of the avenues which I have discovered. Hopefully, this will in turn inspire others on a similar journey to contribute their experiences. In addition, our ongoing efforts should elicit new discoveries on which we can collectively build in the future.

Essentially, our attempts to harness the power of being will reflect its nature, especially in the sense that there is both an internal and an external aspect to the process. It is internal to the extent that it involves us working on ourselves to develop the capacity for both spontaneous and rational awareness and responses. And it is external in that we interact with our horses and the immediate surroundings in which this occurs. Having noted this, it is absolutely essential that we avoid the trap of drawing a distinction between who we are and what we do, for they are part and parcel of the same being. For this reason I deal with both the internal and external aspects together as we first examine the way in which we can communicate energetically with the horse before going on to look at how we can direct our own energy in relation to the horse and also redirect their energy. Then we explore some of the dynamics of energetical interaction with the horse before ending with a brief survey of ideas to create a more facilitative horse-friendly domain for interaction with these extraordinary fellow animals. But before we go any further, here is one of the most important tips that I have learned in my dealings with horses and one which we may wish to remember while we harness the power of being.

TIP

When in doubt while interacting with a horse, stop everything and reflect.

The occurrence of doubt is a sign that we are no longer spontaneously conscious and consequently not fully present with the horse. In such a situation the wisest course of action is for us to stop doing everything and reflect until we know what we should be doing. Then we can ground ourselves to become spontaneously conscious again.

Energetical communication with the horse

Let us start by acknowledging that the term, 'energetical communication' is to some extent an example of tautology, that is, stating something more than once using different words. This is because communication is by its very nature energetical as it involves the use of energy. We use energy not merely to produce the words or actions that we use to communicate with others but also to express their quality, for example, whether they should communicate calm or vigour, friendliness or hostility. Nevertheless, we shall use the term, 'energetical communication', to emphasise the need to involve the use of energy in our communication with the horse.

If we are to communicate energetically with a horse, there are two key aspects of the process which we need to consider and resolve appropriately beforehand. They are congruence and intent. And once we have resolved them, we may want to consider how we can influence the energy that we have to contend with.

Congruence

It is sometimes said that a horse is capable of mirroring a human in that they respond to a human as they experience the latter rather than as the human seeks to appear to the horse. If there is a difference between how a horse experiences a human and the image which the latter has and projects of themselves, the human may be described as incongruent. This is to say that there is a lack of agreement or harmony between their actual and preferred presence at that particular time, between their nature and their image. The human's actual presence or nature is what the horse interacts with and not the human's preferred presence or image of themselves. To this extent the horse reflects who the human is at that moment and not what the human seems to be. Consequently, it is quite likely that, if the human's image of themself is more favourable than their actual nature at that point in time, the horse's response to them is likely to be a source of disappointment.

It does not end here though. Imagine for a moment that you are that human and the horse is a large feisty animal. You may be afraid but decide to try and conceal your fear by adopting a nonchalant approach. As such, you will not be congruent and the chances are that the horse will see right through your apparent calm and reflect your fear to you. Similarly, if you declare that mutual respect must be the basis of the horse-human relationship and then resort to coercion to elicit such respect, the horse is likely to see through your lip service to respect and expose your behaviour for what it is: crass dominance. By the same token I could be in a similar position. More importantly, if the discrepancy between our actual and preferred presence is large enough, such lack of congruence may be a source not only of disappointment but danger. The horse is likely to respond to us in an unpredictable manner, one which we are by definition not prepared for. The outcome may be injury, not only to our ego but also physical and/or psychological harm. Indeed, the greater the discrepancy between our actual and preferred presence – that is to say, the greater the incongruence between the two – the more likely it is that we will be disappointed and perhaps even harmed.

It is clear that congruence between our actual and preferred presence is absolutely crucial if we wish to avoid disappointment and injury. In this sense it represents the bare minimum for safe interaction between horses and humans or at any rate for us to feel safe in our dealings with a member of that species barring an unforeseen accident. And because it is only when we feel safe that creative interaction becomes possible, it also represents the bare minimum for a human to do anything truly meaningful with a horse without resorting to force or the threat of it.

There is, however, one exception to this and that is where the incongruence is benign. Because horses are also sensitive to incongruence in humans at the energetical level, they are likely to respond in opposite ways to it depending on the type of energy involved. My observations over the years reveal that, where a horse experiences a human's energy as threatening or potentially so, they will resist or avoid connection and maintain their distance if possible, unless proximity appears to be less threatening, for instance, when chased in a confined space (for example, 'join-up', which is more accurately described as 'give up' – for more information about this see my article titled 'Horses and the Myth of Leadership' in my book, *When Horses Speak and Humans Listen*, a description of and links to which you will find at http://www. horsesandhumans.com/mainsite/whsahl-a.htm). The horse will do this no matter how 'friendly' the apparent actions of such a human are. This is an example of adverse incongruence. It is adverse in that it is threatening to the horse and they respond to it accordingly.

In a number of instances I have also seen the opposite occur. Where a human employs gadgets or methods in a way that is designed to inhibit and control the actions of a horse, the outcome may be favourable in spite of this. If the human is nevertheless committed to the well-being of the horse, they carry with them the energy of care, which also accompanies and informs their use of such gadgets and methods. Horses seem capable of detecting this energy and embracing it, especially if it is accompanied by the energy of joy. I have seen this occur often enough in both conventional equestrian pursuits and 'natural horsemanship' training to draw this conclusion. This is an example of benign incongruence. Because the energy is not or not potentially harmful to the horse, it does not elicit any evasive or defensive action from them.

As we have already discovered, if we want to ensure that we are always congruent, the easiest and fastest way is to ground ourselves. If you have been doing this regularly since starting to read this book, you should be very close to being able to do this without the need to use the techniques outlined in the first part of it. At a certain point you should find it a relatively simple matter to move from rational to spontaneous consciousness by simply deciding to do so. Grounding yourself in this way will enable you to enter into a state of spontaneous, intuitive awareness and response at the drop of a hat as it were. In this mode of being it is simply impossible not to be congruent, because it involves the abandonment of every fully rational thought and brings our energy into line with our presence. There is no longer any question of a separation between the two. They are effectively one. And the quiet contentment which we experience in this mode of being and the energy which it encompasses and radiates is welcome to the horse.

Intent

Intent is quite possibly the most misunderstood and consequently underrated quality of being in a human's relationship with a horse. This acknowledgement simultaneously suggests its importance to such a relationship. The reason why it is so important in this context lies in the role which intent or the lack of any plays in relation to our personal energy. Intent is what determines the state, nature, intensity and direction of this energy.

INSIGHT

Intent is what determines the state, nature, intensity and direction of our personal energy. In a word, we are our intent!

The state of our personal energy may be active or latent. It is active when we move and it is latent when we do not. In the latter case our energy is inert yet potentially available should we need it to be active. And it is our intent which determines whether this energy is active or latent. Similarly, the nature of our personal energy may also vary. For example, it may be calming, encouraging or exhortative when we assist another creature. Alternatively, our personal energy may be harsh and uncompromising, for instance, where we are seeking to prevent an accident from occurring. Again, it is intent which dictates the nature of this energy. In the same way, the intensity of our personal energy may differ depending on how we choose to act in particular circumstances. For example, it may be gentle or urgent, or anything in between. Where we direct our personal energy and the means we employ in order to do this also depend on our intent. Directing our own personal energy is an option which is self-evident. Less so is our ability to redirect another creature's personal energy. This we may choose to do rather than simply respond to it head on.

As we have already noted, intent does not exist as a mere rational idea of what we intend to do or refrain from doing, which we implement as though it is something that can exist as an entity separate from ourselves. Rather it permeates and pervades our every awareness, whether rational and wilful or spontaneous and intuitive. At any rate it should do so if it is to be genuine intent. While it is true that intent may start out as a rational idea, when we enter the present with the horse it becomes the spontaneous, intuitive awareness and response which embody this aspect of being. There is no difference between intent and being then. We are our intent. If our intent is to walk with our horse, then we are not merely implementing the idea of walking. Rather, while we are walking, we are the walking in both its intent and its actualisation. Put another way, we do not merely think intent with the horse. Rather we feel, experience and are our intent in every part of our being. As such, our intent is also immediate. It is not a plan which we intend to implement at some stage or in the long term. Rather intent exists here and now with our horse at the cutting edge of being.

Living intent in this way yields two hugely important benefits. In the first place, we are so involved in feeling, experiencing and being our intent that there is no room for anything else. We simply do not have any capacity available for doubt, hesitation, fear or any other thoughts for that matter. We are our intent completely and comprehensively. This is how our horse experiences our *intentful* presence.

Yet almost paradoxically this does not amount to intent at any cost. Because we are fully intuitively aware, especially if this occurs spontaneously rather than rationally (when there may be a risk of thought hijacking our agenda and turning intent into rigid, unyielding bossiness), we are always alert to changes in what we are aware of and we are capable of responding to them as spontaneously and intuitively as our *intentful* awareness. The significance of this cannot be overstated. It means that, even though we are being our intent, we are equally capable changing that intent immediately in response to what we are spontaneously and intuitively aware of. It means that we remain flexible enough to remain part of the motion, change and energy of being just as our horse always is and, as such, capable of adapting to their flow even to the extent of adjusting our intent. This in turn allows us to guide our personal energy and even that of the horse as flexibly as both species interact with each other.

When we live intent as fully as we are discussing here, that intent enjoys our entire focus and, as our intent adjusts in accordance with what we are spontaneously aware of, so too does our focus in equal measure or so it should. What we need to guard against though is the risk of failing to maintain that focus accordingly, shifting it instead to a subordinate part of our intent. Here is an example of what I mean. I have just turned off the shower and I would like to dry my toes with the towel that I am holding in my hands. It is easier for me to do this by raising my feet one at a time rather than bending over. Because I am in a hurry, I would prefer not to have to support myself with a hand against the shower cubicle wall. So I raise my foot and dry it while balancing on the other. My intent is to dry my foot and this what I focus on. Suddenly I feel myself wobble a bit. What should I do? Most of us would immediately concentrate on retaining our balance. Almost predictably, this would be the end of the exercise for we would lose our balance immediately. Either we would fall, put our foot down or lean against the wall for support. Why? Because we have shifted the focus of our intent from cleaning our toes to balancing. We have lost the primary focus of our intent.

So why does this happen? Quite simply because, when we seek to find our balance, we automatically summon our rational, wilful rather than our spontaneous, intuitive consciousness. We are no longer spontaneously and intuitively aware, with the result that we are no longer capable of responding to what we are aware of spontaneously and intuitively. The rational, wilful mind is simply no substitute, for it cannot respond as quickly as our spontaneous consciousness. And because it is premised on the exercise of the will rather than intuition, it cannot respond with feeling either. Our focus is consequently drawn away from our original intent, with the result that it collapses.

So is there a way to avoid this. Yes, and it is actually pretty easy. We simply keep our focus fixed on our original intent while still retaining the ability to be aware and to respond spontaneously and intuitively. In this particular example we would simply ignore the wobble with our rational wilful consciousness and stay focused on our original intent, which is not to balance our body but to dry our toes. Our spontaneous, intuitive consciousness would take care of our balance. If you find this difficult to accept, why not try it yourself?

PRACTICAL EXERCISE

This is a variant of a practical exercise which you may have already done. You learned how to make it easier to carry a full open container of water without spilling any by shifting your focus to something other than trying not to spill a single drop. This time you will do the same but instead of simply focusing on something else, you will be your intent. To do this we carry out the following steps:

1. find a shallow container with a relatively wide diameter. The base of a large plant pot will do just fine;
2. fill the container with water until just under the rim;
3. activate a timer and carry the container to a spot about ten to fifteen metres away and place it on the ground, while focusing on not spilling a single drop;
4. stop the timer when you have completed the task and note down the time it took;
5. now clarify your intent, which is not to avoiding spilling anything but rather to carry the water to the place that you have designated;
6. repeat Steps 1 to 4 but instead of trying not to spill a drop, make every effort to feel your intent throughout every part of you rather than focus on not spilling any water.

You should find that, as in the case of the first exercise, by shifting our focus away from preventing spillage, we are more effective, either completing the exercise without spilling any water and/or doing this much more quickly than when we focused on trying to avoid spilling a drop. Yet the chances are that by feeling your intent and hence becoming it, you are able to perform the exercise even more effectively.

In our interaction with horses this need to focus on our intent is particularly important, as it helps signal to the horse precisely what our intent is. Yet permeating our spontaneous consciousness as it does and hence being susceptible to change if the horse prefers this, this intent remains an element of interaction rather than a command. In our interaction with horses such focus on our intent can facilitate interaction at liberty precisely because it provides gentle but firm clarity about our intent. Suppose, for instance, that I would like my horse to stop grazing in the field and to accompany me to an enclosure, where we can do whatever it is that needs to be done but I would like to do this at liberty, if for no other reason than that I do not have a halter with me. All that I would need to do is calmly walk directly to my horse (avoiding stealth because horses can see through this very easily) and stop. Within seconds my horse will probably raise her head but, if she does not, then I would simply bend down, place my arm under her neck and then raise myself erect energetically, perhaps accompanied by one or more words, directing energy but *not* pressure on her neck through my arm. My horse raises her head, I point to the enclosure with the arm closer to her head while facing my body and the palm of my other hand in the same direction on the other side of me, thrust the base of my pelvis forward and communicate my intent to her with every part of my presence, which I may or may not accompany with a verbal explanation or exhortation (or both). Done often enough, such a series of body language movements becomes a fluid intuitive expression of my intent but remains an invitation rather than that it becomes a command. My horse may decline the invitation, in which case I have a choice as to whether I should extend another invitation or abandon the action. If my horse accepts my invitation, she always gets to move first and I join her at her side.

So what happens if my horse hesitates or stops along the way? Simply remain calm and repeat the communication of my intent. Above all, I must resist changing the focus of my intent, which is that we need to go to the enclosure. The focus must not shift to trying to persuade my horse to walk with me. This is not my intent. It is a given. My intent is that we walk to the enclosure together and that is where my focus must remain. The fact that my horse will need to walk with me if we are to do this is simply part of what needs to happen for my intent to remain a reality.

INSIGHT

My intent concerns what I intend to do and not what I would like my horse to do.

This is another essential aspect of intent and is a lesson taken directly from our horses. While going about my business with them, I sometimes need to ask a horse to move out of the way. In the past I used to assess the situation briefly, conclude what seemed to be the best direction in which I felt the horse should move and then ask them to do so accordingly. Every time the horse would move either in response to a verbal request or to that accompanied by a gentle energetical touch of my hand, usually on the horse's hamstrings or croup but without exerting any pressure. What surprised me though was that they frequently moved in a different direction to what I had envisaged. Eventually, the penny dropped and I realised that, while I was communicating my intent to pass, I was simultaneously asking them something else, namely, whether they would move in a particular direction, which was ultimately not my intent. Now I line up my request with my intent – which is to pass rather than have the horse move in a particular direction – and let the horse decide on the direction in which they would prefer to move. Everything now goes much more smoothly.

Directing and shaping energy with the horse

In as much as horses and humans utilise energy in countless ways, it is impossible to cover every aspect of this. What we can do is examine some of the main ways in which this occurs and how we can shape and direct some of this energy when it does. Here it is helpful to draw a distinction between ways in which we can:

- influence energy;
- lower and raise energy;
- direct energy; and
- redirect energy.

Influencing energy

When we talk about influencing energy, we are referring first and foremost to our own personal energy. It is possible for us to exert a huge amount of influence over our personal energy with relatively little effort. For instance, looking at photograph of a splendid sunset can have a very soothing effect on our energy. This is an example of directly influencing our personal energy. We are already familiar with the concept of influencing our personal energy directly. This is what we do when we ground ourselves and enter into a spontaneous and intuitive awareness of the present. We also know that influencing our personal energy directly in this way can have the effect of indirectly influencing the horse's energy as well.

Yet there are many other ways in which we can influence our personal energy in such a way as to facilitate connection with a horse. Let us explore ways of doing this:

- before going to the horse;
- when going to the horse; and
- while being with the horse.

Before going to the horse

Although horses have shown themselves to be very sensitive to humans with physical, mental or emotional concerns over the years and still do when they are given a choice, it would be disingenuous on our part to suggest that they usually or always enjoy being saddled with our baggage, as it were. We know that horses are highly sociable, inquisitive and playful, and that they thrive on the energy of joy. Knowing this, it would be very tempting not to conclude, that if we really want to have a close connection with a horse, we have a duty to both them and ourselves to be happy, at the very least before we go them. In this way it would be possible to ensure that all lines of contact, communication, confluence and hence ultimately connection are open.

Of course, the very sad truth of the type of life we humans have condemned ourselves to collectively is that such day-to-day happiness is a pipe dream for the vast majority of us and we are not even talking about the possibility of a calamity befalling us. Nevertheless, it is possible for us to use techniques such as grounding ourselves to achieve a feeling of calm contentment within minutes if not moments.

Sometimes though there may be occurrences which shake up our lives to the extent that we may find it difficult to initiate the grounding routine. What may help at such a time is to have ready access to stimuli which soothe and calm the soul before we even contemplate grounding. Nature is one of the most effective of such stimuli so, if you have access to it, you may want to draw on its rejuvenating and invigorating powers as often as you can. And if you do not have ready access to nature, there are a host of other options we may wish to consider. They can be as simple as finding a quiet spot where you can relax, close your eyes, start breathing more slowly and deeply while drawing on pleasant sensations or memories. Or you might wish to call a friend. Favourite paintings, pictures, music or videos may also help.

TIP

Surround yourself with positive energy. This will make it so much easier for you to achieve the calm contentment that we are aiming for in our interaction with horses.

In fact, we may want to consider surrounding ourselves with readily accessible opportunities for and avenues to calm contentment. Indeed, we may even want to avoid contact with disruptive influences. There is a temptation amongst many well-meaning horse people to expose equine abuse by posting pictures and media on social media. Unfortunately exposure to such negativity is contagious and may serve as a distraction from our own attempts to ensure that we have they type of personal energy which is conducive to good relations and interaction with our own and other horses. By focusing on the positive it not only becomes far easier to ensure that our personal energy is appropriate for the type of relationship that we seek with our horses but also helps to create an overall environment within which this becomes much easier for all of us to achieve. Added to this is the fact that in the final analysis judging another human has never helped a horse and in all likelihood will not ever do so.

INSIGHT

Judging another human has never helped a horse, let alone that or any other human. Is there then any point in judging another human?

While going to the horse

If we would like to exploit the power of being in interaction with our horses, then we will need to start the process of going to them by grounding ourselves each and every time. As already mentioned, it is possible to learn to do this so quickly that it can be done while going to the horse. We can conduct a quick internal awareness scan of ourselves, hold on to that awareness by extending it to include the immediate surroundings through which we are passing and then include the horse upon our arrival. As we know, grounding ourselves also has the effect of calming and relaxing us. It rids us of tension, lowers our energy and our centre of gravity, and ensures that our upper body is relaxed and our arms move as little as possible. This is the spontaneous, intuitive awareness of calm content and this awareness is permeated with the intent of care for and commitment to the horse and what we plan to do when we enter our horse's presence, all without expectation.

And what we intend to do with our horse when we enter their presence is to do all that we would expect of ourselves as a partner, provider, protector and friend to them. Our immediate intent on our way to our horse encompasses the essence of these roles. As a partner, we will be looking forward to pleasant, supportive contact with each other. As a provider we will be keen to know if the horse lacks anything and how we may remedy this. As a protector, we will want to satisfy ourselves that they are safe. And as a friend we would like to share the joy of being with our horse.

Such intent may start off as a rational thought but by the time when we are about to enter the horse's presence, that rational thought will have matured into *intentful* awareness. By this stage we will be fully in the moment with them and both horse and human will be ready to engage with each other in greeting and rediscovery. This ritual should become so commonplace that it simply evolves into a very natural part of going to our horse. Within a relatively short space of time we will know no other way of joining our horse in the present.

Being with the horse

By the time we reach our horse, we are so spontaneously and intuitively present and full of the intent of a partner, provider, protector and friend that we radiate the energy of all of these roles. Consequently, within moments there is contact, communication and confluence between and of horse and human, with the result that connection between the two is restored. There is absolutely no need to expect or force it. If our energy reflects our presence, the horse will respond accordingly for no other reason than that is the nature of the beast. If we are a friend, our horse will greet us as a friend. Yet even if we are not a friend but reflect the appropriate energy, the horse is more likely than not to enjoy being and interacting with us, for they are sociable by nature and also seek to be with those who truly provide for them and protect them.

What we are called upon to do is to allow this to happen by letting the horse take the initiative as far as possible. When we go to our horse, we try to ensure that we are not the one who initiates the contact, even if this means walking right up to and standing next to them without trying to make direct contact. Because we have grounded ourselves and are fully present, we have no capacity available to entertain expectations. This is important, because if we expect anything of the horse, we are likely to be denied. After all, a horse *chooses* to be with a partner, provider, protector and friend precisely because they see a benefit in doing so. Any expectation would be likely to call such perceived benefit into question. Initially, this approach may not yield a response. If it does not, even after we have waited a while, we leave and try again later.

Alternatively, we may choose to stand or sit somewhere in the horse's immediate surroundings and spend time enjoying what is available to enjoy, especially our horse's presence. The energy of joy is contagious to horses, so whatever approach we adopt, we would like to ensure that we have an abundant supply of it. Grounding ourselves before we go to our horse can really help with this. At some stage or another the horse is likely to want to satisfy their curiosity as to what exactly is responsible for this energy and will wander over to us to find out. This is when we can share the joy in any way which the horse appreciates.

As of that moment, whenever we go to our horse, we will want to ensure that the horse takes the initiative to seek contact with us rather than the other way round, even if this means that we walk right up to within arm's reach without contact occurring. If the horse does not make the final move to initiate contact, we can simply conclude that our energy is not appropriate. Now we can simply back off and try again, once we feel that our energy is appropriate. And once the horse makes contact with us, we will find a way to share our joy with them, even if it only takes the form of a scratch with the soft tips of our fingers, moving in a fashion similar to the movements which horses make when they groom each other.

Allowing the horse to take the initiative as far as possible and hence to express themself accords with their nature as followers by choice rather than by inducement. This, as we know, is in line with their nature. To this extent, we also make it easier for the horse to find some 'reward' for their actions in those very actions. As such, the reward is in the doing. And, like us, where a horse finds pleasure in doing something, they are likely to want to repeat the activity. This is an essential aspect of sociability. We socialise because, amongst other things, it is pleasurable to do so and so do horses. The activities which we undertake with our horses may consequently occur within the context of sociability rather than 'work', an approach which offers far more of an incentive to both horses and humans than the concept of yet another chore to be done.

Allowing the horse to take the initiative is not only in line with their nature. It is also empowering. I have watched our own horses grow in self-assurance as a result. This is reflected not only in their dealings with us but also in their relationships and interaction with others of their own species, especially in a herd. And when horses are more self-assured, they also tend to be calmer and more disposed to a gentler form of interaction with a human who is fully present with them.

While with a horse it is also possible for us to do much more than influence our own personal energy. We are also able to influence the horse's energy by varying our own. Animals are very sensitive to variations in energy. Many of us have noticed this in our dogs. And as we have already noted, horses are exceptionally sensitive to energy and even the subtlest variations in it. Consequently, they are able to detect the slightest modulation of energy within us. This ability on the part of horses to detect the energy within us and to respond accordingly is something we need to be particularly aware of when we share space and time with our horse. This is because the energy within us has the power to draw the horse towards us, to drive the horse away from us, to make the horse indifferent to us or to elicit every shade of behaviour in between. Put another way, because we always have active energy within us while we are alive, we are always influencing our horses' energy, even when we are not aware of doing so.

Lowering and raising energy

Let us consider the two main ways in which we can harness our personal energy, namely, lowering and raising our energy level before going on to examine how we can direct our personal energy both directly and indirectly.

Lowering our energy level

It is a relatively simple matter to lower our personal energy level. All we need do is simply feel any intent which has the effect of calming or soothing us or bringing us to rest. Yet, while it is essentially a simple matter, I must stress that it involves feeling and not merely thinking intent. The feeling of such intent must be so complete that we effectively become our intent and its realisation. For instance, when we ground ourselves, we effectively lower our personal energy level entirely, so as to come to rest completely. Although focused in our core, this energy is inert but harnessed and ready to be used when required.

Lowering our energy level can also be employed to good effect while interacting with our horse (and any other creature for that matter). This is possible because we are capable of varying the way in which this occurs to some extent. We can alter the pace, intensity, frequency and degree with which it occurs. For example, we may opt to drop our energy level completely from one moment to another while moving or only partway. A partial fall in energy could immediately be followed by a raised level and then another partial drop to create a series of rising and declining energy levels. Numerous alternatives are possible. Why not experiment with your horse, feel their response and respond accordingly?

Raising our energy level

Similarly, raising our personal energy level is also a relatively simple matter in itself. Like lowering our energy level, it involves intent and feeling it so completely that we become our intent and its realisation. However, unlike lowering our energy level, it can be done in a far greater variety of ways. The simplest is raising our energy levels in response to a perceived need not only to be fully aware but also capable of responding in any possible way. This has the effect of transforming our entire being into the equivalent of a loaded coil wound up tightly and ready to unleash in response to the slightest trigger, much like a horse monitoring a potential threat or signal to play.

Yet we can also raise our personal energy level as part of the process of directing or redirecting energy internally or externally in the myriad of ways in which this can occur.

Directing energy

In our interaction with other creatures, be they horses, humans or any other animal, we can direct our personal energy in a variety of ways. More often than not we do this unwittingly or inadvertently rather than consciously and with intent. But what would be possible if we could learn how to harness our personal energy and direct it consciously and with intent when we interact with our horses? The simple answer is a great deal.

Directing energy directly

The term, 'direct energy', is the one that I use to refer to the personal energy which we can use to influence the horse's energy and movement by directing it directly at the horse. When we do this, we can direct our personal energy directly from our core or through another body part. Let us explore ways in which we can do this and what effects they are likely to have.

Directly from the core

The core, as you may recall, is that part of our belly which is located about a hand's width below our navel. It is to this spot that we locate our breathing and lower our centre of gravity, when we ground ourselves, relaxing every part of our body above it. It is through this spot too that we can draw on our personal energy when we want to exert ourselves. It is also the main point in our body from which we direct energy directly at an external target.

We can draw on our personal energy and direct it either internally or externally. Grounding ourselves is an example of the internal direction of our personal energy. When we ground ourselves, we direct our personal energy away from our upper body and concentrate it in our core and its connection with the earth beneath our feet. It becomes inert and dormant, albeit only temporarily, for it lies ready to be harnessed in a flash.

Similarly, we can direct our personal energy internally while interacting with a horse to bring ourselves to rest, even if only briefly. This can be put to good effect while interacting with our horse, as we will explore in the section titled *Energetical Interaction with the Horse*.

More often than not, we will probably find ourselves directing our personal energy directly from our core while interacting with our horse. This is because this type of personal energy use is particularly effective for the purposes of conscious interaction with a horse within the context of a trusting relationship and even more so at liberty. It can help us to communicate our intent very clearly yet very gently, while still being open to changing tack at the drop of a hat in response to what we become aware of during our interaction with the horse.

When we direct energy from our core, we need to feel rather than think our intent. If we think our intent, we are far more likely than not to strain as part of a rational attempt to project our energy. The result is almost inevitable that we tighten and tense the muscles in our core. This has the effect of doing the opposite of what we intend. Tight, taut, tense muscles in our core simply block the release of energy and confine it to our body, thereby compromising communication and confluence with the horse. Communication between horse and human is undermined, if not destroyed.

We can avoid this by feeling our intent and by adjusting our breathing and the angle of our pelvis at the same time. When we direct energy from our core, we do so when we exhale. Simultaneously, we tilt the base of our pelvis forward to line up our core with the external target of our energy. This could be the chest of the horse when asking our equine friend to move back without any physical contact between us. Alternatively, it may be the shoulder to seek shoulder-in while interacting on the ground. Whatever the case, what we are trying to do is direct our pelvis while breathing out with our core muscles completely relaxed. Initially while we are learning to do this, it may seem contrived. It is but, as it slowly becomes part of our experiential vocabulary, the coordination of the physical and the energetical will increasingly feel more natural until we no longer notice it and can immerse ourselves in feeling and being our intent in the moment with our horse.

Through another body part
Very often we will not direct energy at an external target directly from our core. We may want that energy to exit through another body part, such as our hand. In such a case our energy will always emanate from our core, where we harness it. We direct this energy

internally from our core to the body part in question, in this case our hand. The body part through which we direct our energy may line up with the direction in which we project our energy but it will always remain relaxed enough to allow the energy to pass through. And as in the case of energy directed at an external target directly from the core, we also release our energy when we exhale, tilting the base of our pelvis forward as may be required while directing it from our core through the relevant body part towards our target with the appropriate intent.

You may recall that we employed this technique when we asked our horse to raise their head while grazing. Similarly, we can also employ it whenever we would like our horse to do something for the purposes of which it would be more appropriate to direct our energy through a body part rather than directly from our core. It works whether we are lightly touching the horse or not at all. While writing the first draft of this section, our vet came to conduct an ultrasound abdominal and a rectal examination on our gelding, Farinelli. It was possible for me to position and hold the horse on a loose lead throughout by using this technique to direct energy through my hands as and when required both without any contact and while lightly touching him at times, all the while reassuring him with a calm, reliable presence, firm in intention but relaxed in approach. Fortunately, the examinations also yielded nothing to be concerned about.

Directing energy indirectly

In the same way that we can direct energy directly at a horse, it is also possible for us to do so indirectly. Rather than direct our personal energy directly at the horse from our core or through another body part, we can direct it elsewhere but in such a way that it also affects the horse but does so indirectly. In this case we can draw a distinction between indirectly directed energy which deliberately targets the horse (targeted) and that which does not deliberately do so (untargeted).

Untargeted indirectly directed energy sounds like an awfully complex concept. Actually, it is very simple. All it refers to is the fact that a horse is affected by our personal energy indirectly but without us consciously targeting the animal. This would occur, for instance, if I were to make my way directly through a group of horses to open a gate, access a water trough or anything else. They sense the energy of purpose and intent, move out of the way but are not unduly perturbed. Although I am conscious that the horses are affected by my energy as I move through the group, it is not my intention to target them.

Horses normally yield to such untargeted, indirect energy. This occurs not because the horses feel targeted by such energy but precisely because they do not. In this case they defer to our energy because they experience it as something over which they are incapable of exercising any control yet which they do not experience as an actual or potential threat. To this extent it resembles the energy of a perceived provider and/or protector.

I use this type of energy extensively when I feed our horses. Within a trusting relationship in which our horses recognise me as a provider in this role, it is possible for me to carry buckets of feed amongst them without fear of being mugged. They simply step out of the way to the side or backwards as I make my way amongst them and place the buckets in the various locations in which they eat.

Targeted

It is also possible for us to direct our personal energy indirectly with the aim of targeting a horse. In this case we direct our energy directly at something other than the horse but with the intention of affecting the horse. This is a hugely effective way of communicating our intent to the horse in the absence of any indication which could be viewed as actually or potentially threatening. As such, it is particularly useful to facilitate communication and confluence with any horse in which trust is still fragile and more of a commitment rather than an established aspect of the horse-human relationship. Yet it can also be used within a stable, mutually trusting relationship between a horse and a human with tremendous effect.

By way of illustration, let me mention an example of how I sometimes employ targeted, indirectly directed energy with our horses. There are times when Anaïs feels that the feed in front of another horse (usually Pip) is actually far superior to hers and that she is therefore entitled to take it herself. Pip readily defers to the more generously proportioned mare, which is not a good outcome for either of them as far as I am concerned. Pip would lose out on her nutrition and Anaïs would extend her sizable girth. For this reason I intervene gently but firmly by simply stepping between the two mares while directing my energy straight ahead rather than at Anaïs and then stop and occupy the space between them. Her majestic rotundity immediately draws to a halt, while Pip visibly relaxes her raised head, drops it and resumes her meal. In the past Anaïs would then try to edge round me on either or both sides and I would simply adjust my position between her and Pip, intent on occupying my new space rather than impeding her. Nowadays she no longer tries this. Instead, within a minute or so, she visibly relaxes and retreats to her own feed. Although my intent is to occupy the space between them and my energy is directed at doing this, Anaïs is of course the target of the exercise. However, because my energy is not directed at her directly, she does not feel threatened and is able to accept responsibility for her own actions and to act accordingly. No one tells her to return to her own feed. She decides to do so herself.

Redirecting energy

Instead of directing our own personal energy, we may find it helpful to redirect the horse's energy in certain circumstances. In this respect we can draw a distinction between responding directly to the horse's energy and rerouting it as it were.

Direct response

When we respond directly to a horse's energy, we are also directing our personal energy but we are not doing so solely on our own initiative. Instead, we do this in response to the horse's energy, which we perceive to have been directed directly at us. As a result, it seems as though we are reflecting the horse's energy back at them.

The clearest example of this is when a horse approaches us directly and we feel a need to have the horse slow down or stop, using nothing more than our personal energy coupled with body language to do so. When we are fully aware, preferably spontaneously rather than rationally conscious so as to be able to feel into the horse's energy rather than analyse it, we can raise ourselves up directly in front of the horse and project our energy in response to that of the horse using the techniques which we have discussed. How much energy we project will depend on what we wish to achieve. To slow the horse down we would need to project less energy than that of the horse approaching us but enough to induce the horse to reduce theirs. If we would like the horse to halt we would need to project enough energy to match that of the horse. Depending on the speed with which the horse is approaching us, we may also need to move forward slightly and even raise our arms over our head to make ourselves look bigger. Whatever we do though, we need to resist the temptation to wave and gesticulate wildly. Sure, we will stop the horse from continuing their approach by doing this but we will also fail to achieve any meaningful form of communication, let alone connection.

Rerouting
This particular form of redirecting a horse's energy is not only potentially safer than a full frontal response, it is also more empowering for the horse and easier for the human to achieve. Instead of confronting the horse's energy full on and seemingly reflecting it back at the horse in the form of a direct response, we can make use of that energy to redirect it and hence also the horse into a different direction. This we can do by simply stepping to the side to allow the horse to pass us and, as they do, by then using our body language and energy to influence and direct the horse's energy using any of the techniques which we have dealt with so far not only to

change the horse's direction but also the pace at which this occurs. Again though, this is not merely a matter of employing techniques but of doing so within the context of full spontaneous awareness and connection with the horse. Without this context there is only the potential for disappointment, for it is simply impossible for us to respond with the intricacy and effect in the absence of spontaneous consciousness with the rational mind in control.

Energetical interaction with the horse

It is in our day-to-day interaction with our horses that everything which we have discussed so far comes together. This is the cutting edge at which the power of being defines the dynamic interface between horse and human. It is here that we can consciously be all that we have learned and absorbed to the point of having it 'in our fingers' in our everyday interaction with horses. Because the various principles, techniques and methods which we have considered rationally have now become so commonplace as part of our being, we are able to employ them effortlessly and even without rationally thinking about them while we are spontaneously conscious.

If we then reflect on how this occurs, we will notice certain occurrences and patterns, from which it is possible to draw conclusions in relation to:
- feeling;
- synergy;
- self-incentivisation; and
- supportive strategies.

Feeling

When we interact with our horses energetically, we may be rationally conscious when we start. For instance, we may briefly review what we are planning to do before starting to do it by grounding ourselves. In the course of such grounding though we immerse ourselves fully in the present. Being becomes our *modus operandi* rather than thinking and, as we now know, thinking and being are not the same thing, however much Descartes may have insisted that they are. In this ongoing process of being we are spontaneously rather than rationally conscious, which means that we are fully aware in every part of our being. We perceive, sense and experience our immediate surroundings. And within those surroundings we can *feel* the presence of the horse through the energy expressed in them, that of their being.

INSIGHT

Feeling is both the vehicle and the fuel for energy, the energetical expression of intent, and when we feel, we are the feeling.

Everything that we do, being aware and responding, starts with feeling. It is simply impossible to be fully aware without feeling. And without feeling it is similarly impossible to time, initiate and calibrate our response to what we are aware of in the split-second gaps that advance our way while interacting with our horses. Feeling is both the vehicle and the fuel for energy. Without it, all that we are capable of is the mechanical and the mechanistic. That is the path to a breakdown of connection between horse and human, because it requires us to rely on rational consciousness and prefabricated rational methods, gadgets and gizmos created on the premise that all horses are identical, in need of being trained (conditioned) and that the same mechanical tools can be successfully employed with all horses.

We know that connection is essential for any meaningful interaction between horse and human. We also know that connection cannot be trained, because it relies on gut-level awareness and response. And it is feeling which makes such gut-level awareness and response possible. It is through and with feeling that we harness and direct energy with intent when we interact with the horse while spontaneously conscious and calmly content. We *feel* the horse making space for us when we enter their personal domain with feed and they do so. We *feel* the horse raise their leg while we run our palm down the front of it to pick out the hoof. We *feel* walk when we are about to step forward with the horse on a slack lead or at liberty and they start doing so, usually moving before we do. We *feel* a change in direction and the horse moves accordingly. We *feel* a collection of energy to move into a faster gait and the horse, again usually doing so before we can move with them if we are inclined to. We *feel* a slight relaxation of energy and the horse shifts down to a slower gait. We *feel* rest and the horse draws to a stop, usually coming to a halt a split second before we do. And so it goes … we *feel*!

In this sense, feeling is the energetical expression of intent. To the extent that it is, feeling – like intent – is not divorced from us. We and our feeling are not two entities. When we feel, we embody the feeling. Put another way, we are the feeling. And whatever the nature of feeling at any particular point in time, because it is an expression of our response to what we are spontaneously aware of, that nature may change depending on any variation in what we are aware of. If the horse expresses something else that we become aware of from one split moment to the next, we are capable of responding to it equally fast in what we feel. It is the spontaneous nature of our awareness and response which makes this possible, for it permits gut-level awareness and gut-level responses instan-taneously. This is something which rational consciousness with its dependence on the rational processes of the brain cannot offer us. The circuit from stimulus to response is too long and allows room for doubt and questioning. Feeling eliminates this while facilitating dynamic intent and action.

The power of voice

There are some who claim that we should not speak to our horses and that we should remain silent because horses do not communicate through voice or at least not through speech. This approach is premised on the belief that we need to behave with our horses as though we are members of the same species. It is also symptomatic of an approach which is based on the assumption that our horses are incapable of drawing a distinction between a horse and a human. I do not know about your horses but mine and all of the many others with whom I have been privileged to interact, be it for the purposes of equine bodywork, saddle-fitting or anything else, are smart enough to know that I am not a horse. Indeed, I would dare to say that they are very grateful that I am not and that I am capable of doing things to help them which no horse is able to do.

Those of us who deal with horses every single day know that horses do use their voice to communicate with each other and do so frequently. Amongst other things, horses whinny or neigh to declare their presence and to ascertain that of their companions. They squeal to express disquiet, snort or blow to express heightened awareness, grunt to indicate contentment, groan to reveal stress, roar or trumpet their fear or rage, sigh their contentment and nicker their pleasure and affection. There is little or nothing to suggest that the various sounds we humans produce do not have an effect on horses. Even if the words are unintelligible to a horse, the sounds that we produce convey the nature and intensity of our energy. To this extent, our voice is a significant indicator and communicator of our state of being and therefore important in our interaction with our horses.

INSIGHT

Talk may be cheap but with horses it is invaluable! This is because talking to a horse can help us communicate our intent.

Yet there is another, even more compelling reason why we may want to speak to our horses, namely, to communicate our intent. I talk to our horses frequently precisely for this reason while interacting with them. In the beginning I would be astonished to note that they seemed to understand what I was saying, from a mundane request to step aside or move back to directions yelled to Pip on a hill from a distance to help her find her mate, Anaïs, below. You can read about this and other examples in my blog post entitled *Horse Training: Do We Not Hide Behind It?* at http://horsesandhumans.com/blog/ 2019/08/17/horse-training-do-we-not-hide-behind-it/. While I have no evidence to show that horses, understand the meaning of what we say, their responses seem to indicate that the use of my voice helps them understand my intent. This may be due to the nature and intensity of the sounds that I produce. More importantly, I feel that the articulation of my intent also facilitates its expression. The enunciation of feeling appears to enhance and clarify it, with the result that it is easier for the horses to interpret my energy and understand my intent. Talk may be cheap but with horses it is invaluable!

Being human for horses

One of the most important advantages of the overall approach described so far is that it allows us to create an incentive for our horses to choose to be and interact with us, one which is internal rather than external to ourselves. Our task is to interact with our horses as their partner and friend, who is also their protector and provider. If we manage to do this as the being we are learning to become, we will discover that our horses increasingly do what we ask of or suggest to them without expectation either on their or our part. No mechanical tools or mechanistic methods are required. Training, gadgets, gizmos, methods and techniques become redundant. There is a very simple reason for this and it is this. As we have already learned, it is in the nature of horses to want to engage in interaction with their partners and friends, provided that such interaction is interesting and enjoyable. And it is in the nature of horses to want to be with their protector and provider. If we manage to be fully present and *intentful* with our horses as protector, provider, partner and friend, our horses will derive an incentive to interact with us from the very nature of that interaction. If horses require a reward as is done as part of the most successful form of behaviourist training, namely, positive reinforcement, then the reward is in the doing! It is by being the kind of human with whom a horse enjoys being – being human for horses, as it were – that we create an incentive for the horse to be with us.

The reverse is naturally also true. If we fail to be a human with whom a horse enjoys being, the horse will not have an incentive to spend time and interact with us. Put another way, if our horse is reluctant to be with us, it is more than likely that the reason is to be found in us and not the horse. Of course, it is possible to circumvent this difficulty by resorting to and relying on training and the attendant gadgets, gizmos, methods and techniques. If we were to do this though, would it not be an admission of failure, of confessing that our horse is making it very clear to us that we are simply not enough? And is this not a challenge to us to step back for a moment before again seeking within ourselves the means to be a human for our horse?

At the end of the day we are all capable of keeping a horse with us and of making them do or not do as we want. We only differ in terms of the nature of and extent to which we rely on the training, gadgets, gizmos, methods and techniques that we employ for this purpose. This is not really what it should be about. The real challenge lies in finding it within ourselves to help the horse find joy in being with us and in doing or refraining from doing what we ask or suggest. We have already acknowledged that the horse has a choice and may not want to spend time or interact with us. Similarly, we have also recognised that such choice should not be equated with laissez-faire. It is not a free-for-all, where the horse gets what they want. Rather, it is choice within parameters, some of them external and others internal to the horse. It is the internal parameters which concern us more for they are determined by the nature of the species. And we know that it is in the nature of a horse to want to be with their protector, provider, partner and friend. For us humans then the choice becomes as simple as it is to the horse. Are we able to be a protector, provider, partner and friend to our horses?

We also need to realise that if we want the horse to have a choice and we decide to rise to the occasion to be their protector, provider, partner and friend, this does not mean that we choose to descend into the realm of *coochy coo*. To do so would be a disservice to the horse, because it would entail that we would be incapable of playing any of these roles. Quite simply, there are times when, while being gentle, we need to be very firm, if we are to play some of these roles effectively, in particular, those of friend and protector. For instance, this might occur should we feel that urgent action is required to avoid an accident which could endanger our horse or ourselves. You could probably think of several other examples yourself. Horses readily sense the energy of urgency in a creature whom they trust, such as a caring human, and they usually respond accordingly. This is my experience anyway.

INSIGHT

Whatever clarity and firmness of purpose we express needs to be accompanied by the energy of commitment and care. Ultimately, this is one of the defining features of being human for horses.

Indeed, many if not most horses prefer clarity and firmness of purpose, albeit accompanied by acceptance and loyalty, if not an underlying commitment to mutual care, as exhibited in the small bands of horses that make up a herd. The alternative to such clarity and firmness is to be left in a grey area of indecision, uncertainty and vacillation. On the whole horses do not respond well to this and they do not do so precisely because they are followers and not leaders. Then again, we need to bear in mind that they are followers by choice and not compulsion, the implication being that they most certainly do not appreciate bossy behaviour. They draw a sharp distinction between the urgency of protection and the bossiness of ego. The former they will voluntarily yield to, while the latter they will resist or reluctantly resign themselves to en route to learned helplessness. As such, whatever clarity and firmness of purpose we express needs to be accompanied by the energy of commitment and care. Ultimately, this is one of the defining features of being human for horses.

Synergy

The horse's natural predilection for cohesion and synchronisation when interacting with other members of their own species is something which we humans can utilise very effectively in our interaction with them, especially at liberty. Being fully present with our horses makes it possible for both them and ourselves to sense and respond to each other energetically, feeling into and feeding each other's awareness and responses. This is similar to a human couple of long and intimate standing dancing together. The partners are so aware of each other's energy and movement through both sensitivity and familiarity, that each can virtually anticipate the other's next move. The absence of any synchronisation of movement is all but impossible to consider. At the same time, this sensitivity and familiarity, coupled with the trusting relationship which the dancers have with each other, draws them together while simultaneously encouraging them to find their own boundaries, thereby enhancing their cohesion and desire to move together. In such an interplay of being between horse and human with its constant flow of motion, change and energy, it therefore comes as no surprise that many of us refer to this as 'dancing with horses'.

Although such cohesion and synchronisation can also occur as part of the mundane interaction of everyday routines, it is in the dance at liberty that the horse and the human are capable of co-creating a confluence of interspecies motion, change and energy whose overall impact on the horse, human and any spectator is greater than that of the sum of its parts. Think about it. On their own, a horse is able to capture our attention through their beauty, movement, power, any other aspect you may be aware of or a combination of these. Add one or more horses to the mix and their impact seems to increase exponentially. If you have not witnessed a large group or a herd of horses moving as one in real life, you may have seen this in a video. The effect is often jaw-dropping. So too is the video footage of a horse interacting energetically with another species. Examples are available on social media and have usually gone viral. And so too have images of a horse and a human dancing at liberty in a wide open space or the former riding the latter without any tack in the wild. For those of us who live and breathe horses such images portray a dream that we would like to turn into a reality. Such is the impact of horse and human making magic together and the power of horse-human synergy.

Cohesion and synchronisation also make it possible for the spontaneously conscious horse and human interacting with each other to influence each other's movements by altering the intensity and direction of their energy as they respond to each other in the intensity of the moment. The occasions on which I have experienced this most emphatically have been with Pip while interacting at liberty. While walking with her I sense her sensing me, as though we are both on the lookout for a signal from each other. Then suddenly it seems opportune to collect as much of my energy as possible in my core and to feel the intent of trot while still walking, albeit slightly more quickly. Being fully present with Pip allows me to sense her pace and almost instinctively match it to synchronise with hers as far as it is possible for a two-footed creature to accomplish this with a four-footed one. Raising the pace, hers and mine, then becomes a pushover. I raise my energy and direct it towards boosting our pace. More often than not my mare breaks into a trot first and I have to leap into a run to keep pace. Something similar occurs during the downward traditions from trot to walk and then from walk to halt. Only now I focus on lowering my energy while synchronising with Pip's movement. Dropping from trot to walk is a bit like feeling a half-halt, relaxing somewhat while maintaining sufficient impulsion to keep moving. Halting together simply involves full relaxation accompanied by the sense of coming to rest. It is truly an awesome feeling to experience the power of intent and energy in this or any other similar situation. It is sometimes difficult to say who is following who in this energetical interplay of the species. Ultimately, does it really matter? After all, does the synergy of the combined movement of horse and human not seem to create a new entity, much like two dancers uniting in a harmonious flow of motion, change and energy?

LIVING THE POWER OF BEING

If we are to live the power of being in our dealings with horses, we need to be humans for horses. There are two main ways in which we can do this. The first and most important is internal to us, while the second is external in its implementation. In both cases we require a paradigm shift. Sure this sounds very trite and clichéd but then some of the most inconvenient truths are.

HARNESSING THE POWER WITHIN

The internal paradigm shift which we need to make if we are to be humans for horses requires us to move the focus of training from the horse to the human. It is not the horse that needs to learn how to harness the power of being. After all, they do this all the time. Rather, we humans need to train ourselves to learn how to harness the power of being. This is the central theme of this book and represents the internal paradigm shift which we need to make.

This may sound like a tall order but really it is not. It is a process which starts with the decision to adopt the ground position. This is the first small but so utterly important initial step. There is no need to think beyond it. Indeed, it is highly advisable not to, for every step leads to the next and what it exactly is will depend on the nature of the human taking it and the conditions in which this occurs.

In itself, this approach may seem to be simplistic or far too simplistic. If it were, this book would not have been written, for it clearly shows that it is anything but simplistic. This is because it is always developing in the moment. It does this dynamically rather than as a set of rules which need to be implemented or used mechanistically like a predetermined method. Nevertheless, it is an approach which is disarmingly simple precisely because it is dynamic, which means that it can be employed by anyone who chooses to do so right from the very moment when they decide in favour of this.

It should also be clear that my description of how energy may be harnessed to live the power of being with horses is fairly basic. I am under the impression that I am merely scratching the surface of what is possible when we employ energy in our dealings with horses. Indeed, there may be humans out there who are more advanced down this path than I am. If so, I would like to hear from them so that I may learn from them. Learning is an indispensable part of this experiential approach to horse-human interaction. If we stop learning, we close the door to what is possible.

INSIGHT

If we stop learning, we close the door to what is possible.

SHARING THE POWER WITHOUT

The second important way in which we can be humans for horses lies in undertaking to share the power of being with them more fully by opting for a husbandry regime that enables our horses to live in accordance with their intrinsic nature in captivity as far as is possible to do so. Such an undertaking would involve an external paradigm shift. Essentially, this would entail breeding and keeping horses in conditions which accommodate their nature as physiological, cognitive, energetical, sentient, rhythmical, emotional, sociable and trusting beings. Such conditions would therefore largely seek to emulate those in which horses live in the wild but to the exclusion of any threats posed by predators. As far as possible, this might entail allowing horses to live as part of a 'herd' which is large enough to permit the organic formation of bands within it in an area which is sufficiently extensive so as to permit widespread movement over varying terrain. In principle, the horses would be kept barefoot without rugs and fly masks, provided that it is safe to do so and is conducive to their health and well-being. Feeding would occur as regularly as possible to accommodate their need for smaller, frequent meals and with sufficient abundance so as to reduce competition for resources as far as possible. Although this description is far from exhaustive, it is indicative of the emphasis that we would place on efforts to confine the stress of captivity to a minimum and to foster overall health and well-being.

Such an external paradigm shift can benefit horses not only in easing the constraints of captivity for them. By doing so, it can also make it easier for horses to exercise choice and to choose to be and interact with us when doing so. We have noted the innate sociability of horses in the wild and how they exercise choice by choosing which members of their band to follow. Little imagination – or logical reasoning for that matter – is required to conclude that the existence of similar circumstances in captivity could be conducive to allowing horses to make similar choices in relation to humans. My experience and that of our horses strongly suggests that this is the case.

Eight years ago we relocated our horses from conventional livery and moved them to a yard where they became part of a 'herd' of about twenty horses. We had already abandoned bits, rope halters, and all other tools of restraint and instruments of coercion with the exception of soft leather cavessons, comfortably lined webbing halters, soft, lengthy rope leads with small connectors and dressage whips. Unfortunately, we still needed the whips to keep our horses in check when we took them for walks in the forest. Now, however, our horses were no longer stabled or separated from their equine companions. Instead, they were free to choose whom to be and interact with in the 'herd' and whether they preferred to be indoors or outdoors and when. We made a point of being at the yard every single day to groom and care for our horses, which included Equine Touch bodywork sessions. I also did a hoof-trimming course and learned how to maintain Pip's hooves under the guidance of an equine podiatrist.

As the months passed in this new environment, we noticed that our horses came to be far more relaxed overall and that they welcomed the opportunity to join us when we invited them to do so. Apart from general care, joining us involved a variety of activities from just hanging out to 'gymnasticisation' exercises, straightness training, equine bodywork (often at liberty) and frequent walks in the forest. Within months we no longer required a whip while we were out and about with the horses and increasingly we found ourselves doing everything with them on a loose lead. This experience seemed to confirm what I came to expect when our horses moved to a yard with a similar approach and a 'herd' of roughly the same size, namely, that such conditions, which seek to emulate those one might expect to find in the wild, are more conducive to equine conviviality than conventional livery. It seemed that these more 'natural' conditions reduced the stress that is so commonplace amongst horses in conventional care, with the result that they were more open to connection with humans. Alternatively, the reason might have been found in our self-development. Of course, both factors could have been responsible for this.

INSIGHT

The way in which we keep horses may have a hugely beneficial effect on the relationship between horses and humans.

Whatever the case, our horses' next experience appeared to confirm that the way in which we keep horses may have a hugely beneficial effect on the relationship between horses and humans. When our existing livery yard was forced to close, we were fortunate to find another. There our mares came to be part of a 'herd' of up to forty horses in an area of about seven hectares. Although arguably insufficient, the land was large enough and so was the herd to permit the horses to separate into individual bands of their own choosing. While conditions were far from perfect and the herd included the unnatural phenomena of geldings, mutilated horses that do not exist in the wild, they were designed to approximate natural conditions and this appeared to have a calming effect on the 'herd'. There was little or no evidence of the stress and conflict which frequently occurs between horses in captivity. An important contribution to this relative calm lay in ensuring ready access to resources such as feed and water and reducing competition for resources in general. There were ample troughs and feeding times saw hay put down in a sufficient number of piles spread out over a large enough area to ensure that there were always a few to which horses could move if they wished to avoid a needy neighbour. In between meals the horses also had access to vegetation growing in the large field which they inhabited.

As far as I was concerned, the highlight was when a late-gelded male whom our mares knew from the previous yard was released amongst the horses while they were consuming hay. Pingo made his way through the 'herd' and within twenty-four hours had assembled a 'harem' band comprising about seven mares in addition to himself. Over the next few days this band stabilised at about four or five mares with the others joining the group at odd intervals. Our two mares constituted the core of the 'harem', with Pip enjoying Pingo's very blatant preference and overtures. What was also endearing to witness was the tenderness which this elderly couple treated each other. Never before or since have I seen my mare so radiant and content. It was as though she had only just discovered romance and sex at the ripe old age of nineteen, the equivalent of a forty-nine-year-old human female. Has anyone ever told humans that horses have such desires and needs as well? The experience raised her self-esteem, gave her more confidence to trust me and to relish the activities which we engaged in during my daily visits. It was during this time that she allowed me to ride her out with just a bareback pad and a cavesson, until I could find a saddle to fit her lopsided body. I never managed to find a saddle which fit her and part of me was happy that I did not. She had had more than her fair share of being ridden by humans and it could not have been a pleasant experience if the pain in her body when she came into my life was a reliable indicator.

So why am I telling you all of this? Precisely because the more our horses' desires and needs were catered for, the easier and smoother our interaction with them became. As the stress of captivity fell away, our mares became far more open to joining and interacting with us every day when we arrived. More often than not, they would accompany us at liberty to the exit, sometimes after we had waited for a few minutes until they were ready to do so. When we did use a halter, it was of the soft, webbing variety always connected to us through a loose lead without the need to drive the horse. If there was anything which could be interpreted as reluctance, if not resistance, it was when we passed the field that was home to the 'herd' on our way out of the yard to go out for a hack or a walk. This, I felt, was only natural, for in the wild the mares within a harem band would normally not desert it, unless they were intent on joining another stallion. For the rest, it was possible for our horses to interact with us as we saw fit or to choose not to. Alternatively, we might just hang out with them or groom them, often while they were grazing with the other members of their band. I used to trim Pip's hooves at liberty in the 'herd' or share an Equine Touch bodywork session with her. We also found that our mares' interaction with us outside the 'herd' helped boost their self-assurance amongst the members of their band.

All-in-all, it became very clear to me that the more our horses' living conditions approximated what they might have been expected to experience in the wild with the exception of predators and excessively harsh circumstances, the less stressed they were and the more receptive they were to connection and interaction with us.

Although anecdotal, there is a lesson that I have drawn from these experiences and it is this. The more we humans are able to keep our horses in conditions which resemble what they would be likely to encounter in the wild with the exception of the harshest of risks involved, including that of being eaten, the less stress they are likely to experience due to their captivity and hence the more receptive they are likely to be to connection and interaction with us, especially if we are able to harness the power of being to become and be human and humans for horses. To this extent, such conditions would serve to support us in our endeavours to help heal and empower our horses and, as a result, to experience the synergy of connecting and dancing with them, not because we expect this but precisely because we do not.

To date, the only places where I have found a similar horse-friendly approach to horse husbandry have been in 'natural horsemanship' livery yards. The 'natural horsemanship' approach to horse-keeping has been hugely beneficial to horses and we must acknowledge this without reservation. Unfortunately, the 'natural horsemanship' approach to horse training has not been quite so generous to the horse, as I have explained in my articles, 'Yielding to Pressure: The Reality of the Myth' and 'From Natural Horsemanship to Holistic Horse-Humanship' in my book, *When Horses Speak and Humans Listen* (you can find more information here: http://www.horsesandhumans.com/mainsite/whsahl-a.htm). And equally unfortunately, it is the 'natural horsemanship' approach to horse training which prevails at 'natural horsemanship' livery yards. This means that at present, if we would like our horses to benefit from horse-friendly husbandry in a livery yard, there is a very good chance that we may also be confronted with an approach to training which is significantly less beneficial to the horse.

Apart from this, many of us would prefer to have our horses at home with us rather than in a livery yard. In most cases, however, this would preclude any possibility of keeping our horses in conditions which accommodate their essential nature for reasons of practicability, feasibility and/or affordability. Of the numerous humans who keep their horses at home, very few have the financial and other material resources available to do so in the manner which I have described. An alternative suggests itself in the form of a communal approach to horse husbandry which simultaneously accommodates our own individual living preferences. We may wish to consider the establishment of communities of like-minded horse owners and carers who share a vision for a horse husbandry regime which can accommodate the intrinsic nature of the horse and who are committed to forms of interaction with horses which are in line with that nature. Such a community might take the form of individual homes of varying size and characteristics located on the fringes of a large communal centre, which serves as a gateway to a tract of land comprising cleared and forested sections interspersed with water features, slow-feed stations and shelters of varying sizes, and partitioned at intervals into interlinking fields and tracks that can be joined or isolated as required. The centre itself would include special horse care facilities to accommodate visits by equine veterinarians, dentists, podiatrists and bodyworkers, tools and equipment, and sheds to house them, and might also have facilities for meetings, presentations, social gatherings and meals along with visitor accommodation. As such, it could serve not merely as the point of human access to the horses but also as a venue for social gatherings and learning with input from locals and visitors from other similar communities and elsewhere. Opportunities for communal food cultivation and the use of environmentally friendly energy and technology could also be investigated. The various communities could maintain contact with and help each other using both physical and virtual means.

Although the establishment of such horse-human communities would demand significant initial and ongoing investments, the financial drawbacks would probably be more than compensated for by the obvious benefits of synergy. Establishing a single community would be a joint venture that would require less in the way of individual investment than if each participant were to invest in their own individual home and equine facility. The same applies to upkeep and maintenance, which could be funded jointly using communal tools and equipment, thereby avoiding the need for costly replication. The location of such communities might also yield significant financial benefits. For instance, here in Europe land in the countryside is increasingly becoming more plentiful and affordable, as the youth and others abandon rural areas to seek opportunities in the cities and adjacent urban areas. The land and infrastructure which is left behind could be repurposed for such communal horse-human ventures, possibly in conjunction with local councils intent on resettling abandoned areas with the aid of attractive schemes.

Such horse-human communities would also represent a win-win situation for both the horses involved and their humans in that the intangible benefits could be considerable. As we have already discussed, a horse-friendly husbandry regime would not only benefit the horses but would also be conducive to their interaction with their humans. Because the latter would find themselves living in nature, they would find it easier to live the power of being with their horses and to learn how to do so.

THE PATHS TO THE HORSE

You have read this correctly. I use the plural, 'paths', and not the singular, 'path'. Why? To my knowledge, the approach to the horse that I have set out here has not previously been enunciated in any other book or comparable publication, or at least not as comprehensively as here (although I stand to be corrected). As such, it would be tempting to claim – as has been claimed or suggested in relation to other approaches – that it represents *the* path to the horse. To do so, however, would elevate me to the status of some type of guru and relegate you to that of some type of potential follower. This is anything but my intention. In the course of the self-development that has led to this book, I sold up everything and moved to the other side of the world for the second time in my life in search of myself, only this time I had come to view it as a quest to find the path to the horse with the aid of a guru. I found both myself and a path to the horse but the true lesson suggested itself in the final realisation that I need not have crossed the earth to find it the first time, let alone the second. What I was looking for was waiting within me. My path to the horse was simultaneously the rediscovery of my humanity. I had become a human for horses, human.

The key lesson that I have learned is that, however much any other human may help us on our way and no matter how many horses we may learn from, there is only one human who can serve as our guru in relation to horses or anything else and that is the one whom you see when you gaze at yourself in the mirror. That is the human to whom you answer in relation to your dealings with the horse or anything else for that matter. Only your way can be best for your horse, for it is ultimately the only one you have.

No path to the horse is entirely the same. One human's path may be another's dead end.

Nevertheless, there is at least one factor that is common to every step along the path which effectively leads to the horse and it is this. It is any factor which is in harmony with the natural flow of motion, change and energy. You will know it when it occurs, because it will simply feel right.

The path towards being humans for horses by harnessing the power of being which I have set out in this book reflects the essence of what I have learned from horses both directly from them and indirectly from humans who have studied horses and/or ways in which we can harness this power. Given the nature of the paths to the horse, it does not make any pretence to being comprehensive and exhaustive. It is simply a path that has led *me* to the horse. As such, it is not *the* path to the horse but merely mine. Nevertheless, if, like me, you are someone who needs to work at finding a path and staying on it, I sincerely hope that this book can be of some assistance to you in your endeavours. And if it is, then it will have served its purpose.

A TRIBUTE TO PIP

If you have made it this far, you will be aware that I owe much of what I have learned about horses to ours and, in particular, my mare, Pip. Sadly, while I was busy finalising the text of this book, Pip came down with a devastating bacteria. Utterly ruthless and relentless in its aggression, it took her to impending death by asphyxiation within forty-eight hours. Faced with the inevitable, I took the unenviable decision and she returned to the earth in my arms.

Rather than update the book to refer to Pip in the past tense, I have left the text as it is. Ultimately, the essence of all that I was privileged to learn from and through this magnificent mare is something I carry with me and will continue to do until I too return to the earth. I have written a tribute to Pip titled *Pip and the Pain of Joy*. You can find it here: http://horsesandhumans.com/blog/2020/05/16/pip-and-the-pain-of-joy/.

An invitation

If you have found this book worth reading and are in agreement with the approach towards horses which it advocates, may I invite you to leave a positive review on the website of the retailer where you purchased it. The more positive reviews there are, the more likely it is to be read by other humans who are looking for a more horse-friendly way of being with their horses.

Also available

A large part of the journey which has resulted in the publication of this book is documented in a series of three books entitled *In Search of the Master Who Dances with Horses: Challenge*, *Growth* and *Being*. You can find out more about these books and where to obtain them by visiting the relevant page on the Horses and Humans website at http://www.horsesandhumans.com/mainsite/challenge. htm.

In the course of the journey along my path to the horse I wrote a number of papers, most of which have been published in *When Horses Speak and Humans Listen*. You can find out more about this book at http://www.horsesandhumans.com/mainsite/whsahl-a.htm.

Contact

Feedback is welcome. You may email me at liamsga@gmail.com or contact me through my Facebook page at https://www.face book.com/andrewglynsmail. Horses and Humans also has a publications page on Facebook at https://www.facebook.com/horses andhumans and a group page at https://www.facebook.com/ groups/horsesandhumans/. Please feel free to join the Horses and Humans group and make a contribution to helping people become the kind of human a horse seeks to be with.

The Horses and Humans blog may be found at www.horsesand humans.com/blog/.

BIBLIOGRAPHY AND OTHER RESOURCES

The following are the only books and other resources which I care to recommend at this point in time.

Bevilacqua, Michael, *Beyond the Dream Horse: A Revealing Perspective on Attaining a True Relationship*, Equi-Forme, Quebec, 2010 (www.beyondthedreamhorse.ca)

— *Au-delà du Cheval de Rêve: Comment créer une relation authentique avec votre cheval*, Equi-Forme, Quebec, 2010 (www.beyondthedreamhorse.ca)

— *Freunde Fürs Leben: Ehrliche Partnerschaft Mit Deinem Pferd, Equi-Forme*, Quebec, 2010 (www.beyondthedream horse.ca)

Hurst, Ren, *Riding On the Power of Others: A Horsewoman's Path to Unconditional Love*, Vegan Publishers, Boston, Massachusetts, 2015

Kathrens, Ginger, *Cloud: The Wild Stallion of the Rockies Collection*, Australian Broadcasting Corporation, 2011, (www.abcshop.com.au). The three documentaries on this DVD are also available free of charge to viewers in North America at www.pbs.org. (Be mindful when you listen to the video commentary that the author is not an equine ethologist.)

Kohanov, Linda, *The Tao of Equus: A Woman's Journey of Healing and Transformation through the Way of the Horse*, New World Library, Novato, 2001

May, Stormy, *The Path of the Horse: Taking the First Step* (DVD), Stormy May Productions, 2008 (now available free on YouTube at https://www.youtube.com/watch?v=TQUMAJCh1 fA)

— *The Path of the Horse: From Competition to Compassion*, Our Horses Press, 2012 (www.ourhorses.org)

Rashid, Mark, *Horses Never Lie: The Heart of Passive Leadership*, David & Charles, Cincinnati, 2000

Rees, Lucy, *Horses in Company*, J.A. Allen & Co Ltd, London, 2017. I have written a detailed review of this book titled *An Equine Ethologist in the Company of Horses: A Book Review*, which you may find here: http://horsesandhumans.com/documents/book-review.pdf.

Resnick, Carolyn, *Naked Liberty: Memoirs of My Childhood*, Amigo Publications, Los Olivos, 2005

Ruddock, Jock, *The Equine Touch: From Zero to Hero in Your Horse's Eyes*, The Equine Touch Foundation, 2008 (www.theequinetouch.com)

Tolle, Eckhart, *The Power of Now: A Guide to Spiritual Enlightenment*, Hachette Australia, Sydney, 2004

– *Practising the Power of Now: A Guide to Spiritual Enlightenment*, Hodder & Stoughton, London, 2011

A Tai Chi and Chi Gong or some other body awareness course with reference materials (video and/or book) that you can take home with you. If you can, try and find one which devotes attention to the breathing and energetical aspects.